NEW STORIES FOR OLD

CROSS-CURRENTS IN RELIGION AND CULTURE

General Editors:
Elisabeth Jay, *Senior Research Fellow,*
Westminster College, Oxford
David Jasper, *Reader in Literature and Theology,*
University of Glasgow

The study of theology and religion nowadays calls upon a wide range of interdisciplinary skills and cultural perspectives to illuminate the concerns at the heart of religious faith. Books in this new series will variously explore the contributions made by literature, philosophy and science in forming our historical and contemporary understanding of religious issues and theological perspectives.

New Stories for Old

Biblical Patterns in the Novel

Harold Fisch

First published in Great Britain 1998 by
MACMILLAN PRESS LTD
Houndmills, Basingstoke, Hampshire RG21 6XS and London
Companies and representatives throughout the world

A catalogue record for this book is available from the British Library.

ISBN 0–333–71409–1

 First published in the United States of America 1998 by
ST. MARTIN'S PRESS, INC.,
Scholarly and Reference Division,
175 Fifth Avenue, New York, N.Y. 10010

ISBN 0–312–21250–X

Library of Congress Cataloging-in-Publication Data
Fisch, Harold.
New stories for old : biblical patterns in the novel / Harold
Fisch.
p.   cm. — (Cross-currents in religion and culture)
Includes bibliographical references and index.
ISBN 0–312–21250–X
1. Fiction—History and criticism.   2. Bible—In literature.
3. Literature, Comparative—Themes, motives.   I. Title.
II. Series.
PN3352.B53F57 1998
809.3—dc21   97–38690
                                                      CIP

© Harold Fisch 1998

This book is printed on paper suitable for recycling and made from fully managed and
sustained forest sources.

10   9   8   7   6   5   4   3
07   06   05   04   03   02   01

Printed and bound in Great Britain by
Antony Rowe Ltd, Chippenham, Wiltshire

For Joyce, again and always

Contents

Preface

This book complements my earlier work, especially *Poetry with a Purpose: Biblical Poetics and Interpretation* published by Indiana University Press in 1989. There attention was focused on the biblical text itself, on the patterns (in the sense both of informing ideas and literary structures) which give to the book of Job and the story of the Binding of Isaac, for instance, their disturbing uniqueness. Here we shall be concerned with the reappearance of these same patterns and others in prose fiction from the eighteenth century onwards. They will be seen to have had a shaping influence on the history of the novel. But this influence has been profoundly antithetical: the marvelous stories of Genesis are echoed, but they are also resisted. Abraham and Joseph are the heroes of Fielding's *Joseph Andrews*, but the biblical paradigms are at the same time inverted, satirized. Job is a powerful presence for Dostoevsky, Kafka, and many other writers down to our own time who have grappled with the subject of unmerited suffering, but there is an adversarial quality in the dialogic encounter with the ancient word. The western imagination cannot escape it but neither can it accept it unaltered. What we have in effect, as I shall argue, is a continuing debate with Job.

There is also the question of the language of the novel. The impact of the Bible's characteristic mode of narrative discourse is clear in the writings of Bunyan, Defoe, and Fielding. In fact it is impossible to think of the rise of the novel except in the context of the coming of age of a new literate, Bible-reading middle class. And yet what stands out is also a continuing uneasiness. The prose of the gospels and the Genesis narratives has never been unequivocally adopted as a standard by novelists – with the possible exception of Bunyan. Even Tolstoy who pointed to it as the ideal, failed to provide us with supporting examples in his own fictional practice. This simultaneous acceptance and rejection of the biblical models will be among our central concerns in the ensuing discussion.

The final chapters will be concerned with the contribution of modern Hebrew authors. The problem here is that the biblical patterns are so pervasive (in the language as well as in the *fabula*) that a full account would turn out to be something like a history of the modern Hebrew novel! I have therefore confined myself to two Israeli authors: they are S.Y. Agnon, whose work belongs basically to the first half of our century and A.B. Yehoshua, a leading contemporary writer. Their writings seem to me of unusual interest from the point of view of this study.

The substance of Chapter 2 on *Robinson Crusoe* and Chapter 5 on Kafka's *The Trial* was presented originally in the context of two international workshops held by The Center for Literary Studies of the Hebrew University of Jerusalem (one in 1983, the other in 1991) under the joint chairmanship of Professor Sanford Budick and Professor Wolfgang Iser. I am grateful to the organizers for the stimulus of those remarkable sessions. The Defoe essay, under the title of "The Hermeneutic Quest in *Robinson Crusoe*," was later included in the first volume to emerge from the deliberations of the Center, namely, *Midrash and Literature*, eds. G.H. Hartman and S. Budick (New Haven: Yale University Press, 1986). It is here reproduced in a modified form with the kind permission of the publishers. Several other chapters making up this present study are adapted in whole or in part from previously published essays. Acknowledgment is hereby made to the publishers and editors of the following items, listed chronologically. The numbers in square brackets after each item refer to the chapters of this book: "Biblical Imitation in *Joseph Andrews*." In *Biblical Patterns in Modern Literature*, eds. David H. Hirsch and Nehama Aschkenasy. Brown Judaica Studies, No.77. Chico, California: Scholars Press, 1984 **[3]**; "Biblical Realism in *Silas Marner*." In *Identity and Ethos: A Festschrift for Sol Liptzin*, ed. Mark H. Gelber. New York: Peter Lang, 1986 **[4]**; "Biblical Archetypes in *The Fixer*," *Studies in American Jewish Literature*, 7, no.2 (1988): 162–76 **[7]**; "Bakhtin's Misreadings of the Bible," *HSLA* 16 (1988): 130–49 **[1]**; "Being Possessed by Job," *Literature and Theology* 8 (1994): 280–95 **[6]**.

In Chapter 9 I have quoted extensively from a volume of studies in Hebrew devoted to A.B. Yehoshua's novel, *Mr Mani*. It is *In the Opposite Direction: Articles on* Mr. Mani *by A.B. Yehoshua*, ed. with an Introduction by Nitza Ben-Dov, © Hakibbutz Hameuchad Publishing House Ltd, Tel-Aviv, 1995. My thanks are due to the contributors concerned, including Mr Yehoshua himself, who is the author of two of the extracts, as well as to the editor and the publisher, for permission to reproduce this material in translation.

Finally, I would wish to thank the many students and colleagues – too numerous to call to mind individually – who have, over the years, by their comments and criticisms, helped me to see the subject of these chapters more clearly. The occasion for the last and most sustained of these conversations was a seminar on this very subject that I gave at Yale College as guest lecturer in the fall and winter of 1991. I would like to acknowledge how much I was helped by those very lively class discussions.

This would also be the moment to express gratitude to Chaim Seymour for his help with the index and to Carola Luzann who very kindly volunteered to transcribe some of the early chapters into the computer.

HAROLD FISCH Jerusalem,
anno mundi 5758 (October 1997)

Part I
Introductory

1

Dialogue and Repetition

The telling and retelling of stories is no incidental feature of the Hebrew Bible. It sometimes seems as though there is nothing of greater importance. The Exodus from Egypt is we may say the "primal scene" of Israelite history, and also, so it has been argued, a fundamental point of departure for the political history of western nations.[1] But the Bible is not simply concerned with telling us what happened; in two places in the book of Exodus – 10:2, and 13:8 – it enjoins upon its readers the duty of retelling the story to their children and grandchildren. There is thus a narrative and a meta-narrative, an account of what occurred and a fore-grounding of the account itself as a primary outcome of the occurrence. Which matters more, we may ask, the Exodus or the relating of the Exodus? This becomes a nice question for the exegesis of the two verses in question. The Rabbis tended to put their emphasis on the narration and the attendant ceremonies as the ultimate value, the end-purpose so to speak of the whole historical process. They read 13:8 as: "And thou shalt relate to thy son on that day saying: It is for the sake of this [relating and the visible symbols that accompany it] that God so did to me when I came out of Egypt."[2]

Historical discourse, as philosophers and historians have become increasingly aware, is inseparable from story-telling. The "facts" cannot be represented without an element of narrativity. And this means inevitably the ordering and moralizing of those same facts.[3] But whilst admitting this, most objective, "scientific" historians would maintain that the object of historiography is history; the *data* are what really matter, the story as story is secondary. The Bible it would seem inverts this order: the "telling" is all important. Things happen in order that they may be told about! And not only told but retold "in the ears of thy son

3

and thy son's son." These in turn would relate the story to *their* own children and grandchildren.

It follows from this emphasis on retelling that what is valued is not only the story, but the ongoing life of the story, including the potentiality for change inherent in the process of recapitulation. Clearly, when it is repeated from age to age, it will not be quite the same story each time; it will have been interiorized, experienced afresh as the new generation brings its own historical experience to bear on the record. The retelling thus achieves two functions simultaneously – it gratifies the fundamental human need for novelty and also for sameness, for a constancy of meaning.[4] Repetition, as Paul Ricoeur reminds us, involves an existential deepening of our sense of time.[5] When a story is retold its previous tellings echo down the memory. But repetition not only points backwards in time; it also points forward, gratifying our need for continuity, affirming an openness to the future. The reader too, like those who took part in the first Exodus, is booted and belted for the road, ready to start out on an ongoing interpretive journey. In retelling the story, he or she affirms its unexhausted possibilities and meanings. There is a sense in which such a tale is never concluded, for readers are encouraged to insert themselves into the narration. "Everyone is obliged to see himself as though he too had gone out of Egypt."[6]

The story thus remains alive for future generations; it haunts them like a revenant. Sometimes it seems that they cannot forget it even if they would like to. Like the Ancient Mariner they are seized with the need to repeat the tale of fear and wonder or like Horatio they are commanded to assume the role of continuing witness and narrator:

> In this harsh world draw thy breath in pain,
> To tell my story.

In the biblical models the reader becomes a witness and the story, a testimony that he is charged to deliver. "Witness" and "testimony" are in fact the terms which Moses in Deuteronomy uses to define the reader's response to a poem, the poem he is about to introduce which would focus on the desert experience:

> And it shall come to pass, when many evils and troubles have befallen them, that this poem shall testify against them as a witness; for it shall not be forgotten out of the mouths of their seed.
> (Deut. 31:21)

Such an ongoing testimony, enjoined upon the Israelites in regard to the Exodus and the journey through the wilderness, indicates a particular hermeneutic stance, a particular relation assumed between reader and narrative. If the tale is never completed it is because the reader has an active role still to perform. His retelling is of the very matter of the story. Nor is this hermeneutic of "ongoing testimony" only a mark of the Passover celebration; we may claim it as relevant also to the subject on which we are embarked, namely, the retelling and re-echoing of Bible stories by writers of fiction from the eighteenth century onwards. And perhaps it is relevant to the poetics of the novel in general which is characterized to so great an extent by visions and revisions as earlier fables are constantly recycled.

Absence of closure as we have remarked is implied in the necessary relationship between an original narrative and its subsequent retellings down the ages, but in the case of Bible stories it is implied very often in the structure and context of the original narratives themselves. Bible stories seem to resist closure. The Exodus may seem to have a clear beginning (Egypt), a middle (the wilderness trek) and an end (arrival in the Promised Land). This would give it an Aristotelian shape. But the arrival in Canaan when it comes seems more like a beginning than an ending. There is a dynamic forward movement which takes little account of the supposed exigencies of narrative form which we are told demands an ending.[7] There is no real ending. As though to make this clear, the people on their arrival in Canaan perform the passover ritual with its re-enactment of the Exodus. They also partake of the first corn of the Land (Joshua 5:10–12). The whole occasion suggests the beginning of a new era.

Likewise, the story of Joseph and his brothers has often been seen as having a classical shape, beginning with the enmity which as a youth of 17 he aroused among his brothers, proceeding through his trials and difficulties in Egypt and ending with his triumph as vice-regent of Egypt and his restoration to his father. But if the story is read in its context, there is no such neat closure. Even Joseph's death is no terminus. Significantly, his bones will accompany the people on their pilgrimage through the desert. And their interment in Shekhem (Joshua 24:32) will mark something of a new beginning – the beginning of the turbulent history of the northern kingdom of Ephraim, the "children of Joseph," with its uncompleted vistas, its still-awaited fulfillments.

It follows from this typical ongoingness of the biblical narratives that Apocalypse is not its characteristic mode. The book of Daniel, the prophecy of Zechariah, the last chapter of Isaiah speak of the last days, and of course much of the Apocrypha as well as the book of Revelation belong to this genre. But the narratives in Genesis, Exodus, Samuel and Kings – to which modern storytellers from Fielding to Hardy have so often been drawn – are more concerned with this-worldly endeavor, with trial and error in the historical present, with accidental courses and purposes mistook. Men and women are tested, they pass or fail the test, and then they try again.

To judge by the use that they have made of the biblical narratives, what has impressed modern writers of fiction has most often been the realism, the accessibility to everyday human imaginings of these powerful stories. They demand to be related to the history that we know. Of course they can be read in a transferred way also – as "types of the Apocalypse." The author of the Epistle to the Hebrews read the Old Testament narratives as prefigurations of greater matters which lay beyond the world of everyday. Thus the material sanctuary which Moses erected in the wilderness is a shadow of a "more perfect tabernacle not made with hands" (Hebrews 9:11). In *Paradise Lost* Milton's hero is instructed in such typologies: Joshua becomes a type of Jesus –

> His Name and Office bearing, who shall quell
> The adversarie Serpent, and bring back
> Through the worlds wilderness long wanderd man
> Safe to eternal Paradise of rest.
>
> (XII, 310–13)

No longer are we concerned with a this-worldly struggle in the dust of history, but with a metahistorical conquest of a metaphysical Canaan. Our material aims and failures are eclipsed and higher aims take their place. Robinson Crusoe toys with such models of transference. He frequently compares his lonely ordeal on the island with the sojourn of the Children of Israel in the wilderness. But in meditating on this ordeal and his longed-for escape from it, he oscillates as we shall see in his interpretation of the biblical word "deliverance." Sometimes he wonders whether what he really desires is not deliverance from sin, that is, from a metaphysical wilderness such as that which Michael alludes to in the passage just cited from *Paradise Lost* Book XII, rather than deliverance from his island prison, that is, his physical wilderness.

There is clearly great fascination in such metaphorical dis-placements – they enable writers to glimpse the seemingly eter-nal forms in the everyday. But whilst many poets, among them Dante and Milton, have been attracted by this kind of figura-tion, writers of prose fiction have been drawn on the whole to the realism of the biblical narratives, especially those to be found in the historical books of the Old Testament. These stories seemed to them to have reference to an order of time and place relatable to their own world; they did not affirm the absoluteness of a super-natural order. The story of Ruth and Boaz, for example, ends with the birth of Obed, who is to become the grandfather of David. This event is greeted with the cry: "A son is born to Naomi." If in line with Christian typology we change the lower-case "son" to "Son," then we get a suggestion of the final consummations of Apocalypse; the more mundane order is transcended and a supernatural order takes its place. But typology is not history and in the fictive re-echoings of this story (for instance in George Eliot's *Silas Marner*), novelists have been drawn to it as *exemplum* rather than as prefigurative sign. It has moral power, truth to life and a certain archetypal simplicity but it does not burden the imagination of the late-born writer with the weight of predetermined doctrine. The new story evokes the old, bears witness to it, but it is not eclipsed by it. Nor does the new strive to eclipse the old. To use a term which has been given currency by the Russian theorist Mikhail Bakhtin, we may say that the relation between them is dialogic, just as the relation of the reader to the oft-told tale is dialogic. He inserts himself as witness into the ongoing record. In that way it never loses its actuality, its rootedness in the here-and-now and its applicability to our own moral dilemmas.

2

The study and appreciation of the novel in recent years owe much to the work of Bakhtin.[8] In his emphasis on the constant commerce in the art of the novel between the world and the word, Bakhtin has helped to save students of that genre from the effects of a sterile formalism. Specifically, he has injected into the discussion of the poetics of the novel the notion of the "chronotope" – a scene of meeting rooted in time and place. It might be there-and-then, that is, some place and time beyond our own, but it always has reference also to the here-and-now, to our contemporary reality.[9] The interaction between these two modes of imagining he terms dialogue. Thus *Don Quixote* exhibits a dialogic conjunction of the world of romantic adventures of which the Don himself is the chief representative and the material world of everyday objects and concerns typified in the thoughts and conversation of Sancho Panza. The actual personal dialogue between the two characters – in which much of the novel is conducted – is thus part of a larger encounter between two different world-views – the one idealistic, the other realistic, the one anachronistic, the other contemporary. We have also the crossing of different languages, a dialogic interchange between different styles, the one "high" the other "low" in which the one is set off against the other. Bakhtin lays emphasis on the element of parody in such "heteroglossia." The language of everyday realism is meant to undermine the high speech of traditional romance or epic. From this point of view, the novel genre is in a deep sense anti-literary; it brings us down to earth and questions the received categories of the literary and the poetical.

Bakhtin finds the ritual equivalent of the novel in folk festivals and carnival, and its literary prototypes in Menippean satire and, later on, the writings of Rabelais. Surprisingly, in discussing the origins of the novel, he excludes the Bible.[10] He tends to treat the biblical material as that which is satirized and parodied (as frequently in Rabelais) or else he finds it embedded in the text as "pious and inert quotation that is isolated and set off like an icon."[11] This constitutes his chief criticism of Tolstoy's *Resurrection* – a novel which, he says, develops a number of abstract theses propped up by quotations from the gospels.[12]

Whilst this view of the biblical text may have some relevance to the history of the Russian novel and may owe something also to Marxist concepts of social realism current in Russia in Bakhtin's time, it surely ignores the powerful formative presence of the Bible in the English and American novel genre from Bunyan to Hardy and Melville. In the examples we shall be discussing, the biblical presence is manifested in at least three ways: first, as authorizing the moral code by which the characters are perceived and judged; second, as undergirding the plot structure; and third, as the model for a particular kind of narrative realism. The novel

was – we need scarcely remind ourselves – the literary instrument of the new Bible-reading, Protestant middle class. If it gives
us the voice of the common man as against the elevated and
hierarchical voices heard in the romance and the epic, this is largely
because the Bible, which formed the staple for the new reading
public, had a tendency to undermine such formal divisions. As
the medieval English rhyme has it: "When Adam delved and Eve
span,/ Who was then the gentleman?" Erich Auerbach has taught
us that Augustine's adopting of the biblical model led to his radical
questioning of the prevailing doctrine of stylistic hierarchies going
back at least to Cicero. From now on humble things like a cup of
cold water can be spoken of in the lofty mode of sublimity and
"the highest mysteries of the faith may be set forth in the simple
words of the lowly style which everyone can understand."[13] And
as Auerbach makes clear, such a radical mixture of styles, such a
confusion of *genus grande* with *genus humile*, is recommended by
Augustine on the authority of the gospels, the Psalms of David
and the narrative portions of the Old Testament. It was to have
the most revolutionary impact on European literary culture in
the Middle Ages and beyond. The early history of the novel testifies to that impact.[14]

To this revolutionary mixture of styles to which he drew our
attention, Auerbach, had he known it, might have applied Bakhtin's
term "heteroglossia" (*raznojazychie*). For Bakhtin too had discerned
in the Europe of the Middle Ages a popular culture which radically
called in question the traditional divisions of style, thus prepar-
ing us for the mixed mode of the novel as it was to develop later
on. And there is here, as Tzvetan Todorov rightly notes, a remarkable closeness between Bakhtin's perceptions and those of
Auerbach.[15] But where Bakhtin relates the phenomenon to the
model of the carnival and the Menippean satire, Auerbach relates
it to the Bible.

But this mixture of styles and with it the implicit questioning
of the formalities of traditional modes of discourse, is not only a
characteristic of European literatures – typically, the novel – when
exposed to the influence of biblical realism. It is worth pointing
out that the Bible itself affords examples of the same phenomenon, thus permitting us to make an even more radical extension of Bakhtin's thesis. Stephen Prickett pointed some years ago
to the conjunction of different linguistic and cultural strands –
Mesopotamian, Egyptian, Canaanite – in the Old Testament

writings and also to the way in which the vernacular Aramaic of
the New Testament writers had been, through translation,
refocused for a Greek-speaking audience with different cultural
expectations. "The Bible," he concludes,

> not only illustrates Bakhtin's thesis , but actually provides one
> of the supreme examples of the way in which discourse arises
> and takes its meaning from the intersecting of contextual and
> linguistic boundaries.[16]

More recently Walter Reed has devoted a full length study to
the application of Bakhtinian dialogics to the biblical texts in their
full extent – narrative, law, wisdom and prophecy. In all these
he finds a "struggle for dominance" between different narrative
aims, different sources, or different cultural positions dialogically
engaged with one another.[17]

If modern myth criticism, notably that of Northrop Frye, has
tended to discern in the Bible a single overarching pattern, a
kind of monomyth,[18] other readings have emphasized rather the
decentered nature of the text, the dialogic interplay of different
voices and genres. Powerful support for such readings is provided
by Meir Sternberg in his 1985 study, *The Poetics of Biblical Narrative*.
Sternberg does not refer to Bakhtin but he cogently demonstrates
the richness and complexity of what he calls the Bible's
"multifunctional discourse."[19] He notes, for instance, in the story
of Saul's downfall and rejection in I Samuel 15, the distribution
of authority in the telling of the tale between three voices, three
points of view: that of the narrator, that of God, and that of the
prophet. The reader transfers his sympathy from one point of
view to the other, sometimes seeking to reconcile them, sometimes suffering the tensions between them, always entering into
the narrative as an active dialogic partner. Sternberg, for instance,
notes the gap between the divine judgment of Saul's fault and
that of Samuel in the following passage:

> And the word of the Lord came to Samuel saying, I repent
> that I have made Saul king, for he has turned away from
> following me and has not performed my commandments. And
> Samuel was enraged and he cried to the Lord all night.
>
> (I Samuel 15:10–11)

The reader's sympathy (like that of Samuel) is drawn to the tragic figure of Saul. We likewise are enraged at the divine judgment. It becomes a task of some difficulty and one requiring all the narrator's rhetorical skill, to persuade us to see the situation otherwise.[20] We are involved in the story, our point of view by no means consistently and rigidly predetermined. Such shifts and dialogic variations closely resemble the characteristics to which Bakhtin directs our attention in his favourite authors and he defines them in almost identical terms. In Dostoevsky he finds "polyphony"; in *Don Quixote* he finds "double-voiced, internally dialogized discourse." These are emphatically the attributes of the biblical narratives also.

We could demonstrate the "dialogic," multivocal character of the Bible equally from poetic texts. The vision of the underworld in Isaiah 14 is an example of what Bakhtin terms "authorial unmasking." All the kings of the nations, we are told, rise up from their thrones in Sheol to meet the newly arrived king of Babylon. In a mocking lament on his fall, the prophet likens him to Helel ben Shahar, the god of the dawn, who is thrown down by Baal in the Canaanite mythology.

> Sheol from beneath is moved for thee
> to meet thee at thy coming:
> it stirs up the shades for thee,
> all the chief ones of the earth;
> it has raised up from their thrones
> all the kings of the nations . . .
> Thy pomp is brought down to Sheol,
> the sound of thy harps;
> maggots are spread under thee,
> and worms cover thee.
> How art thou fallen from heaven,
> O bright Star, son of the morning!
> How art thou cut down to the ground,
> that didst rule over the nations!

(Isaiah 14:9–12)

The voice here that is ironically echoed is that of some Canaanite theomachy.[21] But the lofty style, suited to the high wars of the gods and suited also to the high and proud pretensions of the king of Babylon, is here undermined by a process of mock-epic reduction and parody. One does not begin to understand the passage in which this verse occurs if one remains with the high epic style of the myth. There are at least two other voices engaged here: one is that of parody, almost one might say, comic travesty. To be sure the prophet is echoing the epic style, but he is also undermining it, reducing the grand vision of a mythical underworld where the great kings sit on their thrones to a foul pit of worms and maggots. In verse 11, such mockery becomes explicit:

Thy pomp is brought down to Sheol,
the sound of thy harps;
maggots are spread under thee,
and worms cover thee.

It is not only the king of Babylon who is reduced to dust; so is the high poetry ("the sound of thy harps") in which such kingship is normally celebrated. But behind the epic and mock-epic voices and, at the same time, refracted through them, there is a third voice, namely that of divine indignation. The prophet declares that God will cut off the name and remnant of Babylon, turning it into a desert "and I will sweep it with the broom of destruction, says the Lord of hosts" (verses 22–3). The homely image of the broom not only serves to sweep away the remnants of Babylon but also the remains of the poetic system which the prophet has been echoing. There is here in this hybrid mixture of voices a dialogic encounter between different languages which of course also represent different belief-systems. And the final effect is reductive, we are brought down to earth, to the common fact of death – death without honor and without mythological trappings.

It can be claimed that this passage from Isaiah is as richly dialogic in Bakhtin's sense as the episode of Epistemon's visit to the underworld in Book 2, Chapter 30 of Rabelais's *Gargantua and Pantagruel* which Bakhtin so much admired. There we see Alexander the Great darning old hose and Cyrus attending to the cows.[22] The visit to the Underworld, an august *topos* in Homer and Virgil, becomes in Rabelais part of a carnival, a riot of gross imaginings. Now, there is no carnival in Isaiah, no celebration of the lower bodily functions, but there is a remarkably similar mock-epic drift and a comparable realism, as the figure of the Babylonian king is stripped of its glory and his body is trodden underfoot.

Such "double-voiced, internally dialogized discourse" is more characteristic of biblical literature than is commonly realized. In general, the Bible is by no means so "inert" a text as Bakhtin thought. Isaiah 14 is of course poetry, whilst our business in this study is more particularly with prose narrative. In the memorable first chapter of *Mimesis* ("The Scar of Odysseus")[23] Auerbach pointed to the unadorned simplicity of the story of the Binding of Isaac as the standard of biblical realism. It was the polar opposite of the realism of Homer with its epic richness, its fullness of descriptive detail and prodigality of episode. This is a fundamental insight to which we shall return from time to time, and yet it is by no means adequate as an account of biblical narrative. The stylistic situation is more complex than Auerbach had supposed. The book of Esther for instance is more like a novel than the brief and enigmatic story of the "Binding." And like the novels discussed by Bakhtin, Esther too is characterized by a conspicuous mixture of styles.[24] It impresses us at first as a tale of oriental opulence, of royalty and feasting. The descriptions are elaborate as the story moves forward with a certain slowness and repetitiveness:

> And when these days were fulfilled, the king made a feast for all the people that were present in Shushan the capital, both for great and small, seven days, in the court of the garden of the king's palace: there were hangings of white, of fine cotton, and blue, fastened with cords of fine linen and purple on silver rings and pillars of marble: the divans were of gold and silver, upon a pavement of alabaster, marble, pearl and precious stone.
> (Esther 1:5–6)

Homer could not have been more elaborately descriptive. But then this festive style is undermined in the story itself. Esther and her uncle Mordecai, whilst accommodating themselves to the manners and "style" of the court, bring into the novel another world-view and another language. In the account of Mordecai's doings we note that economy of detail which Auerbach perceived as the mark of Hebrew realism. The very few things that we know of him (for example, his refusal to bow down, his overhearing of the plot against the king, his putting on of sackcloth) are utterly necessary and utterly significant, unlike the superfluity of detail in the account of the feasting and the customs of the palace and the harem in the first two chapters. The silences of Mordecai and Esther turn out to be more eloquent than the prolixities of Haman and his associates (for example, 5:10–14). In short, the book of Esther gives us a Hebrew "counterplot" in contrast to the main "Persian" narrative and exhibits the dialogic interplay of two world-views as well as of the two modes of language that go with them.

3

In spite of all this it may be objected that the Bible directs us to a reality "beyond" the here-and-now of the Bakhtinian chronotope. It insists surely on a process of salvation aimed at transforming the world we know. Martin Buber anticipated Bakhtin in his insistence on the centrality of dialogue[25] but ultimately such dialogue is for him grounded in the relationship between Man and God. Is there not here an irreducible barrier separating the art of the novel as Bakhtin understood it, from biblical story-telling and from the experience of biblical Man? *Heilsgeschichte*, salvation-history, would seem to be in the end irreconcilable with chronotope.

Against this objection it should be insisted that there are different ways of understanding salvation. If the first epistle to the Corinthians declares that "flesh and blood cannot inherit the kingdom of God" (15:50), then the book of Deuteronomy by contrast urges that the commandment is not in heaven neither is it beyond the sea (30:12–13)! Salvation is near at hand, within the realm of human possibilities or, as Buber would say, rooted in community. For him the I/Thou dialogue seeks materialization by being "embodied in the whole stuff of life."[26] Buber was particularly fond of Psalm 73 which for him held the key to the primal encounter. Verse 25 of that psalm is usually rendered: "Whom have I in heaven but thee? And there is nothing on earth that I desire besides thee." Buber read the verse a little differently as: "Whom have I in heaven? And being with thee I desire nothing more on earth." This is to rid the verse of its metaphysical suggestions; God and Man encounter one another not in heaven but on earth.[27] Salvation-history, in short, belongs to the world of everyday.

The book of Ruth can be taken as an example of salvation-history in this sense. There is an unfolding divine plan reaching back to the patriarchal age as in the speech of the elders (4:11–12) and reaching forward to the birth of David. But fallible human beings are involved and if they advance the process, they do so, as we noted earlier, by indirections, by trial and error. There is no clear sense of an ending. Instead attention focuses on every-day events – a hot day in the fields during the barley harvest, a chance meeting between Ruth and Boaz, a transaction involving a parcel of land, a marriage and a birth. The story has the epic momentousness of an episode in covenant history but it is also firmly anchored in the quotidian and the mundane. The two combine to form a "double-voiced" narration which is profoundly dialogic. There is an implicit divine "guidance" both here and in the book of Esther, but there are also human beings blindly groping for some kind of assurance. Moreover, there is no question of one mode "undermining" the other. We are not speaking of a parodic relation between the two "voices" in dialogue. We are speaking rather of a cooperative dialogue, wherein Man is addressed and summoned to respond. But this transaction takes place in the visible diurnal sphere, amid the randomness and discords of our human situation.

It is necessary to stress that the characters enjoy a certain auton-omy, a freedom, we might say, from authorial control. In the story of Ruth such freedom finds expression in the famous exchange between Ruth and Naomi on the road from Moab to Bethlehem (1:11–18). Naomi seeks to dismiss the two daughters-in-law; one of them leaves her, the other remains. But it is not alone the characters who are independent: the narrative itself is in a sense undetermined; it is free to move in the direction in which the characters wish it to go, without authorial intrusion. Moreover, the reader is also involved as a free agent in dialogue with the narrative; as such, he is implicitly invited to weigh the actions of the characters. He may, for instance, judge the mid-night visit of Ruth to the threshingfloor as a bold move cunningly contrived to "catch" Boaz whilst his heart is merry with wine (3:7), or again he may see it as an act of self-sacrifice and of loyalty to the living and the dead – which is how Boaz himself sees it (3:10).

The striking parallel with two other Old Testament stories, that of Tamar and Judah (Genesis 38:13–30) and that of Lot's daugh-ters (Genesis 19:31–8) would seem to reinforce the less noble view of the encounter between Ruth and Boaz. Those are also stories of assignations initiated by women left without husbands with a view to compelling an older male kinsman to "lie with them" so as to perpetuate the clan. Moreover, the three stories are linked as part of the same family history. Lot is the ancestor of the Moabites from whom Ruth is descended and Judah, through Tamar, is the father of Perez, the ancestor of Boaz. There is in fact a pattern of repetition, for repetition is not only characteristic of the ongoing history of Bible stories – stories begetting other stories – it is also a characteristic of the interior rhythm of the stories themselves and the interrelationships between them. The Bible tends to focus on what Robert Alter terms "type-scenes." Michael Fishbane speaks more loosely of "inner-biblical midrash" – as when different passages echo and comment on one another.[28] The third chapter of Genesis recording the sin and expulsion of Adam is followed by the sin and expulsion of Cain who becomes a wanderer in the Land of Nod "east of Eden" (4:16). Similarly, in two later chapters (21–2) we have the account of the exposure and near death of Ishmael followed by the "Binding" or near sacrifice of Isaac; in both cases a voice from heaven intervenes to save "the lad." Such "dialogic revoicing," as Walter Reed terms this technique, is more frequent than is generally realized.[29] In the instance that we are presently discussing, the story of Ruth and Boaz echoes that of Judah and Tamar (Genesis 38) whilst the latter is also echoed with much ironical contrast in the story of Joseph and Potiphar's wife which immediately follows it (Genesis 39). Again, the story of Joseph's interpretation of Pharaoh's dreams is clearly recalled for the reader by the account of Daniel's similar performance in a later generation for a later monarch (Daniel 2).

We return to what may be termed the Ruth corpus. When the three stories – that of Lot and his daughters, of Judah and Tamar, and Ruth and Boaz – are put side by side, what stands out is not only the remarkable similarity between the three narratives, but equally the striking differences in tone and atmosphere. The story of Lot is one of cave-dwellers (19:30). With a crude directness and without any ceremony at all, the older sister proposes to the younger that they should make their father drunk and each lie with him so as to bear offspring from their father. In the case of Judah and Tamar we have a pastoral, nomadic community (Judah is celebrating a sheep shearing). Tamar waylays Judah at the roadside disguised as a prostitute. Minimal forms are observed and there is payment for services rendered; moreover, Judah justifies her actions in retrospect (38:26) and the dialogic exchange attains a higher moral tone than that of the Lot story. By the time we reach Ruth and Naomi, we are in a settled agrarian society with delicacy and rules of decorum to go with it. Ruth's secret visit to the threshingfloor where Boaz is sleeping is preceded by a ceremony of washing and anointing and in due course their union is sanctioned by the elders at the gate in accordance with the well-established custom requiring the redemption of the property of the dead by a near kinsman (4:2f). The male partner is no longer the father (as in the Lot story) nor the father-in-law (as in the Judah-Tamar story), though he is a father figure and one linked by kinship to Ruth's father-in-law, Elimelech (2:1).

In short, there are different perspectives from which to view the story of Ruth and Boaz. The parallels are significant but they are not imposed on us. The characters are as Auerbach would say "fraught with background," but the effect of that background is not completely unambiguous. The author makes no direct comment, his point of view being refracted rather through the discourse of the characters, and his voice becoming perhaps just audible in the brief genealogical parentheses already alluded to.

The story of Joseph is one whose moral thrust is relatively direct and this made it easier for Fielding to subject it to burlesque treatment in *Joseph Andrews*. But it is nevertheless "polyphonic" in a subtle way or, at least, craves a polyphonic interpretation. The lack of authorial comment, the silences of the text at critical moments, all invite us to discern a hidden dimension – an occulted guilt for instance in Joseph, by no means expressed in the words of the story but nevertheless derivable from it.

4

At this point where interpretation becomes something more like a reinventing of the story, a creative extension of its possibilities generated by the dialogic exchange between the text and the reader, we leave the Bakhtinian model behind. It becomes necessary to invoke another category, namely, that of *midrash*.[30] "Midrash" is the name given to the mode of biblical commentary practised by the Rabbis of late antiquity. Those teachers, pondering on the story of the attempted seduction of Joseph by Potiphar's wife, wondered what really lay behind Joseph's "refusal" to agree to

her solicitation (Genesis 39:8). Perhaps it was not so determined
a refusal after all! The Hebrew word *wayema'en* – "he refused" is
punctuated in the received masoretic text by the very rare accent
known as *shalshelet* – a drawn-out undulating note which suggests
a very reluctant refusal indeed. The midrash reads the story with
an eye to such ambiguities. If the text finds it necessary to stress
that Joseph was so good looking (39:6), perhaps this suggests
that he preened himself – "he began to eat and drink and curl
his hair," says one midrashic source. Then again, what is the
meaning of that rather cryptic phrase, "and he went into the
house to do his work" (v. 11)? Among the Rabbis there were two
views on this: one was that he had work to do around the house;
another view was that he went into the house to accomplish his
desire with Potiphar's wife, knowing, as the same verse pointedly tells us, that there was no one at home except his mistress.
Only he was deterred at the last moment by the sudden recol-
lection of his father's face.[31]

These are not extravagant notions but the elaboration of meanings which the text seems to authorize and even invite, once the
reader's imagination allows itself to range freely over it and within
it in a dialogic give-and-take. The result is something between
interpretation and a new invention, for biblical narratives, by virtue
of their polyphonic character, as well as their pregnant silences,
are peculiarly suited to beget other narratives. And this makes
midrash directly relevant to our immediate concern in this study
of modern novels based on biblical patterns. Such novels may be
viewed as an extension of the midrashic mode, which combines
an act of reading with the fertile play of the imagination. They
are the effect of a radical hermeneutic, an interpretive bounty,
whereby new and independent narratives are generated out of
the dialogic encounter with the prime text of the Bible. And it
may be claimed that the reinterpretation or "reinvention" of Bible
stories after this fashion became a central feature of the history
of the novel from the time that it first came into existence in the
form that we recognize it. The Joseph story is a particularly good
example. I will argue in Chapter 3 that Fielding's *Joseph Andrews*
(1742), which he saw as inaugurating a new genre, that of the
"comic epic poem in prose" – is a kind of "midrash" on the biblical story of Joseph and his brothers.

Thomas Mann's famous trilogy of *Joseph and His Brothers*,
appearing two hundred years later, is even more obviously a

"midrash." In fact, it uses a great many traditional midrashic interpretations to fill in the gaps and round out the human contours of the biblical narrative. Whilst the biblical text merely mentions that Potiphar's wife spoke to Joseph "day by day", Mann supplies the actual conversations! The text leaves Joseph's reactions as an open question: how did he react to these attempts by his mistress to engage him in conversation "day by day"? Mann's narrator provides one possible answer: he did nothing to avoid these exchanges! His face, as he urges his argument for restraint, is flushed with excitement and desire. Almost unconsciously, the narrator tells us, he is employing his charm on the woman whilst convincing himself that he is only acting the schoolmaster! He enters the house when no one but his mistress is there, hardly recognizing the strength of the urge which leads him to do this. In true midrashic style, Mann's narrator compares the provocative use of Joseph's charm in arousing his mistress's passion with the provocative use of the same charm, earlier on, in arousing his brothers' hatred. For both Joseph will pay the penalty.[32] And finally, in a playful fashion Mann introduces the actual midrashic story of Jacob's image appearing to Joseph at the critical moment.

> This it was which saved him. Or rather, he saved himself – for I would speak in the light of reason and give credit where it is due, not to any spirit manifestation. He saved himself in that his spirit evoked the warning image. In a situation only to be described as far gone, with defeat very nigh, he tore himself away – to the woman's intolerable anguish, as we must, in justly divided sympathy, admit . . .[33]

Mann is writing a modern, somewhat sceptical midrash, but he is employing a dialogic method which enabled him, as it enabled the authors of these medieval commentaries, to exercise his imaginative autonomy whilst drawing upon the power of an ancient writing which still resonates for later generations of readers.

In speaking of "imaginative autonomy" we must of course bear in mind that nevertheless the ancient text exercises a certain constraint. Playfulness, variety, rounding out, new perspectives, all manner of additions and interpretive modifications, parallels with other literatures and mythologies and with other episodes in the Bible itself – all are to be found in Mann's novel and, in varying degrees, in the other biblically-shaped novels we shall

be considering. But the source text nevertheless remains somewhere in the background of the story as an unsubverted, indeed
obsessive point of reference. There are unlimited possibilities for
new readings, but they are new readings of a textual constant
which remains to be joyfully re-encountered or else, in some cases,
to be fought against and resisted. Either way the Bible is a presence not easily put by; it asserts its authority with a certain importunacy. All this yields a dialogic situation clearly different from
that implied by the Bakhtinian model. If midrash as we have
said gives the reader a more creative role in the interpretive process,
it also paradoxically places him under greater constraints. He is
subject to a kind of control unknown to Rabelais or Dostoevsky
(or their readers), for he is responsible to, coerced by, a source
text which cannot be ignored or set aside. Here again we have
left behind not only the Bakhtinian categories but also the assump-
tions of much post-structuralist theory, predicated as that is on
the absence of a firm and unalterable source of meaning behind
or beyond the text.[34]

From this point of view, Mann's novel is a highly reflexive
discourse, often adverting amusingly to this very situation. Thus
when Joseph tries to argue the lady (and himself) out of giving
way to their passions, he does so by urging upon her the need
to remain true to the sacred record which governs the story of
which they are a part!

> Hearken, Eni, and in God's name recall your understanding
> for that which I would say, for my words will stand, and when
> your story comes into the mouths of the people, so will it sound.
> For all that happens can become history and literature, and it
> may easily be that we are the stuff of history. . . . Much could
> I say, and give words to many involved matters, to resist your
> desire and mine own; but for the people's mouth, should it
> come to be put into it, will I say the simplest and most perti-
> nent thing, which every child can understand, thus: "My master
> hath committed all that he hath to my hand: there is none
> greater in this house than I; neither hath he kept back anything
> from me but thee, because thou art his wife. How then can I
> do this great wickedness, and sin against God?" These are the
> words which I say to you for all the future, against the desire
> that we have for each other.[35]

Joseph's speech here with its embedded biblical text may be play-fully ironical, but it is not absurd. The biblical passage is here not "inert" quotation but part of a dialogic exchange between different worlds and different cultures. In Mann's reconstruction the dialogue between Joseph and Potiphar's wife becomes indeed the focus of a confrontation between the fertility religion of Isis and the religion of the biblical patriarchs. Whilst the author freely rereads that religion in accordance with a somewhat limited view of ancient Israelite belief, based on the anthropologists of the "myth and ritual" school, the text nevertheless retains its literary power and its commanding authority as an ancient word which cannot be ignored or completely trivialized in spite of the mani-fold ironies which surround it.

It may be suggested that here our classic analogue is *Don Quixote*, another inaugural text in the history of the novel and of course a book to which Fielding looks back in *Joseph Andrews*. Cervan-tes's hero feels himself bound to recall at all points and indeed to act out, the deeds recounted in the literature of chivalry. He is in a manner constrained by this body of writing, encountering it at every turn and forcing the other characters to encounter it with him. This dialogic stance could serve as a paradigm for the situation I am here seeking to define, Cervantes presenting through his hero's devotion to the tales of chivalry something like a hermeneutic key to the use of biblical sources in modern fiction. Moreover, this may be more than mere coincidence. Marthe Robert has plausibly suggested that behind the symbolism of the tales of chivalry Cervantes is pointing to the attachment of the con-temporary believer to his sacred texts. *Amadis de Gaul* is Don Quixote's Bible. Sacred writ is here masked as romance, and the "inspired fanatic," whether given to persecuting or crusading, is masked as "a harmless maniac."[36] Such satirical, or at least comic reference to current beliefs had necessarily, in the period of the Inquisition, to be disguised. And Cervantes disguises it and dis-guises himself in the process.[37] But if such is the disguised theme of *Don Quixote*, then it is necessary to add that we are not here in the realm of mere comic parody or satire. There is a serious undercurrent also. The Don as well as being a figure of absurd-ity is also a figure of benevolence and moral passion and he owes this moral passion to the noble tradition enshrined in those same "sacred texts."

This we will find is true in general of the writers to be considered in this book down to our own century. The biblical source may be reflected with irony, it may come to seem as absurdly out of place as the literature of knight-errantry in the "real" world that we inhabit – but it will nevertheless retain a certain moral authority for reader and narrator alike. Kafka in *The Trial* is much preoccupied with the Book of Job, but he is preoccupied above all with the way that it does not work for the modern victim of a metaphysical wager. Joseph K. hears no answer out of the stormwind, there is no vindication, and above all, no happy ending. Like the Man from the Country he will never gain admission to "the Law." Nevertheless the book continues to haunt him; Kafka cannot escape the Joban paradigm. It remains as a kind of testimony and, as such, it demands to be interpreted anew for each generation of writers and readers.

Part II
Biblical Realism and the English Novel

2

Robinson's Biblical Island

Of the origins of the novel we may say not that in the beginning was the word but that in the beginning was the interpretation of the word. The novel is rooted in exegesis. The dreaming narrator of *The Pilgrim's Progress* offers a series of adventures for us to interpret. The pleasure will not be in the adventures so much as in the interpretation. But not only do we, the readers, interpret his dream; "the man clothed with rags" with whom the dream begins is himself an interpreter. We see Christian in the opening sentences with a book in his hand. "I looked and saw him open the Book, and read therein; and as he read, he wept and trembled." His journey is in essence a quest for the meaning of the words in the book. His wrong turns are essentially misreadings, his victories essentially sound readings indicated by suitable prooftexts in the margins. His escape from Doubting Castle is by means of the Key of Promise – a promise to be found in the same book wherein he read of the imminent destruction of his city.

All these are events in a hermeneutic journey. It is no wonder that, in setting out on his pilgrimage, Christian is early on directed to the House of the Interpreter where he sees signs and wonders and is given instruction in how to decipher them independently. But the sights he sees are interpretations of further hidden matters. For if Christian is a man with a book in his hand, then the figure of the Judge and Savior sitting upon the clouds of whom he hears in the last tableau in the House of the Interpreter is himself a man with a book in his hand! The marginal gloss here directs us to the verses in Daniel (7:9–10) which speak of the Ancient of Days sitting on high on his fiery throne with the Books opened before him, and to the echoing of those verses in Revelation 20:11–12. The Ancient of Days in judging the world is himself a reader and interpreter – which reminds us of the midrash which says that God looked into the Torah and created the world.[1] We do not get beyond interpretation.[2]

Of all literary genres the novel most clearly demonstrates this principle. Todorov carries it back to Boccaccio, remarking that "tout récit renvoie à un récit précédent: le récit est toujours un écho de récits."[3] Novels are interpretations of preceding novels; more than that the novel genre as a whole represents a reinterpretation of other genres, specifically the romance. It is thus a particular kind of fabling, one that is aware of a relation to earlier modes of fabling. The novel in fact, as it has grown up in Europe, is a very reflexive genre: it does not merely tell a story; it is about the act of fabling and about interpretation, sometimes obsessively so. Conrad's Lord Jim sees himself "as a hero in a book" (Chap. 1). Jim's doings become we may say a kind of interpretation of that book. Marlow, the narrator, sets himself to interpret the narrative of Jim's doings. We the readers weigh that interpretration and form our own. We never get to the end of what J. Hillis Miller has called "the self-sustaining motion of an unending process of interpretation."[4] It is the very stuff of the novel, the "yarn" that it spins. That word is Conrad's. Yarn is also the image used by S.Y. Agnon at the beginning of his very midrashic short story "Agunot" where he speaks of the "thread of grace" that the Holy One weaves endlessly in the world. It is a way of talking about the working of providence; it is also a way of talking about the composition of fictional texts. Emma Bovary is not only a character in a story: she sees herself constantly in relation to other characters in other stories of which her story is, so to speak, the latter-day interpretation. We never escape the magic web of intertextuality. That is the peculiar characteristic of the novel.

But to return to origins: Don Quixote's story begins as we noted with the reading (or misreading) of such earlier fictions as *Amadis de Gaul*, *Palmerin of England*, and the romances of Montemayor. Whilst the barber and the priest may regard the Don's readings as mere folly we may be forgiven for treating them seriously, for after all he and his author have created a new genre out of the romances of the fifteenth century, setting down the feet of their knights errant on the soil of everyday and thus transforming their deeds of incredible chivalry into the material substance of the novel. The interpreter, like a magician, rubs his lamp and we have new stories for old.

Such reinvention is more like the true novel than the symbolic interpretations we encounter in *The Pilgrim's Progress*. For in contrast to the allegorical dream which Bunyan offers us, reinvention in *Don Quixote* takes a realistic turn. No matter how enchanted the hero may be, we, the readers never forget that Dulcinea is a village girl, that windmills are merely windmills, and taverns are merely taverns. By the same token Cervantes is nearer than Bunyan to the midrashic mode. The physicality of midrash points to the *Dinglichkeit* of the world we know; it does not, like *The Pilgrim's Progress*, translate the concreteness of the biblical episodes into the realm of abstraction. Pharaoh's dream will do as our model here. The seven fat kine and the seven lean kine are not metaphors, symbols, but graphic instances of the seven years of plenty and the seven years of famine. In like fashion Jacob going down into Egypt is seen by midrash to prefigure future exiles. But he does not *symbolize* those future exiles: he so to speak *participates* in them, he acts them out. He literally goes into exile! It is a case of metonymy rather than metaphor.[5]

In midrash then we "stand on earth, not rapt above the pole." If typology sees the tales of Chaucer as pointing up to the region of the Trinity, midrash – at least as one of its functions – does the opposite: it prevents the lives of Abraham and Joseph from escaping into the stratosphere; it brings those figures down to dwell among men. We remember the midrashic comment on Joseph's resistance to the seductions of the wife of Potiphar. We are told that he might have failed the test except for some physical embarrassments that he had to contend with at the critical moment.[6] As the midrash says repeatedly, speaking even of God and his doings, "To what may this be compared? To a king of flesh and blood."

2

No novel could be more down to earth than *Robinson Crusoe*. Speaking of the metonymic density of the work of the Russian novelist, Gleb Uspenskij, Roman Jakobson remarks that "the reader is crushed with the multiplicity of detail in a limited verbal space."[7] There could be no better definition of the effect on us of reading *Robinson Crusoe*, or, indeed, any other major novel of Defoe's. The weight of *Dinglichkeit* is sometimes overpowering. We are always talking about things, not symbols. It is the *things* that Robinson manages to drag off the wreck that hold our fascinated attention, the *things* that he makes or fails to make with his limited skills. The island itself, which constitutes his material environment, not only imprisons him but somehow imprisons the reader with its manifest substantiality. We may add that it has imprisoned the critics to the point where they have not been able to see the forest for the trees. They have seen Robinson as *homo economicus*, but they have not seen him as what he is also – a spiritual voyager. Only in more recent years have commentators become aware of the elements of spiritual biography and biblical exegesis in the book, in particular of the overarching theme of exile and deliverance.[8] There is Robinson's "Original Sin" followed by his trials and tribulations, his conversion and repentance, marked by dreams and biblical prooftexts as in *The Pilgrim's Progress*.[9] Indeed, Bunyan and Defoe shared the same Puritan literary tradition. And yet *Robinson Crusoe* is not allegory. It is something else – a moral pilgrimage presented in biblical language with an immense amount of biblical allusion and yet having reference to a person as ordinary as the man next door and inhabiting a universe as palpable as our own.

If, as we have said, the volume of material facts in the novel is almost overpowering, much the same is true of the volume of reflections on biblical episodes and passages. Our concern is with the way these two sets of signs relate to one another. I begin with the story of Jonah. This is evoked in connection with Robinson's first voyage. He had gone to sea in defiance of his father's express warning and command. This had been his Original Sin. Like Jonah fleeing to Tarshish, he remains in his cabin in a stupor while the storm rages, coming up to help with the pumps only after he sees the rest of the ship's company at their prayers. Finally, the ship founders off the Yarmouth Roads and Robinson gets ashore with difficulty to be warned by the captain against ever going to sea again: "Perhaps this is all befallen us on your Account, like *Jonah* in the ship of *Tarshish*."[10]

We remember Father Mapple's sermon on Jonah at the beginning of *Moby Dick*. The Jonah story has almost equal significance as a controlling image in *Robinson Crusoe*, except that Defoe's novel remains within the boundaries of the quotidian; it does not, like Melville's novel, engage us with the mystery of evil, or with the wars of the gods. What attracted Defoe to this biblical story was

not the prodigy of the great fish but rather Jonah's essential loneliness. Jonah – alone on board ship, in the belly of the fish, keeping
his vigil not inside Nineveh but outside it, set apart from the
inhabitants – is a figure of radical loneliness. In that he becomes
a key to Robinson's condition on the island. It is worth noting
some of the details of the Bible story. After being saved from
the sea, Jonah proceeds on his journey to Nineveh. The burden
that he carries to the inhabitants is the call to repentance. That
becomes his essential task. We see him in Chapter 4 outside the
city to the east, in the desert in fact, where, like the Children of
Israel in the wilderness, he builds himself a booth (*sukkah*) to
shelter himself from the fierce heat of the sun. And something
else happens to remind Jonah both of his special protection and
his special vulnerability. God prepares a gourd (*kikayon*) to protect
him with its foliage, but the next day the plant is attacked by a
worm and withers to nothing. Jonah is left comfortless, lonely,
and exposed.

The story of Robinson's many trials on the island may be read
as a kind of midrash on Jonah. The island is normally referred
to in the book as a desert or wilderness with frequent, explicit
reference to the wilderness in which the Children of Israel wan-
dered for 40 years. One of Robinson's major preoccupations is
the building of a shelter for himself. He scoops out the earth
from the side of a rock, making himself a kind of cave in front
of which he erects a pallisade containing a tent covered over
with thatch. He has another shelter near the center of the island
which he calls his "bower." In Part II of the novel, Will Atkins
makes himself a home of basketwork. The vulnerability of these
sukkot is dramatized when Robinson's first home is threatened
by earthquake and later when he fears he will be invaded by
wild beasts and by savages. He feels marvelously protected and
terribly endangered in turns, as does Jonah and as do the Children
of Israel in the wilderness.[11] Here is the biblical polarity which
Defoe establishes as the main aspect of Robinson's desert experience
– he is chosen for special protection, but he is also singled out
for special trials. This is the condition of biblical man. And the
question which he constantly asks himself is that of Moses, Job,
Jonah, indeed all the heroes of the Bible, Why am I singled out?[12]

The biblical resonance is specially notable in the matter of the
miraculous growth of the barley. Like the gourd which springs
up for Jonah, or like the manna in the wilderness, the green blades

of barley and rice which Robinson finds springing up in the vicinity of his hut during his first months on the island strike him as miraculous. He is at first moved to thank God for thus providing him with sustenance in "that wild miserable place" (p.63). Later his religious thankfulness begins to abate when he discovers that he himself had accidentally emptied out some grains of barley a few weeks earlier thinking they were merely husks. From these eventually he will reap a magnificent harvest of corn. But, in the meantime, his first attempt at sowing is a failure and, like Jonah's gourd, the entire crop withers by drought – to his great vexation. And it is always threatened by birds and beasts. He has to learn what it means to live by the grace of God; that is the nature of the trial in the desert. The question of the psalmist remains with him to be echoed and interpreted four times, each time with a different emphasis, in the course of his long desert sojourn: "Can God spread a Table in the Wilderness?" (Ps. 78:19). The desert is not Bunyan's Slough of Despond but a material wilderness and the "table," by metonymy, is the material sustenance, the food by means of which he hopes to survive. These actual privations and this actual bounty turn out to be ways of understanding the biblical verse.

Robinson is a modern Jonah in a number of other ways. Like Jonah, he is that man who brings the message of repentance to others and is himself recalled to his duty. In his fever he has a terrible dream; he sees "a Man descend from a great black Cloud, in a bright Flame of Fire, and light upon the Ground." The appearance of the man and the accompanying flashes of fire and trembling of the earth recall the vision of the Ancient of Days described to Christian in the House of the Interpreter. And the purpose is similar. The man threatens Robinson with a spear and cries out to him in a terrible voice, "Seeing all these Things have not brought thee to repentance, now thou shalt die." Like Jonah and the people of Nineveh, his conscience that had slept so long now begins to awake and he cries out mightily to the Lord: "Lord, be my Help, for I am in great Distress" pp.70,73). This recovery of the power to pray is the turning point of Robinson's moral history, having the same force as the parallel moment in the career of Coleridge's Ancient Mariner when, after blessing the watersnakes, he is for the first time enabled to pray. The following day, finding himself somewhat recovered though still very weak, Robinson walks a little way out of his tent towards the shore and, sitting down upon the ground, he gazes upon the sea and sky. Appropriately enough, his religious education now begins with an avowal which echoes the first words of Jonah to the seamen when they ask him to identify himself. Jonah had replied: "I am an Hebrew and I fear the Lord, the God of heaven, which hath made the sea and the dry land." Robinson's searching of divine knowledge like-wise begins with a series of questions regarding his own identity and that of his surroundings:

> What is this Earth and Sea of which I have seen so much, whence is it produc'd, and what am I, and all the other Creatures, wild and tame, humane and brutal, whence are we? Sure we are all made by some secret Power who form'd the Earth and Sea, the Air and Sky; and who is that? Then it follow'd most naturally, It is God that has made it all.
>
> (pp.73–4)

There are of course other biblical sources, such as the New Testament parable of the Prodigal Son, at work in the moral history of Robinson Crusoe. I have tried to isolate the Jonah strand because we are directed to this early on by the captain in his rebuke to Robinson and because Robinson's lonely ordeal first by sea and then by desert exactly parallels that of the biblical prophet, as does the emphasis placed on repentance and the value of prayer. Robinson Crusoe operates for the western imagination as more than a fictional hero; he is a near-universal paradigm. His lonely trial becomes a fundamental myth, a means of articulating our search for self-understanding and our understanding of reality. It is also a fundamental paradigm for the genre of the novel as it will develop later. It is therefore of special interest to note that Robinson is not only called upon to withstand trials by sea and land but to communicate them to us in words which relate them firmly to a preexisting biblical source.

3

So far we have argued that this novel proceeds by means of an exegesis of biblical passages and episodes. We must now go one stage further – to the stage of meta-exegesis. For the story not only interprets, it is about interpretation. It is not only that

Robinson's doings and the things that happen to him are the subject of interpretation by the narrator and the reader: he himself is an interpretant,[13] a hermeneut. In this Robinson goes beyond the Ancient Mariner. In Coleridge's poem it is the marginal gloss which carries the interpretation of the mariner's moral history; here in Defoe the mariner himself performs this role. He is at once the object of divine wrath, the man who repents, the mediator of a saving message, and the interpreter of texts and visions. Interpretation is very much his business. In the midrash on Jonah, the prophet in the belly of the fish is taken on a conducted tour of some of the more mysterious texts of Scripture.[14] But we do not need to go to the midrash: the Bible itself ascribes to its heroes this hermeneutic function. Joseph is the dreamer and, at the same time, the interpreter of dreams. Jonah is asked to interpret the withering of the gourd: Jeremiah is asked to explain the sights shown him at the beginning of his ministry; Ezekiel is charged not only with performing strange signs but with interpreting them. There is a sense in which interpretation is not only a means but an end, a basic property of the spiritual life. This is even more obviously the case with the parables of the New Testament and Jesus' interpretation of those parables.

Defoe's book then is not only about a man who undergoes a moral testing on a desert island: it is about the process of interpretation, its pitfalls and menaces. His success in sowing his corn and reaping his crop after many years parallels his success in making old words yield a new crop of meaning. "Can God spread a table in the wilderness?" – this verse can be glossed: Can Robinson by the grace of God succeed in translating the canonical text of scripture into the words of a modern fable?" The island provides him with a unique opportunity for this kind of exercise. The stage-set is biblical: there is sea and desert, the vision of angels, storm and earthquake. The Bible is placed in his hand and in Protestant fashion he is free to interpret it at will. Indeed, he is left little alternative but to exercise that function. For if he does not find the words and images to comprehend his extraordinary situation, that situation will confound him. Man does not live by bread alone but by the language which he discovers for signifying what is otherwise unsignifiable. And where else should Robinson find that language if not in such a text as Jonah which gives him a key to his own lonely trials and tribulations? It is rather like what Paul Fussell tells us of the desperate need of the soldiers in the trenches in the First World War. They were in search of a language for dealing with their unparalleled sufferings. They found it often in Bunyan:

It is odd and wonderful that front-line experience should ape the pattern of the one book everybody knew. Or to put it perhaps more accurately, front-line experience seemed to become available for interpretation when it was seen how closely parts of it resembled the action of *The Pilgrim's Progress*.[15]

In a hundred memoirs and diaries Bunyan's "Slough of Despond" becomes the precise image for the warfare in the mud and filth of the trenches of Flanders. Here is a case of symbolic interpretation being reversed and something more like metonymy being restored. Bunyan had spiritualized the biblical Wasteland, the Valley of the Shadow of Death of David's struggles (which in the biblical source meant simply a profoundly dark valley) treating them as metaphysical locations; the men of the Great War reinterpreted them as physical and concrete. They restored the historical moment, converting symbol into chronotope.

But to return to Robinson and his assumption of the role of hermeneut. This occurs after his meditation on the seashore mentioned above. As night falls, he walks back to his hut fearful that the fever which had brought on his terrible dream the night before will recur. How was he to treat his fever? It occurs to him that in one of his chests he has a roll of tobacco leaf and that this herb was used in Brazil as a medicine for all manner of ailments:

I went, directed by Heaven no doubt; for in this Chest I found a Cure, both for the Soul and Body, I open'd the Chest, and found what I look'd for, *viz.* the Tobacco; and as the few Books, I had sav'd, lay there too, I took out one of the Bibles which I mention'd before, and which to this Time I had not found Leisure, or so much as Inclination to look into.

(pp.74–5)

The tobacco is not symbolic tobacco – it is the rank weed itself which he uses, laced with rum, to cure his fever. And the words which he finds as he casually opens the book, have as immediate an application to his present condition. They are from Psalm 50:

"Call on me in the Day of Trouble, and I will deliver thee, and thou shalt glorify me." The tobacco, it seems is the material exemplification of the deliverance spoken of in that verse from psalms. And the two, text and referent, are literally contiguous! Of course the two do not always rest comfortably side by side as in this instance. Sometimes the Book will supervene and sometimes the Tobacco. We will sometimes forget the one and find ourselves totally absorbed in the other. To see them in relation to one another and find room for both becomes the aim of the novel – indeed, in a manner of speaking, the aim of the whole genre of the novel which Defoe helped to inaugurate. In Jane Austen's *Sense and Sensibility*, Marianne Dashwood is delivered in her day of troubles; she overcomes her Giant Despair and is rewarded with love and marriage and an income of two thousand a year. Likewise, in *Pride and Prejudice*, Elizabeth Bennet achieves the blessedness of true love grounded in moral virtue – the secular equivalent of Grace – but she also becomes the mistress of the great estate at Pemberley. The reader requires both kinds of gratification and also the assurance that the two can be brought together to dwell side by side like the Tobacco and the Bible in Defoe's novel. It is Elizabeth's achievement that she provides the reader with that assurance, thus mediating between the realms of moral experience and material fact. In this respect, *Robinson Crusoe* stands as a paradigm for a mode of dialogue which will characterize the development of the English novel from now on. But its importance is not only that of a paradigm; it is also an expository model, for Robinson, unlike the heroes of Jane Austen or Charles Dickens, defines the dual nature of his great expectations through an unremitting process of interpretation. His is at bottom a hermeneutic achievement.

Robinson's first attempt at interpreting the words from the Psalms, "Call on me in the Day of Trouble, and I will deliver thee," is according to their literal signification. And the difficulty of this mode of understanding strikes him at once. Was it conceivable that he would pray and then simply be rescued? "The Thing was so remote, so impossible in my Apprehension of Things, that I began to say as the Children of *Israel* did, when they were promised Flesh to eat, *Can God spread a Table in the Wilderness?* So I began to say, Can God himself deliver me from this Place?" (p.75). To expect the verse to implement itself in that automatic fashion seemed illogical and presumptuous. That was on June

28. On July 4 he takes up the Bible again and now, like a good Calvinist, he begins systematically with the New Testament, reading it "seriously" morning and night. This leads him, as he says, to construe the words of that Psalm differently. The key word is deliverance – a Bible word of course – and this becomes from now on the focus for an intense effort of reinterpretation which continues through the novel.

> Now I began to construe the Words mentioned above, *Call on me, and I will will deliver you*, in a different Sense from what I had ever done before; for then I had no Notion of any thing being call'd Deliverance, but my being deliver'd from the Captivity I was in; for tho' I was indeed at large in the Place, yet the Island was certainly a Prison to me, and that in the worst Sense in the World; but now I learn'd to take it in another Sense: Now I look'd back upon my past Life with such Horrour, and my Sins appear'd so dreadful, that my Soul sought nothing of God, but Deliverance from the Load of guilt that bore down all my Comfort: As for my solitary Life it was nothing; I did not so much as pray to be deliver'd from it, or think of it; It was all of no Consideration in Comparison to this: and I add this Part here, to hint to whoever shall read it, that whenever they come to a true Sense of things, they will find Deliverance from Sin a much greater Blessing than Deliverance from Affliction.
>
> (p.77)

Here he has moved in the direction of an evangelical theology. Deliverance has to be understood symbolically as deliverance from guilt. But he is betrayed by the phrase "as for my solitary Life it was nothing." Was it really nothing? If so the very substance of the book he is writing is nothing: the accumulation of the details of desolation and exile, the physicality of his dreary environment – all this is nothing. The neat dichotomizing in the last sentence ("they will find Deliverance from Sin a much greater Blessing than Deliverance from Affliction") does not carry conviction. Neither the reader nor the narrator (for the passage has considerable irony) is taken in by this total spiritualizing of the term "Deliverance."

A little later on, musing on a verse from Joshua, "I will never, never leave thee, nor forsake thee," Robinson takes the evangelical interpretation as far as it will go:

I began to conclude in my Mind, That it was possible for me
to be more happy in this forsaken Solitary Condition, than it
was probable I should ever have been in any other Particular
State in the World; and with this Thought I was going to give
Thanks to God for bringing me to this Place.

I know not what it was, but something shock'd my Mind at
that Thought, and I durst not speak the Words: How canst
thou be such a Hypocrite, (said I, even audibly) to pretend to
be thankful for a Condition, which however thou may'st endeav-
our to be contented with, thou would's rather pray heartily to
be deliver'd from: so I stopp'd there.

                                                              (p.90)

He dangles the purely spiritual notion of deliverance before our
eyes. But good sense prevails over the radical doctrine of Grace
and he pulls himself up in time – "I stopp'd there!" That line of
interpretation will not get him off the island nor will it get him
to the accomplishment of the kind of bourgeois fiction on which
he is embarked. He will pray rather for deliverance in a sense
compatible with all his actions on the island – his attempts to
grow corn, the building of his house, his yearning for society,
the desperate and continued boat-building. In fact, like the heroes
of many other novels of Defoe, he oscillates between two kinds
of understanding. In moods of relative contentment with his lot,
he embraces the spiritual, transferred meaning of deliverance;
he finds comfort in the doctrine of Grace, in the thought that
through the Book he will achieve deliverance from sin. At other
times, especially when the dangers of his situation press closely
on him, he seizes upon the historical sense of the words; he is
filled with what he terms "the eager prevailing Desire of Deliverance" which he said "master'd all the rest" (p.156).

In the 24th year of his stay on the island, he reviews his condition, mental and physical. In spite of religious comforts, he is
now constantly disturbed by thoughts of the unwelcome guests
who from time to time visit the island to engage in their canni-
bal feasts. His mind is set wholly on escape: "I look'd back on
my present Condition, as the most miserable that could possibly
be, that I was not able to throw myself into any thing but Death,
that could be call'd worse" (p.154). But how to compass his deliverance from the island without compromising his deliverance
from sin? For the only practical plan of escape seemed to him to

involve slaughtering a group of natives as they landed on the island and seizing one of their number as his slave. Robinson, we must remember, is now a converted Christian, not a savage nor any longer a blaspheming English sailor. He has discovered not only the Tobacco, but also the Book, and from now on his life will necessarily be guided by the Book. But how was it to be interpreted? He will not be saved by the literal meaning pure and simple. He is not likely to be delivered if he simply calls on God in the day of trouble when the savages step on shore. He must also act. But he must act in response to the right signs, the providential signs. It is a little like Hamlet's mood in the last act of his play. "There is special providence in the fall of a sparrow . . . The readiness is all." He must be ready to take up the prompting of that providence.

Interpretation now takes the form of an active cooperation, an active reading of signs. Robinson must learn to act in accordance with the Book and yet he must adapt the Book to his own particular circumstances. This is akin to the casuistry taught by proponents of practical divinity in the previous century, such as Jeremy Taylor and Joseph Hall.[16] We see Robinson engaged in weighing the response required of him to the arrival of the cannibals. It was difficult to see how he could manage without killing a great many of them: "and this was not only a very desperate Attempt and might miscarry; but on the other Hand, I had greatly scrupled the Lawfulness of it to me; and my Heart trembled at the thoughts of shedding so much Blood, tho' it was for my Deliverance" (pp.155–6). He concludes with the sentence already quoted above: "The eager prevailing Desire of Deliverance at length master'd all the rest; and I resolved, if possible, to get one of those savages into my Hands, *cost what it would*" (emphasis added). The last phrase shows him abandoning for the moment the attempt to find a moral interpretation for his proposed actions or a moral basis for the term Deliverance. He will, like so many of the new colonial settlers in their war against the Indians, give up the attempt to square his actions with his conscience or seek a scriptural warrant for what he wants to do. He will say, with Angelo, "Blood, thou art blood" and proceed to act out his desires. But this is only for a moment. In the end he finds Friday being pursued by two men intent on killing him. This solves the problem for him. "I was call'd plainly by Providence to save this poor Creature's Life," he declares. He promptly kills the pursuers and saves

Friday. This exercise in casuistry is conducted not without a certain irony on Defoe's part.

Robinson faces a similar casuistical problem later on, in his 27th year on the island, when he and Friday, armed to the teeth, go to attack six canoe-loads of Indians. Again he asks himself, "What Call? What Occasion? much less, What Necessity was I in to go and dip my Hands in Blood?" (p.181). Friday might act because his tribe was at war with theirs. For himself he knows no personal cause to attack them. This is his problem. He decides he will go as near as he can and observe them, gun in hand, and "act then as God should direct." Defoe's irony is unmistakable. Coming close, Robinson finds them about to kill one of their prisoners who is a white man! This "fir'd all the very Soul within me." It was the sign he had been waiting for and so he and Friday attack. They release the prisoner, who turns out to be a Spaniard, and then the three of them fall upon the savages, killing 18 out of the 22 who had come ashore. Another of the prisoners whom they release turns out to be Friday's father. So all is well, the island is now peopled, the enemy is destroyed, and the problem of dealing with the words in the Book has been solved, though at the cost of some little self-deception and a fortunate, ex post facto justification. It is the history in miniature of the Christian settlement of the New World.

Robinson never really solves the hermeneutic problem. We are left with the feeling that if the transferred, symbolic meaning of "deliverance" is no answer, the direct appropriation of the word to his own immediate needs may likewise result in distortion. He is impaled on the horns of a dilemma. It is of course the Puritan dilemma resulting from the antinomy of Grace and Nature. When we have separated Grace from Nature, Nature will tend to run away with us, as in Paul's letter to the Romans (7:19), and we will sin no matter how hard we try not to. Robinson strives to bring the two together but does not quite succeed. One thing, however, is clear; as long as he is on the island he does not escape the need to grapple with this antinomy, the need to come to terms with the Book which provides him with the indispensable words and images needed to make sense of his situation. There is no alternative to hermeneutics. It seems sometimes that his imprisonment on the island (the term "imprisonment" is obsessively frequent) is also an imprisonment in the text. His island experience constrains him. The role of interpreter is not a comfortable role: it involves him in agonizing choices and contradictions. He will inevitably oscillate between one reading and another. The need to escape from the island becomes, indeed, at one level, the need to escape from the burden of interpretation, from his confinement to the role of interpreter. If only, Robinson seems to say, I could get away from this island, I could be an adventurer like any other adventurer, I could get into a different kind of book entirely, without carrying on my back the burden of biblical interpretation.

Indeed this is what happens to a great extent in the sequel. In Part II of *The Life and Adventures of Robinson Crusoe*, published in 1719, Robinson, having been delivered from his island, no longer spends many hours each day musing over his sacred texts. He has tucked his religion somewhere out of sight and pursues his adventures with a certain innocent reliance on the guidance of Providence and instinct. There is less agonized self-questioning (and also less narrative tension). The task of preaching repentance to the unbelievers on the island is transferred to a French Catholic priest, the Mr Great-Heart of this novel.[17] The Bible words now seem to flow easily, together with a certain enlightened self-interest. Of course, there is also the danger of self-betrayal. At one point, ironically, we find Robinson, the hero of the faith, the Christian pilgrim of Part I, being pursued as a thief on a stolen ship. It is only his resourcefulness which prevents him from ending his life in ignominy. In Part II there are also renewed references to that Original Sin of wandering which sent him off to sea in the first place. We are made to feel that, unlike Jonah, he has not quite learned the lesson of his trials at Nineveh. His repentance is less than complete. The denouement is also unlike that of Jonah. Jonah, we remember, is left in the desert at the end to work out an answer to the unanswerable questions of the text – we are denied closure. In keeping with the requirements of a Puritan, middle-class imagination, however, Robinson ends his days in peace with a sizable income from his investments in Brazil and his equally profitable adventures in the Far East.

Defoe oscillates then between at least two exegetical poles. There is a third part to the *Life and Adventures*: his long *Serious Reflections During the Life and Surprising Adventures of Robinson Crusoe* (1720). This little read work takes us away from metonymy into the direction of symbolism and allegory. Defoe had been attacked for inventing so many of the episodes in the original *Life and*

Adventures of Robinson Crusoe. His defence is to say that the "Story though Allegorical, is also Historical" (Preface). He prevaricates a little, never defining precisely the boundary between "allegorical" and "historical." He insists, however, that the dreams and other similar episodes in the account of his lonely hero's stay on the island all have a "higher" meaning, and are "designed . . . to the most serious Uses possible." Faith is always served. He ends his *Serious Reflections* – a midrash, if you like, on his own earlier novel – with an account of a visionary journey to the "Angelic World," to the Sun and the Planets, citing the example of Milton before him who had used his imagination to envision things quite other than those found in the world we know. He escapes, in short into outer space.

   Read me, he seems to be saying, for the higher truth. But even whilst Defoe affirms this faith in the higher function of the novel, he seems to have his tongue in his cheek. For it is after all not the vision of the Angelic World that we take away from *Robinson Crusoe*, but the vision of a man like ourselves struggling to find a meaning in his lonely existence and doing so with the Bible in one hand and the Tobacco in the other.

3
Biblical "Imitation" in *Joseph Andrews*

Bakhtin had a keen appreciation of what he calls the "English comic novel" in Fielding, Smollett and Sterne, with its radical mingling of languages and modes of discourse, its grossness, its liking for clowns and rogues, its picaresque looseness, its impatience with ideology.[1] In all this there was a deep resemblance to Rabelais whose work was for him a fundamental prototype. Now, clearly such a position has great cogency; it would seem applicable in particular to the comic genius of Fielding. Not surprisingly, one of Bakhtin's prime examples is Fielding's *Tom Jones*, a text which, in its ribald humor, lends itself rather well to treatment as a kind of carnival.

Bakhtin does not, however, discuss Fielding's first novel, *Joseph Andrews* – in the Preface to which he in fact developed his definition of the new genre. In a way that text could have suited his purpose equally well. Though it is based on a biblical story, that of Joseph and his brothers and, more particularly, Joseph's escape from the amorous designs of Potiphar's wife (Genesis 39), the treatment is wildly comical. The joke is to present a healthy young man of the eighteenth century seeking to preserve his "virtue" by heroically withstanding the sexual advances of his mistress. So far this is pure parody and would serve as an example for the "comic-parodic reprocessing" of biblical texts to which Bakhtin draws our attention in Rabelais. But this does not exhaust the significance of the biblical typology in *Joseph Andrews*, nor is parody its main aspect. I will argue that there is also a genuine process of accommodation and imitation. This aspect of *Joseph Andrews* would evidently not have agreed so well with Bakhtin's view of the limited role of the Bible in the history of the novel.

Let us note first the nature and extent of Fielding's use of the biblical analogy. Critics have paid somewhat perfunctory attention to the clear indications given early in *Joseph Andrews* that its hero is meant to recall the career of his biblical namesake. When Joey is called to Lady Booby's bedroom early in the book, we are told that "for a good reason we shall hereafter call [him] JOSEPH"[2] – the good reason being that he is going to act the part of Joseph in the Bible resisting the seduction of the wife of Potiphar. The second indication comes from Joseph himself in the second letter he writes to his sister Pamela after he is dismissed from his situation as a consequence of resisting Lady Booby's advances:

> I hope I shall copy your Example, and that of Joseph my Name's-sake; and maintain my Virtue against all Temptations.
>
> (I, x)

This puts the biblical story on the same level as Richardson's *Pamela* as a shaping influence on the novel. The biblically conscious reader (which of course means Fielding's average reader in 1742) would have seen Joseph from the beginning as fulfilling the role of the biblical knight of Chastity. If he had been especially alert, he might even have noted that, like his biblical namesake at the beginning of his career (Genesis 37:2), Joseph Andrews too was 17 years old when he was promoted to be Lady Booby's footboy.

Martin C. Battestin has given more attention than others to this dimension of the novel, noting that Fielding is following the pattern set by the latitudinarian divines of his day and earlier (notably Isaac Barrow and Samuel Clarke) who had proposed Joseph and Abraham as paradigms respectively of Chastity and Charity, or "Faith expressed in works."[3] Here we have the key to the functions of the twin heroes of Fielding's novel. Abraham Adams, like Joseph, is clearly linked to his biblical namesake. In Book IV, Chapter 8, with explicit reference to the trial of Abraham in Genesis 22, he will be morally tested by the reported death of his son Jacky. Like the story of Joseph and Potiphar's wife, this episode of the 'sacrifice' of Isaac too is handled in low-mimetic, the extravagant grief of Adams comically belying his earlier sermon on fortitude in the face of disaster. But surely Battestin is right in claiming that Fielding, in drawing upon these figures from the Genesis narratives, is developing a kind of "Christian epic"; the intention is not wholly or chiefly to burlesque the biblical characters and episodes but to promote a Pelagian emphasis on the value of innocence and active philanthropy as a religion for ordinary folk in the world of everyday.[4]

Battestin has here pointed the way to a correct reading of the novel but the web of biblical allusions is even more sustained than he has indicated. As we shall see, it goes far beyond the episode of Joseph and the lustful wife of Potiphar and encompasses the novel as a whole, its frame and composition. It may even be suggested that Fielding's use of the biblical model has implications for the novel genre as such, of which *Joseph Andrews* is an early, crucial example.

2

Shortly after his dismissal from Lady Booby's service, Joseph, having set out on foot from their London home, is waylaid by two thieves in a narrow lane. They strip him naked and cast him into a ditch (I, xii). The parallel with the adventures of the biblical hero (Genesis 37:23,24) who is set upon by his brothers, stripped of his coat and cast into a pit is patent. The motif of the divesting of Joseph in Fielding's novel in fact begins with the (twice-mentioned) stripping of his livery earlier on (Chapters ix, x). The livery will remind us of the biblical Joseph's "coat of many colours." Indeed, the liveried servants of the town with whom Joseph had become acquainted in Chapter iv are there described as "party-coloured Brethren." After being beaten and left naked in the ditch by the robbers, Joseph is soon rescued (Chapter xii) and given a ride in a passing stagecoach (though with great reluctance on the part of the travelers and the coachman). The stagecoach is surely meant to recall the caravan of the Midianite merchants who, in the biblical narrative (37:28), "drew and lifted up Joseph out of the pit" and took him down to Egypt. Joseph Andrews is now taken by his rescuers to Tow-wouse's inn where he is presumed close to death. His clothing is later discovered in a bundle which had been tossed to the side of the road and the livery which it contains is recognized by Parson Adams who thereby identified the "dying" man, again reminding us of the continuation of the biblical narrative where Jacob recognizes the coat of his supposedly dead son (37:33). This is not the first nor

is it the last time that Adams acts toward Joseph *in loco parentis.*
But of course Joseph Andrews has a real father too, Mr Wilson,
from whom he had been cruelly separated for many years, precisely
as Joseph had been separated from his father Jacob. In Fielding's
novel too the child had been kidnapped at an early age (like his
biblical namesake) "by some wicked travelling People whom they
call *Gipsies*" – the witty modern equivalent of the Ishmaelites or
Midianites involved in the biblical story of the sale of Joseph into
Egypt. The reunion of father and son after the lapse of years
and their tearful embraces (IV, xvi) will mark, in the novel as in
the Bible story (46:29), the happy ending of the narrative. But
before that consummation is reached there are additional episodes,
especially concerning the divesting and reinvesting of Joseph,
which bear on the analogy.

   In Book IV, Chapters iv and v Joseph and Fanny are about to
be committed to Bridewell through Lady Booby's machinations
(Potiphar's wife all over again) when unexpectedly Joseph is raised
to eminent social rank through the discovery that he is now directly
related to Lady Booby through the marriage of his sister Pamela
to her nephew. In this dramatic change of status, special emphasis is given to the matter of clothing. Joseph Andrews is invested
in splendid clothing which Squire Booby produces from a
Cloakbag; these include "Linnen and other Necessaries." Parson
Adams's delight at Joseph's great good fortune is especially focused
on the sight of his "new Apparel." Beholding it, he

>   burst into Tears with Joy, and fell to rubbing his Hands and
>   snapping his Fingers, as if he had been mad.
>
>   (IV, v)

In the parallel episode in Genesis, Pharaoh had raised Joseph
from prison to be his viceroy and as a sign of this elevation had
placed his own ring upon his hand, had *arrayed him in fine linen*
and put a gold chain about his neck. (41:42). In fact the whole
sustained motif of dressing and undressing, so central to Fielding's *fabula*, has its origin in the Bible narrative of the career of
Joseph.[5]

   So far the details of the analogy are fairly straightforward. There
is however, one subtler application of the clothing motif in which
the story of Potiphar's wife is again seemingly adverted to, though
now from an unexpected angle. In fact it seems at first sight to

be a parodic inversion of the Bible story. In the final night-adventures in Booby Hall (IV, xiv) there is a great deal of coming and going between the ladies' bedrooms. It begins with Beau Didapper, the upper-class rake and scoundrel, who decides to make an attempt on Fanny's chastity by presenting himself to her in the dark as Joseph. He mistakes the room and leaps into bed instead with Mrs Slipslop. She tries to capitalize on the opportunity offered but when Didapper, now made aware of his mistake, tries to escape the clutches of the aging but lustful Slipslop, she determines to prevent him and expose him, thereby seeking, like Potiphar's wife to regain a reputation for her injured virtue:

> At that instant therefore, when he offered to leap from the Bed, she caught fast hold of his Shirt, at the same time roaring out, 'O thou Villain! who hast attacked my Chastity, and I believe ruined me in my Sleep; I will swear a Rape against thee, I will prosecute thee with the utmost Vengeance.' The Beau attempted to get loose, but she held him fast . . .

He makes his escape after the precipitous entrance of Parson Adams and the confusion which ensues. Later in the evening, Lady Booby, trying to sort out the tangle of misunderstandings, sees a fine pair of diamond buttons and the torn piece of laced shirt on the floor of Mrs Slipslop's bedroom. "To whom belongs this laced Shirt and Jewels?" she cries. All this will remind us not only of the angry wife of Potiphar but also of the coat which Joseph leaves in her hands before fleeing and which she later produces in evidence. Didapper, it would appear, has taken over the role of Joseph, as he wants to, but in an upside-down context where a far from innocent "Joseph" is involved, in a sexual episode with a mistaken partner. One might want to argue that Fielding is not only echoing, but also exploding the Bible story of Joseph and Potiphar's wife.

This, however, is not quite so. For the truth is that something like this same inversion occurs in the biblical source as well. For in the interpolated story of Judah and Tamar (Genesis 38), Judah (an antitype of Joseph) has relations with his daughter-in-law, Tamar (the latter being disguised) and leaves behind him in pledge three items of his accoutrement: his signet, his bracelets and his staff. Lady Booby's question "To whom belongs this laced Shirt and Jewels?" seems to echo Tamar's challenge to Judah when her "whoredom" is discovered: "Discern, I pray thee, whose are these, the signet, the bracelets and the staff" (38:25). The link between the two stories, that of Judah and that of Joseph, through the motif of the loss of clothing or other marks of identity is an important feature of this biblical pericope. We are invited to see in the stories of the two brothers a pattern of symmetry and contrast which is more marked in the Hebrew original than in the English translation.[6] What is for Joseph a mark of honor becomes for Judah a mark of shame. When Judah sees his personal effects in the possession of Tamar, he acknowledges that shame (38:26). Conversely, Joseph is only temporarily and outwardly disgraced through the loss of his coat: in the end he will be vindicated. Both in the episode of his being stripped by his brothers and his being falsely charged by Potiphar's wife he will shine out to the reader as the just man. Through his loss, he proves his rightdoing; through a similar loss, Judah proves his wrongdoing.

Fielding it would seem has sensed the dialectical relation between the two figures: he has Beau Didapper pretend to be Joseph only to have his true identity exposed through the loss of his buttons and lace garment. There is perhaps a wider, almost Marxist reverberation here. The stripping of the "Beau" is for Fielding and for us more than just one of the night's adventures in Booby Hall; it is the symbolic end of a type and of a mode of writing which have fallen into decay. We have here another example of a biblical story mediating for us the dialogic encounter, as Bakhtin would term it, between different languages and different social orders. All that is left of the grand cavalier of an earlier day (and of the romances of an earlier day) is his torn laced shirt and diamond buttons. He has departed in nakedness and ignominy. Joseph Andrews, whose rise he had sought to prevent and whose identity he had usurped, will gain the prize and he will do so without the need for false accoutrements. The loss of Joseph's livery in the early part of the book turns out to be no disgrace but the prelude to the disclosure of his true merit and standing in the world, a standing which will ultimately be confirmed by his being invested in appropriately honorable dress.

3

What all this suggests is that we have here a patterning of episodes by the well-known Augustan device of "Imitation". The reader enjoyed recognizing the links with a classical source drawn from antiquity and given a witty but not entirely frivolous application to contemporary life. In like fashion, the eighteenth-century reader enjoyed the systematic echoing of Juvenal's Third Satire in Dr Johnson's "London" or the same technique in Pope's *Imitations of Horace*. Earlier on, Dryden had wittily applied biblical narrative material to a contemporary political situation in "Absalom and Achitopel" (1681). The pleasure was in recognizing the well-known contours of the biblical story in the doings of people of one's own society. In the mode of realism that Fielding chose to practice, the device of "Imitation" was necessarily less direct, the borrowed episodes more deeply buried in the texture of his narrative. But they are there just the same. And it is more than a matter of detail: it is a matter of the total movement and shape of the source as Fielding and the latitudinarians understood it. He is writing a moral fable in which injustice and inhumanity will finally be overcome and Charity will prevail. Adams amusingly falls asleep during Joseph's sermon on Charity – a key passage in the novel (III, vi) – but the discourse in itself is not a joke, as Joseph, clearly speaking for the narrator, is at pains to emphasize:

> I defy the wisest Man in the World to turn a true good Action into Ridicule. I defy him to do it. He who should endeavour it, would be laughed at himself, instead of making others laugh.

Fielding is writing a novel in which the reviled and the lowly are raised above their enemies, in which true virtue is rewarded, not in the next world but in this. These were the directions taken by the Genesis narratives of Abraham and Joseph and they become a principle of order, at once moral and aesthetic, in the novel as Fielding conceived it. Abraham Adams is the righteous man of the first Psalm who walks not in the counsel of the wicked nor sits in the seat of the scornful. His life bears witness to the notion that goodness will prevail and that it is the business of fiction to see that it does.

Fielding's novel is thus a kind of "Pilgrim's Progress" but unlike

Bunyan's masterpiece it develops its moral fable in terms of everyday choices in the world we know. Bunyan's heroes only seem
to have adventures on the road – that road is really a mystic
path leading to the heavenly Jerusalem. In *The Holy War* Bunyan
gives us the Old Testament imagery of battles, the noise of the
soldiers and the shouting of the captains; he echoes Psalm 68 in
the phrase "he hath led captivity captive." But these images are
employed as trope, divorced from their physical and historical setting. There is no real war; the warlike doings of men are
transcended, even condemned as vain. Their only value is as
symbols for the victory of Emmanuel (Christ) over Diabolus (the
Devil). Fielding's procedure is in this more like that of Defoe;
his heroes are not shadowy types, they belong to our own world.
And if, at the same time, they demand to be related to Joseph
and Abraham in the Bible, it is because those biblical figures themselves are perceived more as *exempla* of virtue than as types, *figurae*.
Every charitable man has a touch of Abraham and every chaste
youth, a touch of Joseph. This is the way of metonymy; it works
not by symbolic substitution, but by a direct concrete relation
subsisting between a master narrative and its derived narratives.
The substantial reality of neither is transcended.[7]

There are of course Christian overtones in *Joseph Andrews* which
bear a typological interpretation. Ignoring the more obvious
parallel with the story of Joseph and his brothers, William Empson
insisted that

> Fielding never made a stronger direct copy of a Gospel par-
> able than in *Joseph Andrews* (I, xii) when Joseph is dying naked
> in the snow and an entire coach-load finds worldly reasons
> for letting him die.[8]

In this episode the postilion who gives Joseph his overcoat is
acting the part of the good Samaritan in the gospel story (Luke
10:30f). And that allusion is surely there. Moreover, by being
associated with the story of the Good Samaritan, Joseph no doubt
becomes here a type of Christ just as the biblical Joseph, sold by
his brethren, had become a type of Christ in some of the early
writings of the Church. Nevertheless, the main narrative model
here and elsewhere in the novel is the story of Joseph in the
book of Genesis; other symbolic patterns are grafted onto that.
There is a similar conflation of sources in the episode of the final

discovery of Joseph's identity. When Mr Wilson identifies the
strawberry mark on Joseph's breast, Parson Adams rubs his hands
and cries out, "Hic est quem quaeris, inventus est." The reference is to the story of the Prodigal Son (Luke 15) as well as to
the meeting between Jesus and Mary Magdalene beside the empty
tomb (John 20:15). But here again these are surely no more than
overtones; the prime analogy is with the reunion of Joseph with
his father Jacob which, whilst it could bear a transferred Christian meaning, retains in Fielding's text its substantiality as an
object of "Imitation." It is less the union of the upper-case Son
and *the* Father than of a lower-case son and father, that is, any
son and father estranged from one another and reunited by the
well-known devices of romantic recognition. These devices are
given added force by the biblical vision which requires that good
men are seen to prosper in an ill world.

   Metonymy versus typology is in a way the point at issue between
the latitudinarian divines and those of a more evangelical bent such
as the Methodists, Whitefield and Wesley. To do good in the
world was for liberal Anglicans (whose views went back to Robert
South and Jeremy Taylor) the way to heaven: one could be aided
by reading the Bible as a collection of commands and moral *exempla*
directly applicable to the worldly space we occupy. A more evangelical approach sees the earthly meanings of the Bible transcended
in the interests of the doctrine of Grace. In Fielding this very
issue of Works versus Grace is debated between Parson Trulliber
and Parson Adams (II, xiv). That chapter should be read as a
debate between Charity as symbol ("I know what Charity is, better
than to give to Vagabonds") and Charity as practical command
linking the doings of the figures of the Bible with those required
of men in the world we know. It should also be read as a debate
between two fictional models, the one aiming at a kind of
inward conciliation, the other seeking a correspondence between
outer and inner events. We recall that *The Pilgrim's Progress*
begins with Christian being warned against seeking salvation by
way of Mount Sinai which is the path of Morality counselled by
Mr Wordly-Wiseman. He must instead pass through the little
wicket-gate of the Covenant of Grace: his victories will be psychological victories. Parson Adams is Fielding's rehabilitation of
Mr Worldly-Wiseman for an audience which had learned from
Tillotson, Hoadly and Clarke to prefer a rational, this-worldly
model of salvation. One direction it would seem is represented

by Richardson and takes us forward to Emily Brontë, Conrad and Lawrence; the other begins evidently with Fielding and points forward to Jane Austen, Dickens and George Eliot. Both can claim scriptural authority and indeed they have their beginnings in two different kinds of "Imitation" of Scripture practiced at the beginning of the history of the novel.

In this connection, students of Fielding have overlooked an important item of bibliography.[9] Five years before the publication of *Joseph Andrews*, the eccentric and highly unorthodox rational divine, William Whiston, a friend of Clarke and Hoadly and possibly the model of Goldsmith's Vicar of Wakefield, published his monumental translation of Josephus's *The Antiquities of the Jews*.[10] This together with *The Wars of the Jews* established itself quickly and would often be found standing on the shelf beside the Family Bible in good middle-class homes. It would be surprising if Fielding had not come across it and indeed a reading of the career of the biblical Joseph as presented in Book II, Chapters ii–viii of the *Antiquities* strongly suggests that Josephus's version as translated by Whiston was in Fielding's mind when he penned *The History of the Adventures of Joseph Andrews . . .*

Josephus gives an extended "novelistic" account of the story of Joseph and his brothers laying special emphasis on the episode involving Potiphar's wife which occupies a long chapter in place of the few verses devoted to it in the biblical text. Josephus offers in fact a midrashic amplification of the episode giving special attention to "his beauty of body", his "virtue" and "chastity" – all terms repeated several times in the course of the story of Joseph's life as told by Josephus. Josephus gives, like Fielding, two separate meetings between Joseph and his mistress. At the end of the first meeting, the effect of Joseph's refusal is summed up:

> But this opposition of *Joseph's*, when she did not expect it, made her still more violent in her love to him: and she was sorely beset with this naughty passion, so she resolved to compass her design by a second attempt.
>
> (iv)

The general similarity of the language to that of Fielding is notable. According to Josephus, Potiphar's wife contrives an occasion for the second attempt on Joseph's virtue by pretending to be sick and is thus left alone in the house with him. Josephus says nothing about her being in bed – this is Fielding's development of the hint – but the notion of sickness had been taken up by Fielding at the beginning of Book I, Chapter v of *Joseph Andrews*. There we are told that Lady B. after her husband's death remained "confined to her House as closely as if she herself had been attacked by some violent Disease."

The second and crucial meeting between Joseph and his mistress in Josephus includes a long speech by Potiphar's wife answered with a equally long statement by Joseph. Some phrases stand out as strikingly similar to Fielding. She tells him that "she was forced, tho' she were his mistress, to condescend beneath her dignity." (We may compare Joseph's reply to Lady B.'s invitation to kiss her: "I should think your Ladyship condescended a great deal below yourself" [Chapter viii].) Potiphar's wife according to Josephus proceeds to warn him against "preferring the reputation of chastity before his mistress." Of Joseph's reply we are told:

> neither did pity dissuade *Joseph* from his chastity; nor did fear compel him to a compliance with her; but he opposed her solicitations, and did not yield to her threatenings, and was afraid to do an ill thing; and chose to undergo the sharpest punishment, rather than to enjoy his present advantages, by doing what his own conscience knew would justly deserve that he die for it.

With less gravity, Fielding has his hero declare

> that he would never imagine the least wicked thing against her, and that he would rather die a thousand deaths than give her any reason to suspect him.
>
> (I, v)

(And in the continuation of Fielding's account in Chapter viii: "'What would you think, *Joseph*, if I admitted you to kiss me?' *Joseph* reply'd, 'he would sooner die than have any such thought.'")

Joseph's speech in Whiston's translation of Josephus though detailed and well reasoned (he introduces some advice about the pleasures she might enjoy by remaining faithful to her husband's bed), has little effect and Josephus continues:

Joseph, by saying this and more, tried to restrain the *violent passion* of the woman; and to reduce her affections *within the rule of reason*: but she grew more ungovernable, and earnest in the matter: and since she despaired of persuading him, *she laid her hands upon him* and had a mind to force him. (emphasis added)

The conjunction of "violence" and "passion" occurs several times in Fielding's handling of the story but specifically in Lady B.'s exclamation following her second interview with Joseph – "Whither doth this violent Passion hurry us?" As for the notion of Potiphar's wife laying her hands on Joseph, this is a detail originating in Josephus; it does not occur in the biblical text which only speaks of her seizing his garment. Readers of Fielding will recall that Lady B. in her first and also her second interview with Joseph "accidentally laid her hand on his" and in the chapter that follows, Mrs Slipslop, a burlesque version of the wife of Potiphar, "prepare(d) to lay her violent amorous Hands on the poor *Joseph.*"

Fielding remembers Josephus again towards the end of the novel in the scene describing the reunion of Joseph and his father, Mr Wilson (IV, xv). Not being yet aware of the circumstances of their relationship, Joseph did not express at first the same "extravagant Rapture" as his father though "he returned some Warmth to his Embraces." This same distinction as to the intensity of feeling expressed by father and son respectively is made by Josephus (it is not in the biblical account) who remarks that "*Jacob* almost fainted away" whilst Joseph, though he was likewise moved by the encounter, "yet was he not wholly overcome with his passion, as his father was" (Josephus II, vii).

4

The details of the indebtedness to Whiston's Josephus are of less interest than the affinity itself and its implications for the kind of art form that Fielding was developing. What was it that attracted Fielding about the version of the story given by Josephus? Why did he not just make do with the Bible story? We are here I think at the heart of Fielding's problem as a latter-day cultivated Englishman forging a new literary genre with the help of the narrative resources of the book of Genesis. The Bible is important,

indeed indispensable, for the new middle-class literary sensibility, and yet somehow it won't do. The whole tradition of
epic and romance revolts against it. Longinus taught the men of
the eighteenth century to appreciate the sublimity of "God said,
Let there be light." But what was one to do with "Moab is my
washpot"? And how was one to handle the brutal directness of
the Joseph story – "His master's wife cast her eyes upon Joseph;
and she said, Lie with me"? Tolstoy admired the simplicity and
boldness of that verse. How much better it was, he remarked,
than the way of the modern writer who would feel it necessary
to describe

> the pose and attire of Potiphar's wife and how, adjusting the
> bracelet on her left arm, she said, "Come to me."[11]

All such details were, he claimed superfluous. Nevertheless, in
his novelistic procedure Tolstoy himself provided a wealth of just
such accordant effects – they were evidently far from superfluous for him even when writing a simple tale like *Father Sergius*.
The problem was to tap the power of the Bible story, what
Auerbach calls "the intensity of the personal history" of Joseph
who is, he says "really in the pit"[12] and yet somehow overcome
its harshness. This harshness is a matter of diction but it it also
much more than that; it is a matter of tone, sentiment and mores.
There is an incompatibility to be overcome when the western
sensibility confronts the undiluted text of scripture. That text is,
in a word, too naked. Now Josephus had found a way of cover-
ing its nakedness. He had performed this service for the Hellenized
Jews and gentiles of his time and in Whiston's translation with
its Augustan flavour (as in the example of Joseph trying to "reduce
[the lady's] affections within the rule of reason") he could help
to do the same for Fielding's generation. In balancing the Bible
story against the "midrash" of Josephus, Fielding had found a
strategy for dealing with the tension governing the relation of
the western writer to the biblical text. For Josephus had introduced a certain opacity to reduce its glare, a smoothness to miti-
gate the harshness of its contours, a mode of amplification to
arrest the suddenness if its transitions and an ease of manner to
reduce the severity of its moral judgments. All this is of greater
importance than the narrative particulars which Fielding evidently
drew from Josephus. It is hardly an exaggeration to say that

Josephus helped Fielding solve the main problem of designing a "comic Epic-Poem in Prose."

It may be worthwhile returning for a moment to that definition of Fielding's. It occurs of course in the "Author's Preface" to *Joseph Andrews*. What does he mean by a "comic Epic-Poem in Prose?" In its context the phrase is designed to make us think of the novel as a kind of comic version of the *Odyssey* (with heroes like mock versions of Achilles or Hercules); it may also rightly be explicated by reference to the mock-heroic in *Don Quixote*, a model to which Fielding is demonstrably attached here and elsewhere. He announces on the title page after all that he is imitating the manner of Cervantes. But much of the emphasis should be on the last word. The new form which Fielding (like Richardson and Defoe) was developing was essentially one that brought down the high matter of poetry and rhetoric to the homely accents of *prose*. In this it was in line with the new scientific spirit of the age which called for a correspondence of words to things. "The function of language," says Ian Watt, "is much more largely referential in the novel than in other literary forms."[13] And as we have noted earlier, the new prose discourse for the novel may also be traced back to the style of simplicity, the *sermo humilis* of the early Middle Ages which, as Auerbach has so well illustrated, was often modeled on the biblical narratives.

And yet Fielding does not quite give us the *sermo humilis*. It is there and it is not there. His narrative voice is not really like that of the chronicler of the martyrdom of Perpetua quoted by Auerbach. Nor is it like Augustine's who tells us in his *Confessions* that when he became a Christian and turned his mind to the scriptures he had to learn to "bend down [my] neck to its humble pace . . . for the swelling of my pride could not bear its humility."[14] Fielding does not bend his neck. His humility is tempered with the archness of the mock sublime. If we examine his definition carefully we shall see that it contradicts itself. The new kind of narrative will be "Prose" but it will also be "Poem"; likewise, the term "comic Epic" suggests that there will be both inflation and deflation. Immediately after offering us his definition, he finds it necessary to qualify his insistence on prose. It will evidently not be quite Wordsworth's "language of men". Whilst excluding the high manner from his *sentiments*, he will reintroduce it, he says, into his *diction* in the form of Burlesque. All this suggests a certain ambivalence towards the *sermo humilis* as well as an ambivalence to the text of the Bible as its source and authority. That ambivalence finds its expression in the way that Fielding leans simultaneously on Josephus and the Bible itself.

There are other ways of expressing this dialectic. We should consider in this connection the foregrounding of the motif of dress throughout the novel. At all points we seem to have to do with the putting on and putting off of clothing. Early in the story we have Joseph being stripped of his livery and soon afterwards, as we have noted, he is left naked by the robbers; the novel ends with Fanny putting off her garments as she prepares herself for her bridegroom – "for as all her Charms were the Gifts of Nature, she could divest herself of none" (IV, xvi). As in *King Lear* nakedness signifies vulnerability, but also truth, authenticity and . . . Nature. The sight of Edgar's nakedness had been the occasion for Lear's fundamental anagnorisis – he confronts "unaccommodated man" himself. And yet dress is necessary too for authenticity; often it is the only evidence of our true identity:

> Allow not nature more than nature needs
> Man's life is cheap as beast's

– declares Lear. This is true of Fielding's novel also. Joseph Andrews does not represent "unaccommodated man"; he achieves his true place in the world when he is invested in appropriate garments. Beau Didapper will be stripped of his false honours whilst Joseph will be clothed in scarlet. That is in a way the high point of the story. It may be suggested that we have here a reflexive use of this metaphor, Fielding seeking through it to reconcile the contrary demands of nakedness and ornament implicit in the genre which he is seeking to shape. In the same Author's Preface, Fielding actually speaks of the "Dress of Poetry" in analogy of "the Dress of Men." It need hardly be said that such terms as "ornament" and "nakedness" were an inseparable part of the discussion of prose rhetoric both in Fielding's day and earlier. In the oft-quoted passage from Thomas Sprat's *History of the Royal Society* (1667) we hear of the Society requiring from all its members "a close naked, natural way of speaking . . . preferring the Language of Artizans, Countrymen, and Merchants, before that of Wits, or Scholars.[15]

It will be seen that we have here something like a four-term homology in which simple is to artificial language as nakedness is to dress. We could go further and suggest that they both correspond to a further antinomy, that between Artizans (and Merchants) on the one hand and Wits (or Beaux) on the other. In short there is a class distinction implied in the passage from Sprat as the new middle class appropriates to itself the style of nakedness and the upper classes are condemned for their false ornaments. That sociological distinction is present in Fielding's novel also as an aspect of the confrontation or confusion of styles. From this point of view the novel accords with Bakhtin's notion of social dialogics.[16] But it is not as simple as that. Didapper and Joseph also exchange roles. If at one point Didapper aspires to take the place of Joseph, as we have seen, so Joseph aspires to take the place of Didapper, assuming some of the dress and symbols of the upper class. In this inevitably he will betray the ideal of simplicity. Like Shakespeare, Spenser and Milton before him, Fielding has been caught in the inevitable dilemma of the Hebraic versus the Hellenic components of western literary tradition. Milton's hero in *Paradise Regained*, Book IV condemns Greek ornament and lavishes his praises on Hebrew nakedness but he does so in all the lofty terms of art. If Milton could not resolve the paradox, we should not expect Fielding to resolve it either.

However if Fielding ultimately leaves us with a paradox, we should be grateful to him for having defined its terms as clearly as he does. His ultimate statement comes by way of the pastoral mode. This is the mode evoked in the description of Fanny stripping for bed in the final chapter of the novel:

> She was soon undrest; for she had no Jewels to deposite in their Caskets, nor fine Laces to fold with the nicest Exactness. Undressing to her was properly discovering, not putting off Ornaments; For as all her Charms were the Gifts of Nature, she could divest herself of none. How, Reader, shall I give thee an adequate Idea of this lovely young Creature! the Bloom of Roses and Lillies might a little illustrate her Complexion, or their Smell her Sweetness: but to comprehend her entirely, conceive Youth, Health, Bloom, Beauty, Neatness, and Innocence in her Bridal-bed; conceive all these in their utmost Perfection, and you may place the charming *Fanny's* Picture before your Eyes.
>
> (IV, xvi)

The irony of this passage is that the language puts on its finest dress, its ornaments of style, whilst at the same time and at exactly the same place Fanny divests herself of her dress and ornaments. The language is here the most brocaded, the least naked in the book and we should add that it is at the greatest remove from the simplicity and directness of the Hebrew narrative from which the story of Joseph had been taken. Pastoral here brings Art to the aid of Nature. The passage seeks to deceive us by the cunning inversion of its signifiers, but we are not deceived. Perhaps in this it acts out the nature of dress itself which half reveals and half conceals. Even as it denies Fanny's need of them the passage piles up before our enchanted gaze the riches of Caskets, Laces, Charms and Gifts. We know it is the triumph of words only, but we revel in it as we escape the self-denying ordinance which the Royal Society had imposed on its members or which the Puritan orators had imposed on themselves. The climax of inversion comes in the magnificently self-contradictory sentence:

Undressing to her was properly discovering, not putting off Ornaments: For as all her Charms were the Gifts of Nature, she could divest herself of none.

The ambiguity of "discovering" is a masterstroke. It signifies uncovering as well as revealing. What we thought to be uncovering we "discover" to be the displaying of treasures. We have exchanged Fanny for "the charming Fanny's picture," that is, Fanny fixed and immortalized in a literary tradition which she can share with those shepherdesses who always turned out to be ladies in disguise. Through her, Fielding defines a nakedness which will not require us to divest ourselves of Charms, Gifts or Ornaments. They are all in the passage. Indeed, like Fanny, we have not put them off, we have put them on. We have put them on even more grandly than before, because from now they will be signs not of Artifice but of Nature. As such, they can be draped charmingly over the horns of our dilemma.

4
Natural Piety in *Silas Marner*

1

In Genesis 40 Joseph interprets the butler's dream: the three vine branches are three days; after three days he would be restored to his office as Pharaoh's cupbearer. But the Rabbis in commenting on this chapter creatively enlarged Joseph's interpretive range; instead of the single exposition of the dream given in the biblical text, they proposed at least eight alternative interpretations, all of them different and all of them valid. Joseph, seen as the midrashist *par excellence*, knew them all but kept quiet because these interpretations were intended not for the butler but for different audiences![1] This, it may be noted, is the nature of "midrash." The text becomes the point of departure for a multiplicity of interpretations none of which is held to be final or exclusive. In this midrash sharply differs from allegory; there is no single "correct" midrash. Essentially, as Max Kadushin has argued, each midrash implies "that other interpretations are possible." This he defines as "the principle of indeterminacy." David Stern finds "indeterminacy" (with its post-modern connotations) misleading. He prefers to speak of "midrashic polysemy." But all agree that this mode of exegesis is marked by openness and bounty – a capacity to include multiple and even contradictory meanings.[2]

The works we have been considering exhibit and seem to allow for precisely this fertility of invention in regard to their biblical sources. *Robinson Crusoe*, a kind of midrash on Jonah, implies Melville's freedom of invention in the following century. *Joseph Andrews* is a reading of the Joseph story embodied in one concrete human instance, one contingent situation or tangle of situations and, paraphrasing Kadushin, we could say that it implies the possibility of any number of other readings, involving other

tangles equally human and equally contingent. It implies Thomas
Mann's freedom of invention in relation to the same story two
hundred years later. In short every such interpretive fiction is a
new beginning. It says, "Read me: I am saying what has not been
said before; and read me too because I will remind you of what
you have read before; and read me too because you will be
reminded of me when you read the next story that reminds you
of what I remind you of."

But again we may ask ourselves, is not such intertextuality the
mark of prose fiction generally? Why insist on a special category
for biblically inspired novels? Do not novels constantly remind
us of other novels? Conrad's *The Secret Agent* is demonstrably
indebted to Dickens's portrayals of nineteenth-century London.[3]
Arnold Bennett's *The Old Wives' Tale* professedly emulates the
example of Guy du Maupassant's *Une Vie*. Saul Bellow borrows
the name of his hero and many other features of *Herzog* from
Joyce's *Ulysses*. It would seem that a web of intertextuality linking
novels with other novels that precede and follow them, is the
rule rather than the exception. Novelists rewrite their predecessors.

What would then be the justification for selecting and setting
apart a group of novels built on biblical models? And if we have
given this particular mode of "imitation" the term "midrash," is
there anything to distinguish such midrash from the creative use
of fictional models generally? The answer is that for the works
we are considering, the biblical source is more than a model on
which one may base one's own free invention; it is a text to be
interpreted and reinterpreted, to be returned to obsessively as
the vessel of still unrevealed meanings. The repeated attempts
of Defoe's hero, Robinson Crusoe to understand the meaning
of a verse from Psalm 50 in light of his ongoing experience
suggests that we have to do with a source which compels, which
exercises authority. The relation to it will be more genuinely
dialogic than the relation of Bennett to Maupassant, because the
source text will be urged to speak, will be argued with, listened
to, or resisted. It will have an independent voice in the discourse.

Father Mapple's sermon on Jonah, standing near the beginning of Melville's *Moby Dick*, would do as a paradigm. Here the
interpretive relation is foregrounded and the image of the great
whale, the controlling, multivalent symbol of the book as a whole,
is set before us as a text to be expounded and remembered.
Moreover, the theme of the sermon is the impossibility of escape.

The story of Jonah as related by Father Mapple symbolizes not only sin, retribution and repentance; it also symbolizes what we may term hermeneutic constraint. There is no escape from the biblical source text; it compels our attention as the preacher compels the attention of his audience; it haunts us, it confines us much as Jonah is confined "in the sides of the ship" or in the belly of the whale. This is like the situation of Robinson on his island or of Malamud's "Fixer," Yakov in his prison. They too are "imprisoned" in the text. From this point of view, Kafka's *The Trial* where Joseph K. is held in bondage by a writ of condemnation, the contents of which are never divulged, is not only a kind of midrash on Job, as Northrop Frye has observed;[4] it is also a midrash on midrash. It comes to tell us that we are not totally free. The biblical source has a power which energizes and liberates the imagination, but it also has an authority which limits and compels. It is this dialectic of freedom and authority in the relation of the late-born author to an originary text which is never lost sight of, that distinguishes "midrash" from other freer modes of invention or reinvention.

What should be emphasized is that this peculiarly obligating power of the biblical source or sources is not conditional on the author's personal commitment – his acceptance for instance of the divine origin of those texts. I will argue that *Silas Marner* is probably the most biblically-charged and biblically-haunted novel of its century, and yet George Eliot at the time of its composition in 1860 was and had been for some years, a professed agnostic. The issue seems to be the nature of the ancient text itself and the kind of contract with the late-born author which it seems to require. It demands importunately to be interpreted and reinterpreted.[5] Other texts, ancient and less ancient, do not make such demands on us, nor do they make such offers. The biblical text holds the reader with the promise of some further meaning still to be disclosed in the future if he will continue to give it his unremitting attention.

2

In this respect the hero of *Silas Marner* is like the author of his book. Silas, the weaver of Raveloe, whilst he had broken with evangelical Christianity, had not rejected the Bible along with that.

Paradoxically, the biblical language is used to express the break itself! In speaking to Dolly Winthrop in Chapter xvi, Silas recalls the evil done to him by his friend William Dean when they were both members of the Lantern Yard conventicle, an iniquity which left him friendless and bitter for many years. There was no longer a God of righteousness in whom he could believe. "That," he said, "was what fell on me like as if it had been red-hot iron." And he continues:

> because, you see, there was nobody as cared for me nor clave to me above nor below. And him as I'd gone out and in wi' for ten year and more, since when we were lads and went halves – mine own familiar friend in whom I trusted, had lifted up his heel again' me, and worked to ruin me.

The biblical language and parallelism ("nobody as cared for me or clave to me") give the passage its particular solemnity, but this is not just a matter of general coloring: there is also the literal echoing of Psalm 41 where the relevant verses read:

> All that hate me whisper together against me: against me do they devise my hurt. An evil disease, say they, cleaveth fast unto him: and now that he lieth he shall rise up no more. Yea, mine own familiar friend in whom I trusted, which did eat of my bread, hath lifted up his heel against me.
>
> (verses 7–9)

Silas here formulates his troubles in the language of the Psalms. Whilst his bitterness at the outcome of the casting of lots and the evil which he had met from the members of the Lantern Yard community had led to the loss of his faith (as he says: "there is no just God that governs the earth righteously"), it had manifestly not led him to abandon the biblical sources of that faith.

Indeed we may see Psalm 41 as a key to the understanding of Silas's crisis and its outcome. The novel as a whole becomes, in one sense, an interpretation of that psalm. In particular, as the story develops, we are made to feel the force of the continuation of the verses quoted above: "And as for me, thou upholdest me in mine integrity, and settest me before thy face for ever" (12). Silas does not cite this verse, but it nevertheless seems to shape the novel, so that it becomes a moral history in which there is both judgment and reward. "There's dealings" says Silas, or, as Dolly Winthrop puts it in her more stumbling fashion, there's "them above." Whilst George Eliot had no room in her "Religion of Humanity" for a personal God who enters into a covenant with Man, such relations and concepts are, so to speak forced upon her, or rather they force their way into the discourse through the narrator's dialogic encounter with his biblical sources. The result is that whilst theoretically she might have been a determinist like Hardy or like Ludwig Feuerbach,[6] when she came to construct her personal universe, it turned out to be ruled not by fate or by Hardy's Chorus of the Ironic Spirits, but by the categories of punishment, redemption and reward. Moral decisions are taken with a kind of biblical solemnity. We carry the burden of our past deeds and they will bear down also on our future.

We have spoken of hermeneutic continuity – biblical stories we said demand to be reinterpreted and reunderstood. In this respect the ancient text is, as we noted earlier, a revenant, constantly returning on the late-born author and demanding his attention. But it transpires that such continuity is not only a structural aspect of the discourse, it is also to an important degree the theme of the discourse. When Dolly Winthrop hears of some of the strange practices of the Lantern Yard conventicle, she wonders whether theirs was the same Bible as the one to be found in the parish church of Raveloe. Silas assures her that it was:

> "And yourn's the same Bible, you're sure o' that Master Marner – the Bible, as you brought wi' you from that country – it's the same as what they've got at church, and what Eppie's a-learning to read in?" "Yes," said Silas, "every bit the same."
>
> (Chapter xvi)

The Bible then connects Silas's earlier faith with his life in the present and future. If Eppie, the child of hope, signifies the promise of forward-looking thought – as the epigraph from Wordsworth indicates – then we are here reminded that she has been "a-learning to read" in the same Bible that Silas had known in his dark Puritan past.

The Bible looks back and looks forward, linking past with future through the modalities of moral history. *Silas Marner* defines this mode of continuity in discursive form as in the passage just quoted; it also interprets it through the fictional lives of its characters, at the same time employing in its language the specific kind of realism and economy which marks the Old Testament narratives. Like the Genesis stories or those relating to Samuel, Saul and David, *Silas Marner* is a story of trial, retribution and redemption.[7] The characters are morally tested, forced to acknowledge their trespasses. Faults hidden in the past come to light. Silas, who has suffered from malice and injustice, lives to gain a blessing. The characters come to us weighted with their previous history. Silas's personality is conditioned by what has happened to him in Lantern Yard and earlier. Similarly, Godfrey Cass's past, which he conceals from his wife, will eventually constrain him and there will be a reckoning. Providence works wonderfully and mysteriously, calling the past to remembrance, turning sin and suffering into a path of salvation.

There is throughout a sense of the momentousness of our moral choices, a momentousness too in the doings of simple people – seemingly trivial doings very often, but loaded with "the intensity of their personal history."[8] This is something that Eliot had learned not only from the Bible but, collaterally, from Wordsworth, whose "Michael" (from which she had drawn her motto) provides examples of the same phenomenon. In that poem, too, a simple act by an unlettered shepherd can take the moral weight of the universe. After Michael's only son Luke leaves him, we are told that the old shepherd returns to the sheepfold they had together begun to build:

> many and many a day he thither went,
> And never lifted up a single stone.

The detail becomes momentous, its power a function of its utter simplicity. But this is not strictly a separate influence: for it is clear that "Michael" too in its "high seriousness" recalls the Genesis narratives at every turn. Michael and his wife, with their only child born in their old age, with their simple loyalties and hopes, recall such patriarchal households as that of Abraham and Sarah. The sheepfold of which father and son lay the cornerstone is to be a covenant – "a covenant / 'Twill be between us . . ." When they are far from one another, the heap of stones, like that begun by Jacob at Bethel (Genesis 28:18) in sign of God's promises and his own, or like that raised by Laban and Jacob at Gilead (ibid. 31:51–2), will be a witness to their mutual exchange of vows. When Luke betrays his trust, it becomes the betrayal of a covenant with all the weight of tragic meaning which such a dereliction implies. George Eliot evidently sensed the biblical element in Wordsworth's poem, and she fortified and enriched it with her own first-hand understanding of the imaginative possibilities of the biblical mode of narration.

3

It may be worth pointing out some of the many specific biblical echo-structures in Eliot's novel. In their accumulated force they would seem to have had a shaping effect on the work as a whole. The coming of the infant Eppie to Silas on New Year's Eve bringing to him her gift of love has been termed a "Christ-event"[9] and perhaps there is some such typology at work here, but the biblical episode which is actually evoked in the text is the rescue of Lot from the cities of the plain in Genesis 19:

> In old days there were angels who came and took men by the hand and led them away from the city of destruction. We see no white-winged angels now. But yet men are led away from threatening destruction: a hand is put into theirs, which leads them forth gently towards a calm and bright land, so that they look no more backward; and the hand may be a little child's.
>
> (Chapter xiv)

Like the story of the rescue of Lot, Eliot's tale is one of retribution, redemption and rescue. The angel has been domesticated into a child, but the sense of the wonder and the miracle remains. There is an echo here too of the beginning of Bunyan's *The Pilgrim's Progress* where we are told that Christian fled from the City of Destruction and "looked not behind him." Critics have been right to emphasize the importance of Bunyan's presence in the novel.[10] But here too, as in the example of Wordsworth's poem, we are not speaking strictly of a separate influence, because the same biblical source stands behind Bunyan's text at this point. In the marginal gloss, Bunyan directs us to the story of Lot's escape in Genesis 19:17 as the biblical analogy for Christian's flight from the City of Destruction.

Critical from this point of view is the choice of Hephzibah as the name of the foundling who has come to Marner's door. Dolly doubts whether it is really "a christened name," but Silas retorts by saying that "it's a Bible name." Silas thus establishes the character of his new-found source of comfort by reviving the Puritan fashion of naming. The name, as David Carroll has pointed out, takes on special significance when the biblical source in Isaiah 62 is considered:

> Thou shalt no more be termed Forsaken; neither shall thy land be any more termed Desolate: but thou shalt be called Hephzibah, and thy land Beulah: for the Lord delighteth in thee, and thy land shall be married.
>
> (Isaiah 62:4)

Carroll sees in the name Hephzibah and the verse that it recalls "a reassurance to Silas that his instinctive affection for Eppie will not be betrayed."[11] It is perhaps more to the point that she comes to bring to an end the years in which he has been *Desolate* and *Forsaken*. She represents the promise of joy and delight ("My Delight is in Her"). The giving of a new name – always a covenantal act in the Bible (see Genesis 17:5, 15; 35:10–11, etc.) – confirms and establishes this promise. When Silas goes to church in the village for the very first time, it is for the christening of Eppie. We are told that he finds the Anglican forms entirely alien – "He was quite unable, by means of anything he heard or saw, to identify the Raveloe religion with his old faith" (Chapter xiv). But the biblical name he has given the child, we may say, provides the link. Unwittingly, Silas has found a text which will bind his past and future symbolically together. Not only Eppie but the biblical word by which she is henceforward denominated, has the saving function of binding his days each to each by natural piety. Eppie will compensate him for past sorrows at the same time as she will afford him the joy of "forward-looking thoughts."

Eppie is indeed the focus of the covenantal pattern of the book; she visibly signifies the redemptive process. The high-point in this respect is Chapter xix; there Eppie makes her momentous choice between Silas and Godfrey Cass, giving her loyalty firmly to the adoptive father who has cherished and reared her rather than to her natural father. It has not, to my knowledge, been noted by critics that the high drama of this chapter recalls, and is designed to recall, the story of Ruth and Naomi. In the book of Ruth also, the daughter-in-law chooses her adoptive mother, "cleaving" to her in preference to her natural kin – "Orpah kissed her mother-in-law; but Ruth clave unto her"(Ruth 1:14). Eppie's declaration of attachment to Silas and rejection of Godfrey echo that chapter of Ruth:

> Thank you, ma'am – thank you, sir, for your offers – they're very great and far above my wish. For I should have no delight i'life any more [in other words I should not be myself – "Hephzibah"] if I was forced to go away from my father, and knew he was sitting at home, a'thinking of me and feeling lone. We've been used to be happy together every day, and I can't think o' no happiness without him. And he says he'd nobody i'the world till I was sent to him, and he'd have nothing when I was gone. And he's took care of me and loved me from the first, and I'll cleave to him as long as he lives, and nobody shall ever come between him and me.

The last clause recalls the closing verse of Ruth's declaration to Naomi: "The Lord do so to me, and more also, if aught but death part thee and me" (Ruth 1:17). The effect of this echo is to bring into the novel the memory not merely of the two verses (14,17) which are literally recalled but the entire context of the story of Ruth and Naomi. Naomi who went out full and has come home empty, is the prototype of Silas, robbed of his wealth and bereft of happiness. If Ruth brings a blessing and forward-looking thoughts to the widowed and childless Naomi (see Ruth 4:15), so Eppie proves to be a blessing for barren Silas, holding to him more firmly than a natural child might have done, being better to him indeed than seven sons.[12]

There are also wider reverberations. Eliot seems to wish to endow Eppie's decision in Chapter xix with far-reaching historical significance. In her love and loyalty she represents a fundamental corrective both to the evangelical pieties and superstitions of Lantern Yard and to the purely "organic" or earthbound religion of Raveloe, on the other hand.[13] No less than Hester Prynne and Pearl in Hawthorne's *The Scarlet Letter* of the same period, her heroine is seen as "the angel and apostle of the coming revelation." Eppie's saving message is addressed to natural man, but it signifies the transcendence of the natural in the interests of a higher bond of loyalty. She also challenges a social structure based

on class and inherited privilege, in this hinting at a new conception of the relations between men. This, too, would seem to owe
something to the story of Ruth who is the ancestress of David
and whose story marks the beginning of a history which will
transform a nation.

If Eppie reminds us of Ruth, her father Godfrey Cass reminds
us of another biblical character, Judah, the ancestor of Boaz. He,
too had secretly "come in unto" a strange woman by the wayside; she had then born him a child whom he had ultimately
acknowledged as his own, but only after he had been brought to
admit his fault. The Judah-Tamar story (Genesis 38) and the related
narrative of Joseph and his brothers seem to lurk behind the history
of Godfrey and his brother Dunstan. When Dunstan's body is
found together with Silas's lost gold, the skeleton is identified
by three items of accoutrement. As Godfrey tells Nancy:

> There's his watch and seals, and there's my gold-handled
> hunting-whip, with my name on.
>
> (Chapter xviii)

The discovery of Dunstan's guilt confirmed by these three identifying pieces of property, prompts Godfrey to confess his own
hidden guilt. The Bible-conscious reader is surely reminded here
of Tamar producing the three personal items which confirm Judah's
paternity in Genesis 38:

> By the man, whose these are, am I with child: and she said,
> Discern I pray thee, whose are these, the signet, and bracelets
> and staff.
>
> (38:25)

We have here in non-comic form the same exposure of upper-
class shame as in Fielding's novel. There, Beau Didapper jumps
into Mrs Slipslop's bed leaving his diamond buttons and laced
shirt behind as evidence. The same biblical story of Judah and
Tamar is echoed in both episodes. The acknowledgment of guilt
(and in this instance the acknowledgment of fatherhood) is, of
course, the theme of the whole cluster of narratives relating to
Joseph and his brothers. Immediately following the Judah and
Tamar episode, we are told how the brothers of Joseph are tested
by a series of strange and bewildering mishaps, among them the

seizing of Simeon by the Egyptian ruler. This triggers a process of repentance, causing them to remember their crime of many years previously:

> And they said one to another, We are verily guilty concerning our brother, in that we saw the anguish of his soul, when he besought us, and we would not hear; therefore is this distress come upon us.
>
> (Genesis 42:21)

There is no logical link between the two episodes that the brothers know of, but the chords of memory are struck by the sight of another brother bound and helpless. Similarly there is no logical reason why the discovery of Dunstan's body should have led Godfrey to reveal the matter of his fatherhood of Eppie, but the laying bare of Dunstan's crime triggers off a moral process in Godfrey and causes him to reveal his own guilty secret stemming from the same period. His mood is like that of Joseph's brothers in the above-quoted passage when he says to Nancy:

> Everything comes to light, Nancy, sooner or later. When God Almighty wills it, our secrets are found out. I've lived with a secret on my mind, but I'll not keep it from you no longer.

Lot led by an angel out of the city of destruction; Judah made to confess his paternity; Ruth declaring herself for her adoptive mother against the claims of mere nature – all have something in common. All three stories, those of Lot and his daughters, Judah and Tamar, and Ruth and Naomi are (as we noted in Chapter 1 above) part of a single family history, for Lot is the primitive ancestor of Ruth, while Judah is the direct ancestor of Boaz, the husband of Ruth. All are stories of redemption. Lot's daughters, fearing total extinction, "go in" to their father, becoming by him the ancestresses of the nations of Moab and Ammon. Judah redeems Tamar from her widowed and childless state and a future is assured; finally, in the story of Ruth, redemption becomes the central theme. At the simplest level, a parcel of land belonging to Elimelech, the dead husband of Naomi, has to be redeemed. But in performing this duty Boaz also gains a wife and establishes a line which will culminate in the birth of David. Naomi, too, will be redeemed; Obed, the child of Ruth and Boaz, will

compensate her for her long years of exile and loss.[14] Remarkably, in all three stories the women take the initiative. George
Eliot had a strange insight in bringing these items of biblical
history together within the framework of her narrative. It would
be too much to suggest that she had considered the precise
structural parallels between the three stories, but she must have
sensed their common emphasis on good coming out of pain and evil.

Eliot had, it seems, lost her faith in a personal God whom one
could address in the forms established by the church but, paradoxically, she had not lost her sense of wonder at the mysterious workings of a providence that brings good out of misery in
the long passage of years. It would seem that some such movement was for her if not a religious, then an aesthetic necessity.
The great moments occur when the wonder enters into the
consciousness of the characters themselves. In Chapter xix Silas
achieves his awareness of the wonderful as the stolen money is
restored to him in time for it to serve as a dowry for Eppie –
"It's wonderful – our life is wonderful." And Godfrey, for whom
the past has come back with a sterner admonition, has a sense
of the awfulness and mystery of those same "dealings":

> The eyes of the husband and wife met with awe in them, as at
> a crisis which suspended affection.
>
>   (Chapter xviii)

4

It should be emphasized, however, that the wonder and the awe
that the characters feel do not transport them – or us – beyond
the visible and material world. Coleridge, speaking of Wordsworth's
achievement in *Lyrical Ballads*, remarks that the realism of everyday is heightened by "a feeling analogous to the supernatural"
(*Biographia Literaria*, Chapter xiv). This feeling is just as powerful
in George Eliot's story, but the realism is even greater, for the
medium of the novel is more obviously adaptable to the "unassuming commonplaces" of village life. In the nature of things,
the world of the novel is a prose world, one of material things,
of contingent particulars rather than symbols. The leech-gatherer,
whom Wordsworth describes in "Resolution and Independence,"
was, we know, drawn from life,[15] but in the emphatic imagery of

the poem he achieves a larger-than-life quality – he becomes a prodigy, a portent, his coming and going equally mysterious:

> As a huge stone is sometimes seen to lie
> Couched on the bald top of an eminence;
> Wonder to all who do the same espy,
> By what means it could thither come, or whence.

Characters in a novel necessarily exhibit a more quotidian character than this; their sublimity, if they have it, is pitched nearer to the everyday. Eliot seems to have had a problem here of finding the exact mode of realism to fit her tale. She tells her publisher in a letter dated February 24, 1861, of the way the idea of *Silas Marner* came to her:

> It came to me first of all, quite suddenly, as a sort of legen-
> dary tale, suggested by my recollection of having once, in early
> childhood, seen a linen-weaver with a bag on his back; but as
> my mind dwelt on the subject, I became inclined to a more
> realistic treatment.[16]

A "legendary tale" of Silas would have made him more like the leech-gatherer; indeed, Silas's catalepsy may have been suggested by another passage in that same poem of Wordsworth's:

> Motionless as a cloud the old Man stood,
> That heareth not the loud winds when they call;
> And moveth all together, if it move at all.

But, she was anxious to bring Silas out of the legendary Wordsworthian state into the orbit of ordinary everyday concerns – those of the villagers who sit and converse in the Rainbow where we are not likely to find Wordsworth's huntsmen and shepherds and certainly not his leech-gatherer. This is the "more realistic treatment" she is referring to in her letter.

The felt need to overcome the propensity to the fabulous in the tale as it had originally "come to her" thus becomes a central problem in the strategy of composition; more than that, it becomes in a sense the theme of the novel! We are told in the first chapter how the Raveloe folk had at first found Silas strange and portentous:

for the villagers near whom he had come to settle [his appear-
ance] had mysterious peculiarities which corresponded with
the exceptional nature of his occupation, and his advent from
an unknown region called "North'ard."

(Chapter i)

The word "mysterious" occurs four times in fact in the account
of their first impressions of Silas; they see him as in league with
the Devil, an impression strengthened by Jem Rodney's account
of having met him in one of his cataleptic fits. But the effect of
the narrative as it proceeds is to demystify Silas as he comes
nearer to the people of the village and as they draw closer to
him after the robbery. By Chapter x, the village folk, following
the lead of Mr Macey, the parish clerk, have decided that there
is nothing portentous about him and that he is nothing more
than a "poor mushed creatur." The transition from the legendary to the realistic is here a matter of the attitude of the villagers
to Silas; they now begin to see him as one of them.[17] But, in
the metapoetics of the narration this process of demystification
signifies the determination to adapt and recast the high invention of the ballad of mystery or the "greater romantic lyric" so as
to bring it within the confines of everyday reality. This was the
task the author set herself and it was a remarkably difficult one.

I would wish to argue that the biblical narratives – the parables of the New Testament and, more particularly, Ruth and the
Genesis narratives – provided her with the key to that balance
of the wonderful and the everyday, the fabulous and the realistic, that she was seeking. The story of Ruth has epic overtones;
it situates itself at the crossroads of history "in the days when
the judges ruled" and in the days before a king reigned in Israel.
And yet attention focuses itself on the matters of everyday, on
the gleaners in the field, on legal forms and modes of greeting
in a rural society, on the passage of the seasons from the barley
harvest to the wheat harvest.

Bible stories also exhibit human weaknesses and confusions –
the history they portray is not smoothed over or harmonized in
the manner of a legend. So much, says Auerbach of the Genesis
stories, is contradictory, so much is left in darkness.[18] This is precisely the comment of Dolly at the end of George Eliot's novel:
"It's the will o'them above as many things should be dark to
us." There are loose ends, as in real life, many details being left

unexplained. What became of the people Silas knew in Lantern Yard? Was the secret villainy of William Dean ever discovered? Silas will never know, nor shall we. Only matters that we need to know about are illuminated. And, what is illuminated in the tangle of circumstances which makes up the lives of men and women is the strange twisting path of salvation itself, a path marked out by a very small number of obstinately significant details, such as Silas's catalepsy, or Eppie's golden hair, or Godfrey's hunting-whip. These details stand out because on them, strangely, the whole history of trial and suffering and redemption seems to hinge. Here the fabulous and the realistic combine. They are like Absalom's long hair, or like the ram caught in the thicket in the story of the Binding of Isaac, or the coat which Joseph leaves in the hands of Potiphar's wife, strangely recalling the coat of many colours, which his brothers stripped off him earlier in the story. With such few details, trivial and yet portentous, the Old Testament narratives concern themselves. They give these stories their special kind of realism. Eliot has struggled to capture the same kind of realism in the rigorous selection of details which make up her spare narrative and she has succeeded to a marvelous degree. It is what makes this novel not only unique in her writings, but practically unique in English literature. Joan Bennett asserted that it is "the most flawless of George Eliot's works,"[19] and Walter Allen went even further, claiming that "*Silas Marner* is as perfect a work of prose fiction as any in the language, a small miracle."[20] Again the emphasis is on prose, as in Fielding's definition already cited. We are in an everyday world of struggling men and women, a prose world.

5

The problem of the medium exercised Eliot during the composition of the book; she speaks of the opposing attractions of verse and prose:

> I have felt all through as if the story would have lent itself best to metrical rather than prose fiction, especially in all that relates to the psychology of Silas; except that under that treatment, there could not be an equal play of humour.[21]

The reason she gives here for her choice of prose is somewhat lame, for the fact is that there is little humor in the treatment of her main characters (unlike *Brother Jacob*, another moral tale from the same period) and such humor as there is is mainly confined to the villagers in the Rainbow tavern. What one would want to say is that the special attempt here to capture the "still small voice" of the narrative portions of the Hebrew Bible dictated a style of utter simplicity and directness and an avoidance of artifice. This pointed to prose as the appropriate medium. *Silas Marner* is from this point of view probably more biblically charged and grounded than and other work of fiction in English. Neither Defoe nor Fielding recaptured so completely the *sermo humilis* of the biblical narratives.

And yet the truth is that even Eliot, who uses it as her standard in this novel, does not apply it with total consistency. At some point the literary tradition of the West resists such a radical canon of simplicity. And this applies to this novel of Eliot also. The narrative voice, for instance, with its rational and "enlightened" tone, is not that of the Biblical narrator. Moreover, if we analyze the different stylistic strands in the prose of the novel, we find that the biblical combination of loftiness and extreme simplicity is really specific to Eppie and Silas and the scenes in which they appear. It becomes, we may say, not so much a way of telling the story, as a "criticism of life." The style itself is foregrounded and is beheld in contrast to other styles. In the confrontation in Chapter xix between Eppie and Silas, on the one hand, and Godfrey and Nancy on the other, we become sharply aware of the difference between the modes of expression characteristic of the "upper-class" pair and those of Eppie and Silas.

Let us see how the stylistic aspect of the confrontation is exhibited in that chapter. Godfrey is voluble at first on the subject of the robbery and discusses the hardships of the weaver's life which he would like to do something to ease. The something, of course, is his plan to take Eppie from him, though he says nothing of this at first. Marner's responses are brief and awkward:

Silas, always ill at ease when he was being spoken to by "betters" such as Mr. Cass – tall, powerful, florid men, seen chiefly on horseback – answered with some constraint – "Sir, I've a deal to thank you for a'ready. As for the robbery, I count it no loss to me. And if I did, you coulld't help it: you aren't answerable for it."

Godfrey then reveals the main object of his visit. Saying nothing at this stage about his fatherhood, he proposes simply that, being themselves childless, they take Eppie away to live with them and make a lady of her. Marner would be rewarded for the trouble of bringing her up. The moral insensitivity of this is of a piece with the cultural norms associated with "florid men, seen chiefly on horseback." Matthew Arnold with a similar emphasis on their passion for field sports referred to the members of this class as "the Barbarians."[22] Godfrey concludes:

> she'd come and see you very often, and we should all be on the look-out to do everything we could towards making you comfortable.

Insensitivity here is compounded by the easy clichés which Godfrey uses ("be on the look-out," "making you comfortable"). The narrator's comment draws attention to the clichés:

> A plain man like Godfrey Cass, speaking under some embarrassment, necessarily blunders on words that are coarser than his intentions, and that are likely to fall gratingly on susceptible feelings.

In a reversal of the traditional division of styles as taught in the ancient schools of rhetoric and as practiced in the theater or in the literature of romance, here the upper-class character is the "plain man" whose expressions are "coarser than his intentions," while Silas, the handweaver, has the "susceptible feelings" and the language that goes with them. The reader is now being prompted at every stage to observe the manner of speaking of the different characters. Eppie's first real speech in this meeting is marked by a Wordsworthian simplicity and a biblical cadence; above all, it is free of cliché:

> "Thank you, ma'am – thank you, sir. But I can't leave my father, nor own anybody nearer than him. And I don't want to be a lady – thank you all the same. . . . I couldn't give up the folks I've been used to."

Godfrey, angered by their refusal to accept what he has persuaded himself is a generous offer, now declares the truth about his "natural claim" to Eppie. He is, he says, her real father. The simplicity and truth of Silas and Eppie have now forced Godfrey to reveal his truth, his manifest claim as well as his wrongdoing. But Silas's is still the higher truth, as he angrily opposes to the claims of "nature" – claims long concealed – the power of those august signifiers by which human relations are fundamentally ordered and which are in a sense independent of the natural relations which they signify. In this case the word Father has its own peremptory rights of love and authority, drawn as much and perhaps more from the sphere of the sacred as from biology:

> "your coming now and saying 'I'm her father' doesn't alter the feelings inside us. It's me she's been calling her father ever since she could say the word."

Nature must bow to the language of the heart – is what Silas seems to be saying. And again, the narrator's comment serves to foreground the stylistic aspect of this extraordinary confrontation:

> "But I think you might look at the thing more reasonably, Marner," said Godfrey, unexpectedly awed by the weaver's direct truth-speaking.

He ends by denying that Eppie will really be separated from Marner, even though Godfrey will have taken over the word "father" as his natural right.

> "She'll be very near you, and come to see you very often. She'll feel just the same towards you."

In the great speech which he now utters, Marner exposes the shallowness of Godfrey's sentiments – his upper-class complacency, as well as the idleness of his rhetoric:

> "Just the same?" said Marner, more bitterly than ever. "How'll she feel just the same for me as she does now, When we eat o' the same bit, and drink o' the same cup, and think o' the same things from one day's end to another? Just the same? That's idle talk. You'd cut us i'two."

Again, it is to Silas's simple language with its biblical rhythms that our attention is drawn, a language to which Godfrey is unattuned:

> Godfrey, unqualified by experience to discern the *pregnancy* of Marner's *simple* words, felt rather angry again. (emphasis added)

The express stylistic link with the Bible is made clearer when we find the author commenting in precisely the same terms on the readings she had heard one Sunday in the Little Portland Street Chapel. The letter – to Sarah Hennell – was written in July, 1861, just a few weeks after the publication of *Silas Marner*:

> What an age of earnest faith, grasping a noble conception of life and determined to bring all things into harmony with it, has recorded itself in the *simple, pregnant, rhythmical* English of these Collects and the Bible.[23] (emphasis added)

The confrontation between the weaver and the squire in this chapter implies a far-going socio-linguistic criticism of the British class system. The speech of the weaver in his poor cottage shows the greater delicacy and the greater grasp of reality, whilst the discourse of the "gentleman" reaches its ultimate point of insensitivity when he remarks that if Eppie fails to accept his offer, "she may marry some low working-man." It is this fate that the high society of Godfrey and Nancy with its balls, its horse-riding, and its drinking will preserve her from! The focusing of attention on these two opposed languages, representing two classes, the one in decay, the other discovering itself, seems to me precisely the phenomenon which Bakhtin terms "sociological stylistics" and which he claims to be the distinctive mark of the novel. "Diversity of voices and heteroglossia" he says "enter the novel and organize themselves within it into a structured artistic system." And he adds that such diversity of voices is essentially related to social change and social realities. "Social dialogue reverberates in all aspects of [novelistic] discourse."[24]

But in the example of Silas Marner's speech pitted against that of Godfrey we have social dialogism of a particular kind. For here we have a biblical realism confronting an artificial standard of speech and a false system of values. Nor is it a matter only of opposed languages in the novel. The last-quoted speech of Silas calls attention to a particular instance of "social dialogue" in the Bible itself. Silas speaks of Eppie as eating of the same bit and drinking of the same cup and thinking the same thoughts as he did. These phrases come from the parable of the poor man's ewe-lamb which Nathan the prophet relates to King David. The rich man had exceeding wealth, the poor man had just the one lamb which grew up in his house. And the text goes on to tell us that "it did eat of his own meat and drank of his own cup, and lay in his bosom, and was unto him as a daughter." But the rich man heartlessly covets and seizes the poor man's most precious possession (II Samuel 12:3). Silas echoes the first two quoted phrases, and for him too of course Eppie was "as a daughter." This echo-pattern underlies the confrontation between Silas and Godfrey. Behind Silas is the figure of Nathan and of the poor man in Nathan's parable, whilst Godfrey becomes the rich man in the parable and also in a sense King David himself whose rank and privilege do not exempt him from a fierce moral judgment.

In the end the issue is not "the war of the classes." It is not lower class versus upper class but a questioning of the class system as such. Godfrey and Nancy stand for natural bonds linked to a system of class gradations which are likewise held to be natural. Opposed to this in the dialogue is the biblical, covenantal system of relations which transcends the order of nature, cutting across the rights of class and property. Such a system is implied for instance in Ezekiel's parable of the foundling girl whom the passer-by finds and adopts and finally takes for his wife (Ezekiel 16:5–8) – it is his way of talking about the covenant between God and Israel. And this same higher loyalty finds expression in the story of Ruth and Naomi. It is, of course, the latter text which Eppie's reply immediately calls to mind in the passage already quoted:

> "And he says he'd nobody i'the world till I was sent him, and he'd have nothing when I was gone. And he's took care of me and loved me from the first, and I'll cleave to him as long as he lives, and nobody shall ever come between him and me."

While Nancy still attempts to counter this by an appeal to "nature," "duty," and "law," Godfrey has nothing more to say. He is silent. It is the victory of language, and specifically, the language of those lively oracles which Silas had salvaged from Lantern Yard and brought with him to furnish his onward pilgrimage.

Part III
Job in Modern Fiction

5

Kafka's Debate with Job

1

The book of Job is more than a text to be interpreted and reinterpreted by writers in the West from the Middle Ages on. It is
more like an archetype than a source, a mythic pattern indispensable for rendering a particular category of experience.
Prometheus is such an archetype, Job is another. It would seem
that no writer can begin to explore unmerited suffering and the
posture of rebellion against whatever or whomever is perceived
as the author of such suffering without turning this text to
account. Job thus comes near to claiming the status of a universal
point of reference. Even when not directly invoked, it is there.
Dostoevsky, who had been introduced to the book as a child by
an acolyte at a church service, "remained throughout his life
devoted to Job, who dared to rebel against God."[1] It was a key
to his major fiction. Ivan's major speeches in *The Brothers Karamazov*
turn out to be recapitulations and echoes of Job:

> Listen, I took the case of children only to make my case clearer.
> Of the other tears of humanity with which the earth is soaked
> from its crust to its centre, I will say nothing . . . What comfort
> is it to me that there are none guilty and that cause follows
> effect simply and directly, and that I know it – I must have
> justice or I will destroy myself. And not justice in some remote
> infinite time and space, but here on earth, and that I could see
> myself. I have believed in it. I want to see it, and if I am dead
> by then, let me rise again, for if it all happens without me, it
> will be too unfair. Surely I haven't suffered simply that I, my
> crimes and my sufferings, may manure the soil of the future
> harmony for somebody else. I want to see with my own eyes
> the hind lie down with the lion and the victim rise up and
> embrace his murderer. I want to be there when everyone

81

suddenly understands what it has all been for. All the religions
of the world are built on this longing, and I am a believer.[2]

And yet the text of Job, pervasive as it is, and claiming as it does
a kind of universal application to all times and circumstances, in
fact resists interpretation. For a start, it places formidable difficulties in the way of simple understanding. One of the passages
in Job which Ivan is remembering in the speech just quoted can
be translated, and often is translated as:

> For I know that my avenger lives, and that he who outlives all
> things, will rise when I shall be dust. But whilst I am still in
> my flesh, though it be after my skin is torn from my body, I
> would see God. That I might see him for myself; that my eyes
> might behold, and not another: in longing for that my reins
> are consumed within me.[3]
>
> (19:25–7)

But that text is both difficult and ambiguous. It is possible to
render the word *umibbesari* as above and as in the King James
version (KJB): "whilst I am still in my flesh" that is, whilst I am
still alive I would see God – which is what Ivan is saying. But it
is also possible to translate that term in an opposite sense as in
the Revised Standard Version (RSV), namely: "after my skin has
been destroyed, then *without my flesh* I shall see God." According
to this he will hope to have a knowledge of the truth when he is
no longer "in the flesh." This is clearly not what Ivan is saying.
But it is not unlike what his brother Alyosha maintains. Alyosha
has put off the Old Adam and has been reborn in Grace. Thus
he comforts his young friends at the end of the novel after the
burial of the schoolchild Ilusha:

> "Karamazov," cried Kolya, "can it be true what's taught us in
> religion, that we shall all rise again from the dead and shall
> live and see each other again, all, Ilusha too?" "Certainly we
> shall all rise again, certainly we shall see each other and shall
> tell each other with joy and gladness all that has happened!"
> Alyosha answered, half laughing, half enthusiastic.
>
> (p.838)

Job's words would seem to enter both sides of the equation – they are echoed in the naturalism of Ivan and the supernaturalism of Alyosha. It would seem that only a work of art as complex and as full of contradictions as *The Brothers Karamazov* can begin to interpret such a text.

Then again there is the famous crux at 13:15, rendered in the King James Bible: "Though he slay me, yet will I trust in him: but I will maintain my own ways before him." Following the written consonantal text (*ketiv*) rather than the masoretic reading (*qeri*) the RSV translates this as: "Behold he will slay me; I have no hope; yet I will defend my ways to his face." The New Jewish Publication Society (JPS) version reads the text in a similar fashion. Martin Buber basing himself on the *qeri* interestingly arrives at a third, quite different reading: "He may indeed slay me; I am ready for it, but I will maintain my ways to his face. (Wohl, er mag mich erschlagen, ich harre dessen/ jedoch meine Wege will ins Antlitz ich ihm erweisen)."[4] These are not trivial differences. The KJB gives us the attitude of faith; the RSV gives us the attitude of despair; Buber gives us a kind of acceptance of whatever may come, without the Kierkegaardian leap. Let me add that all these translations are possible and reasonable given the extraordinarily obscure and impacted language here and in other places in Job. The Rabbis, discussing the differences between the *qeri* and the *ketiv* of this verse, argued that we need to retain both in a kind of uneasy balance![5] The text at one and the same time recommends faith *in extremis* and shows us a man confronting the terrors of the universe soberly and without hope. Dostoevsky seems to have interiorized this contradiction. Ivan Karamazov seems to say "Behold he slays me, I have no hope." He remarks later in the continuation of the passage cited above, that he is returning his entrance ticket! His brother Dmitri on the other hand is that man who holds on to his faith in spite of the world's pain and his own. "Though he slay me," he says in effect, "yet will I trust in him." According to Bakhtin, the richness of the dialogic encounter between such different points of view and the antithetical mode of discourse which such dialogism yields, are the very foundation of Dostoevsky's art which is essentially pluralistic and decentered.[6] This made Dostoevsky for him the greatest of novelists. Bakhtin found no such pluralism in the Bible, but it is worth pointing out that in the case of *The Brothers Karamazov* Dostoevsky's achievement may be owing in part at

least to the power exercised over him by Job, and to the felt
need to interpret that most dialogic and at the same time impen-
etrable of biblical texts.

2

But in saying that Job resists interpretation I mean something
more than the difficulty it places in the way of simple compre-
hension. What is more unsettling is that it resists translation from
one cultural ambience to another. More than any other major
source text of western culture, Job is regularly and it would seem
wilfully mistranslated. It seems always to be crossed with another,
adversary text thus creating an inevitable swerve from the direction taken by the biblical book in its received form.

We may consider the crucial issue of the ending. Job after hearing
God's "answer" – or rather his questions – out of the stormwind,
submits to the authority of the divine voice; he "repents in dust
and ashes" (42:6). God subsequently vindicates him and restores
his fortunes. If the self-abasement of Job is a scandal to the Greeks
who expected pride and defiance from their heroes especially at
the end of their careers, the happy ending is a scandal to both
Greeks and Christians. It defeats the dark desire for death which
is so powerful a motif in western mythology and with it the aesthetic perfection of the downward curve of tragedy; it denies us
the logical fulfilment of Job's suffering, that consummation devoutly
to be wished which would have made it consistent with the
Crucifixion.

We are not here concerned with the issue of the integrity of
the text of Job – this scarcely concerned any of the writers we
shall be dealing with and perhaps the questions raised by textual
scholars about the authenticity of the ending are themselves the
effect of the same uneasiness which led writers to swerve from
the happy ending. We are concerned with the way that the writers
almost to a man found in Job an indispensable archetype and at
the same time found that it wouldn't do. The story had to be
redirected, subverted. At the end of *The Brothers Karamazov* we
see Ivan, the most Joban figure in the book, making his demented
but heroic appearance in the court where he takes on himself
the guilt of the world's evil. He is shortly to die. He is Jesus, the
rebel, destroyed by the Great Inquisitor. Dmitri, another Joban

figure, after being convicted of a crime he did not commit, is about to go into exile. Ironically, the only real survivor is Alyosha who is already crucified to the world. Job has become in short a type of Christ, as in so much medieval commentary, but here not so much for the sake of making the story doctrinally acceptable but for the sake of eliminating the untidiness – what I have termed, the scandal – of the way the story ends in the received text. Survivors of Auschwitz have been known to remarry, start new families and open new businesses, but art does not have to be that faithful to real life. It deals, as Aristotle says, not with what is historically possible but with what is probable or necessary. Job's survival is not probable or necessary in terms of the myths by which our culture is largely governed, though it might be argued that it is consonant with Old Testament literary norms which demand not closure, not roundedness, but the ongoingness of a testimony. Job survives just as Isaac survives and just as Lot and Noah survive – as a witness. They live on to tell the tale and in a deep sense their ordeal becomes important only when that tale is told. We are reading the text because they have survived. If Isaac had not survived, there would have been no readers and no text. If the Israelites had not escaped from attempted genocide, there would have been no Exodus and no record of the Exodus!

King Lear is another work of art powerfully shaped by the paradigm of Job, as many critics have observed.[7] There the Joban function is distributed between three notable figures of suffering: Lear, Gloucester, and Edgar. Lear after a moment of submissiveness and penitence in Act IV, seems to be heading with Cordelia for a Job-like ending. Lear promises Cordelia that "we'll live ... and we'll wear out, in a wall'd prison, packs and sects of great ones/ That ebb and flow by th'moon." But then comes the swerve; Lear has to die in defiance and agony to fulfil the laws of tragedy. He gains a Promethean stature at the end as he enters bearing the body of Cordelia in his arms. We are here at a great distance from the Job paradigm. And we are brought hardly nearer by the suggestion that Lear's death is a kind of crucifixion event. "He hates him," says Kent, "That would upon the rack of this tough world/ Stretch him out longer." Gloucester is likewise doomed to die, though his heart bursts smilingly in a concession to the principle of the happy ending.

From this point of view, the original Job pattern is probably most fully realized in the figure of Edgar. In the Folio recension, he is given the final summarizing words of the play as survivor and witness.[8] He suffers the ultimate degradation and the ultimate injustice, but he is vindicated and lives to tell the tale. Shakespeare gives us, we may say, a dialogic encounter between all these modes but there can be no doubt that whilst Job is a fundamental presence in the play, the shape of the fable is controlled by a different aesthetic. The witness function of Edgar is secondary.

Goethe's *Faust* unlike *King Lear* and *The Brothers Karamazov* is explicit in its evocation of the Job model. Part I begins with a Council in Heaven as in Job and as in *Paradise Lost*, Book III. This places the action within the metaphysical frame of a Test, a wager between God and Mephistopheles as to how Faust will behave when tempted. But this Joban pattern is quickly displaced by the more important wager between Faust and Mephistopheles. Here is the Faustian mutation of the Job paradigm. The Test is still fundamental, but the issue is not the mystery of God's dealings with Man, but Man's power to determine his own destiny, to shape a new future. Here is the first swerve – it is not merely that Faust dares to wager his soul; it is rather that Goethe in a spirit of mischief turns Job upside down. He says in effect "Ich bin des trocknen Tons nun satt,/ Muss wieder recht den Teufel spielen." He gives us Job reversed. Job appalled by his human insignificance and helplessness had cried out to God, "What is man that thou shouldst magnify him?" Faust proceeds to find the greatness of man in his own uncurbed powers and possibilities. But there are further multiple reverses still to come. In a brilliant reversal of earlier reversals of Job, the happy ending will be restored. Faust is received with rose petals in heaven, his sins forgiven, his daring rewarded. But this is only an apparent restoration. It is really a way of dismissing, even we may say parodying, both the damnation-myth of the Faust tradition and the salvation-myth of Job. Having failed his test and lost his wager, Faust triumphs over the Job model. No longer needing to humble himself before God, he gains salvation through the service of man. He likewise triumphs over the original Faust story: if he loses his soul in the traditional sense of that phrase, such loss has become an irrelevance. He has gained something better. At least that is what Goethe would ask us to believe. As well as writing a Faust play, he has written an anti-Faust. And he has written an anti-Job also, though an essential nucleus of the original Job remains, namely the questioning and the rebellion.

3

Kafka's writings represent a profound and sustained attempt to render Job for modern men. In Northrop Frye's words they "may be said to form a series of commentaries on the Book of Job."[9] I would add that though Kafka is engaged in a continuous effort of translation and interpretation, an effort more persistent even than that of Dostoevsky, he is no less guilty of displacement. He cannot do without Job but he cannot accept it either. More than that: Kafka, as well as providing his own notable examples of displacement, shows an acute awareness of previous displacements. He has a debate with Job but he also has a debate with previous mistranslations of Job. To start with "The Judgment", published in 1912. Evelyn Torton Beck has convincingly demonstrated that Kafka in this story has taken a deep imprint from Yaakov Gordin's Yiddish play "God, Man, and Devil." This was included in the repertoire of the Yiddish theater troupe which had peformed in Prague during the years 1910–12 and whose performances Kafka had assiduously attended. The relationship between the hero Herschele and his father in Gordin's play is strikingly similar to that of Georg Bendemann and his father; some of the details are directly imported from Gordin's play including the grotesquely comic business of Georg carrying his father to bed in his arms.[10] Herschele had done the same for his father Layzer. In fact, it may be claimed that the theatrical character of so much in "The Judgment" (Georg at one point calls his father a "comedian") and indeed in Kafka's writings generally is owing in large measure to his vivid memories of these Yiddish melodramas.[11]

Now what needs to be pointed out is that "Got, Mentsh, un Tayvel" is a Job play refracted through Goethe's *Faust*. It opens with a Prologue in Heaven in which a Jewish Mephisto, now renamed Mazik, is given permission to try to subvert the moral character of the pious scribe, Herschele. In a reflexive passage this Satan character tells us how he plans to go to work on Herschele:

> You allowed your trusting servant Job to be tested by pain and tribulation; this Jew (Herschele) is not going to be intimidated by troubles of that kind. The learned Doctor Faust sold me his soul for a moment of pleasure. Such dealings are only possible with a non-Jew; a Jew will not pay so dearly for pleasures. Almighty Lord, permit me to tempt him instead with money; with gold I will put him to the test.[12]

Mazik arranges for Herschele to win a lottery and from then on, the richer he becomes the more his soul becomes corrupted. He divorces his wife, becomes alienated from his friends and treats his aged father (who is literally a "comedian" – that is, a professional jester) with diminishing respect. But in a final melodramatic turnabout, he regains his soul – here is the swerve from the Faust model. The son of his best friend is injured as a result of a work-accident for which Herschele feels himself responsible. He debates the issue with Mazik. He finds he is worthless, nothing – his life a fleeting dream. Mazik retorts:

> Yes that is how that Jewish hero, Job, used to drool on, "Man that is born of woman is of few days and full of trouble. He comes forth like grass and is cut down and flees like a shadow . . ." But I much prefer the words of that learned German doctor who said: "I want to take from life everything my eye desires and then to strive for more."

Herschele vigorously rejects the Faustian ideal. "It was no Jew who said that," he declares; the unfulfilled striving for pleasure is not a Jewish ideal. For himself, he has always feared the Day of Judgment; he has always trembled at the thought of the great final blast of the *shofar*.[13] In the end, with the death of the young worker Motele, Herschele is overwhelmed with feelings of guilt and, like Georg in Kafka's story, he finds he can only expiate that guilt by suicide. Thus in spite of his stated preference for the Joban model, Gordin does not adhere to it. After his hero repents in dust and ashes and acknowledges God's righteous judgment, he is not restored to his former state but instead he hangs himself. Here is a radical departure from the biblical plot; Job had been tempted to suicide by his wife but had absurdly chosen life – even the life of total abjection and misery – in preference to death; in so doing he had destroyed the tragic symmetry. Gordin cannot endorse this ending – to be so like Job would evidently defeat the aesthetic ideals to which his work aspires.

Herschele's mention of the Day of Judgment leads us directly into Kafka's text. Kafka's title refers both to the judgment passed on Georg by his father and to Georg's judgment on himself.[14] And the rest of the story seems to follow. Georg's submission to his father's authority like Herschele's repentance would seem to

mark the triumph of the Joban paradigm. And this is followed
by the same swerve from Job in Georg's suicide on "the day of
Judgment." But this would be to oversimplify Kafka's relation to
Gordin's play. In particular it would be to overlook the inversive,
parodic nature of the ending. Kafka is not writing a sentimental
melodrama ending in the judgment and expiatory death of the
hero; rather he is reducing all such judgments and all such
expiations to absurdity. As I have argued elsewhere, a tale in
which a helpless, invalid father pronounces a sentence of death
on a vigorous, healthy son who then immediately runs out and
throws himself over the bridge, is a tale which draws attention
to its own absurdity. Seizing in his hands the myth of the father
who sacrifices his son, Kafka dangles it grotesquely before us
and in so doing he makes his gesture of freedom, a freedom
from all those myths of circularity which demand child-murder
and father-murder, world without end.[15] And perhaps Job, a text
which resolutely, even absurdly denies us the expected consummations of tragedy, helped him to make that gesture.

4

Kafka's most considerable attempt at translating Job into his own
special language is his full-length novel, *The Trial*. The analogy
with Job is in fact a commonplace of Kafka criticism.[16] *The Trial*
is, like "The Judgment," a tale of mysterious and unexplained
condemnation, of guilt imputed to the incredulous victim of "authority."[17] It has been suggested that Uncle Karl, the lawyer Huld
and the painter Titorelli correspond to the three "friends" of Job,
whilst the priest in the cathedral functions in the manner of Elihu.[18]
There are other, more substantial links. In particular, we have a
quality which receives little or no emphasis in "The Judgment,"
namely Job's rebelliousness. Joseph K.'s rebellion dominates the
ending. Like Job (and unlike Georg Bendemann) K. refuses to
commit suicide. It is his most Job-like moment. He will not "curse
God and die." He will remain steadfast in his claim to innocence.
If the "Father" wishes to take his life, it is for him to do it. Joseph
K., like Job, will not agree to become an accomplice in his own
condemnation. He holds on to the end to his integrity – "Far
be it from me that I should justify you", he seems to say to his
executioners, "till I die I will not put my integrity from me. My

righteousness I hold fast, I will not let it go" (Job 27:5–6).

The ending therefore is crucial and more essentially Job-like than "The Judgment" or than Gordin's play. But of course it is also a debate with Job. There is no redress and no vindication, no voice answers Joseph K. out of the storm-wind to save him from his executioners and to rebuke the lawyers, the court officials, the priest and all those who had taken his guilt for granted. He looks out for a vindicator, a last minute rescue. At one point such a figure seems to materialize, framed in the window of a house near the quarry to which his executioners have escorted him. Perhaps he can get into the Book of Job after all and become a survivor!

> Who was it? A friend? A good man? Someone who sympathized? Someone who wanted to help? Was it one person only? Or was it mankind? Was help at hand? Were there arguments in his favor that had been overlooked? Of course there must be. Logic is doubtless unshakable, but it cannot withstand a man who wants to go on living.[19]

But neither art nor historical experience can support such a survival. Job's happy ending remains a phantom-like possibility, a mirage doubtfully revealed to Joseph K.'s fading vision. The logic of the Grand Inquisitor is against him.

The Trial is also a debate with *The Brothers Karamazov* and with many other texts in our western culture. Dostoevsky had staged the greatest trial of all with the decor in place: the judge, the witnesses, the prosecutor and the counsel for the defence. The drama of the courtroom with its great speeches and its moments of astonishment had provided a rousing climax to his great novel. Kafka reduces this to absurdity. Dmitri's trial we may remember had been interrupted and the proceedings had been thrown into confusion by the screams of Ivan who goes mad and, following this, by the hysterical shrieking of Katerina Ivanovna who, to save Ivan with whom she is hopelessly in love, hands the president the ultimate damning evidence against Mitya. It is in effect the end of the case. Kafka gives us the parodic reduction of this when K.'s first interrogation is rudely brought to an end and his grand Job-like speech of defence is broken off in mid-career by "a shriek from the end of the hall."

It was the washerwoman, whom K. had recognized as a potential cause of disturbance from the moment of her entrance. Whether she was at fault now or not, one could not tell. All K. could see was that a man had drawn her into a corner by the door and was clasping her in his arms. Yet it was not she who had uttered the shriek but the man.

(p.46)

The grand drama of Dostoevsky's trial scene has here been reduced to bathos. Likewise, Dostoevsky's great novel had ended with the tragic eclipse of the heroes, their reconciliations, and the account in the Epilogue of the posthumous glory and love which would surround them. The death of Joseph K. is an inversive rendering of this. K.'s clownish executioners like all the other court officials we meet in the novel, are shabby and without grandeur; they wield a double-edged butcher's knife. No grave elegies and no Christian consolations accompany the inglorious death of Joseph K. Instead we are told how one of the executioners grabs his throat whilst the other thrusts the knife deep into his heart:

With failing eyes K. could still see the two of them immediately before him, cheek leaning against cheek, watching the final act. "Like a dog!" he said; it was as if the shame of it must outlive him.

(p.229)

It is *The Brothers Karamazov* done in pantomime.

The theatrical reference in the last quotation should be noted. The executioners become the audience whilst K. is turned against his will into a ham actor. A little earlier on they had been the pantomime actors or clowns with K. as a skeptical and amused spectator:

"Tenth-rate old actors they send for me," said K. to himself, glancing round again to confirm the impression. "They want to finish me off cheaply." He turned abruptly toward the men and asked: "What theater are you playing at?" "Theater?" said one, the corners of his mouth twitching as he looked for advice to the other, who acted as if he were a dumb man struggling to overcome a stubborn disability.

(p.224)

Noticed first it seems by Walter Benjamin,[20] the theater imagery of Kafka here and elsewhere, with its stress on exaggerated gestures and scenic extravagance, points us once again to Kafka's encounter with the Yiddish theater in Prague during his most creative phase. Consisting largely of tragi-comedy and melodrama, these plays relied much on sensational acting and exaggerated effects of all kinds. In his many diary entries on the subject, Kafka sometimes laughed at the actors much as Hamlet laughed at the players in Elsinore. They represented undiluted and unabashed theatricality. But at the same time we need not doubt that he was deeply impressed, even moved not only by the vividness of the performances, but by their central concern with alienation, suffering, justice and injustice, heroism and rebellion. These themes were of course all presented with a great deal of Jewish particularity which is omitted in Kafka's fictional exploration of the same issues.[21] One of the plays which had evidently made an impression on Kafka at the time of the writing of *The Trial* was Avraham Goldfaden's "Bar-Kokhba," a musical melodrama relating the last ill-fated Jewish stand against the Romans at Betar in the year 135. The rows of court officials at Joseph K.'s first interrogation with their white beards, their bent heads, and their "old, long and loosely-hanging Sunday-coats" of black may well have been suggested by the appearance of the elders of the Sanhedrin in Goldfaden's play.

Why is the acting imagery so important for Kafka both here and in his other major fiction? It is not sufficient to say that he had been impressed by the performances he had witnessed and that his writing consequently took a deep coloring from the art of the theater. The phenomenon we are considering is more like a key to Kafka's artistic method. If so many episodes, for example the execution, the scene of the whipper, the priest's address to K. from the pulpit, are markedly theatrical, it is surely because in Kafka's universe existence as a whole becomes a kind of stage play, something like the Nature Theater of Oklahoma in *Amerika* – a universal grand cabaret. We are all walking shadows, poor players, that strut and fret our hour upon the stage. And if Macbeth in those phrases sees life as a play, it is because he has, in the last act, become aware of what may be termed the play-without-the-play. He had thought earlier that he could write his own play, acting the part that he himself had chosen, and assigning their parts to everyone else, that he and Lady Macbeth would "mock the time with fairest show." But now we see the mocker mocked. He is being manipulated by a divine (or diabolical) stage manager; we see him (and he sees himself) as the victim of a plot mounted by the metaphysical Spirits and Powers on the stage of the universe. Indeed, we have all become part of a divine stage play "a spectacle (*theatron*)" as the apostle Paul termed it "to the world, angels and men" (I Cor. 4:9).[22]

Now there is no doubt that the Yiddish plays that Kafka had attended in Prague in 1910–12, naive and melodramatic though they undoubtedly were, all somehow testified to this metaphysical ordering of history. Gordin's "Got, Mentsh, un Tayvel" is probably the most sophisticated piece in the repertoire from this point of view. It is a kind of morality play with God and the Devil struggling for the soul of Herschele on the stage of the world. Herschele has intimations of the metaphysical order which surrounds him and governs his existence; in the cry of the mortally wounded man he hears the *shofar* of the Day of Judgment.[23] Those trumpets we may say would blow the horrid deed in every eye. And of course this awareness of a divine stage play in which men act their part under the testing eye of providence is sharpened for the audience by the adoption of the frame story from the book of Job. Here in the Prologue we have a metaphysical plot set in motion by God and the Angels. The drama that ensues is conducted under the watchful eye of a Providence which has set the stage for the test and awaits the result. The audience in the theater not only participates in the drama of Herschele but is a silent witness to the play-without-the-play; we remain aware of the "watchers" to whom we had been introduced in the Prologue.

The imagery of the theater in the last episode in *The Trial* has a like function. It points to a realm in which all things that we know and do and all things that are done to us are part of a staged performance. There are "watchers" all around us. But if that is what the theater imagery portends, such portents are simultaneously denied, deconstructed by the very theatricality of the presentation.[24] The two executioners are tenth-rate actors, mere clowns. What in Job in Dostoevsky and even in Gordin's play is taken seriously as a *theatron*, a spectacle watched by God and the angels, as in Paul's letter to the Corinthians, becomes a vaudeville, a pantomime. What we might have thought of as a metaphysical frame becomes a parody of all such frames, their final reduction to absurdity, though of course the conception has to be "there" – defined so to speak in outline – if only that its absence might be signified through the system of reductive imagery.

Here we may say is Kafka's fundamental debate with Job. *The Trial* not only omits the metaphysical frame, "the play-without-the-play" – it becomes an expostulation against such frames. God can no longer be conceived as addressing himself to Man. The fleeting image of a saviour figure in the window resolves itself into a mirage and K.'s last questions end with his raising his hands in a gesture of despair:

> Where was the Judge whom he had never seen? Where was the high Court, to which he had never penetrated? He raised his hands and spread out all his fingers.
>
> (p.228)

The very possibility of dialogue is here rejected – that person-to-person relationship which according to Buber constitutes the very heart of Job's meaning.[25] There will be no dialogue between Joseph K. and the forces ranged against him. Indeed the absence of such dialogue is the book's most agonizing concern.

5

Northrop Frye has spoken of *The Trial* as "a kind of 'midrash' on the book of Job."[26] We might prefer to say that it is a profoundly serious attempt to achieve such "midrash." For midrash we are told depends on a measure of assent, "a common accord between ourselves and what is written, and the task of midrash . . . is to bring this accord into the open."[27] Would it not be truer to say that, more than the book is a midrash on Job, it is an announcement that, in the absence of a transcendent point of reference common to the master text and its latter-day interpretation, such midrash is impossible?

The Trial thus raises the whole question of interpretation. Does not the rupture between our secular world and the sacred texts which it has inherited stultify a genuine hermeneutic? It is possible to isolate the human elements in the book of Ruth and the story of Joseph and translate those narratives into artistic form for the modern reader without facing head-on the mystery of a divine lawgiver and stage manager. But can so remorselessly "theo-logical" a scene as the levee in heaven preceding the trials of Job be "humanized" in this fashion, and if it is retained can it be anything more to us than a charade? Can the "testing" of Abraham in Genesis 22 be for us anything more than an anthropological case history, or at best "mere" mythology? Can even the most determined suspension of disbelief enable us to hear in it a divine word addressed to man and a human word addressed to God? Above all can we see it as a testimony involving ourselves? And if not, what happens to the interpretation of such texts by a modern writer?

The question of interpretation is raised as a major issue in Joseph K.'s conversation with the priest in Chapter 9 when the priest, after offering one reading of the interpolated parable "Before the Law," frankly admits that too much attention should not be paid to these readings – "The scriptures are unalterable and the com-ments often enough merely express the commentators' despair." (p.217) ("Die Schrift ist unveränderlich, und die Meinungen sind oft nur ein Ausdruck der Verzweiflung darüber.")[28] This is surely a most revealing comment on Kafka's own enterprise and that of the great authors before him who had attempted to translate Job into their languages. The book of Job is unalterable, a com-pelling presence in western culture – in Goethe, in Shakespeare, in Milton, in Dostoevsky – and yet all their readings express in the end the commentators' despair. Hence the swerve that we have noted as a constant feature of these literary transformations. Ultimately, there is something in the book which makes it unamenable to cultural adaptation. For to take the book seriously as dialogue, is to be obliged to enter that dialogue oneself. And this would be to leave fiction behind, indeed to abandon the sphere of art and enter instead the sphere of testimony.

Writers have betrayed this interpretive difficulty, this uneasi-ness, in their fictions. The unique distinction of Kafka is that he makes it the very matter of his writing; he focuses on the uneasiness itself, indeed he brandishes it before us. "Before the Law" provides the opportunity not merely for varying interpreta-tions but for foregrounding the interpretive process itself, its pitfalls and frustrations. What emerges from the discussion between Joseph K. and the priest on the meaning of the parable is that all readings are necessarily misreadings. We shall never appre-hend with certainty what lies behind the succession of guarded doors which divide us from the "Law." Nor shall we discover with certainty why the man from the country is denied access. This applies also to Kafka's larger parable, namely *The Trial* itself, to which "Before the Law" bears a clear metonymic relation. *The Trial*, like the parable, is about a man seeking access to "the Law" and failing to be admitted. By the same token *The Trial* will resist interpretation. One perceptive student has remarked that we are confronted with "the impossibility of interpretation."

> *The Trial* ... presents itself as message, but for all its tension, for all its straining, it unveils no code, it conveys no univocal meaning. It speaks of its own incompleteness, of its own inviolability. Disguised as a message, it reveals only the form of its disguise.

And he concludes that it is "an act of language founded upon an absence"[29] – the absence, we might want to say, of "the Judge whom he had never seen" towards whom K. stretches out his arms in vain in the last lines of his story. Joseph K. will never see or hear that Judge or understand the Law by which he is condemned, nor will the reader. We will never reach the Castle and understand the nature of the Law by which it governs the people of the village. We are moved to seek the meaning of these figures and institutions. But we shall find only an absence, a closed door which inhibits final interpretations.[30] Jacques Derrida has spoken of this parable of Kafka as exhibiting the inaccessibility to our understanding of the "law" defining the nature of literary narration in general.[31]

But if "Before the Law" dramatizes "the impossibility of interpretation," it also brings us back to our biblical paradigm by being clearly itself an attempted interpretation of the book of Job. It is something like the story of Job reversed. The man from the country who waits patiently at the entrance of the Law wearying the doorkeeper with his importunity is surely an avatar of Job demanding to know how the world is governed and in particular, to know the meaning of God's ways to Job. But whilst Job is finally granted an interview when God addresses him out of the storm-wind, in Kafka's fable there will be no interview, no saving word. The Job paradigm is here reversed as it has been in so many other examples that we have considered. But here the reversal is foregrounded, beheld as a hermeneutic crisis to which attention must be paid. That is the special novelty of Kafka's writing.[32]

What emerges from this is that the man from the country who seeks in vain to penetrate to the interior of the Law is not only Job, he is also, reflexively, the modern reader of Job, convinced that the book holds within it an explanation of its power over him, an answer to his questions. Job in his extremity knows that his Redeemer/Avenger/Vindicator lives, that in his flesh / out of his flesh he will see God. Is such knowledge any longer possible? And if not, is it because the modern reader is unwilling to cross an invisible threshold, or is he actually shut out from the life of dialogue? This is the point at issue in the conflicting interpretations offered by Joseph K. and the priest. K. claims that the man from the country is deceived by the doorkeeper, the priest claims that he is self-deceived. One view would imply that the ancient oracle resists interpretation; it is no longer accessible in our secular age. The other view would imply that the resistance is within us. We are unable or unwilling to come to terms with what lies beyond the door. We could if we liked just enter.

Kafka had felt the full force of the Job paradigm with its questioning of divine justice but he had also endured the modern secular revolution more acutely than perhaps any other writer since Pascal. As a result he exhibited with incomparable intensity the agonizing contradiction set up by the power exercised over us by the biblical text – the need to come to terms with it – combined with our alienation from it. More than that he did what his predecessors had not done – he recorded the very situation itself, he defined the nature of this alienation and this despair.

6

Such a Jacob-like struggle with this mysterious fable suggests then the formidable distance between such a fable and the world of the modern writer. But there is another side to the tension that we are discussing. Astonishingly, the book of Job also provides its own precedents for these interpretive misprisions. In itself it is a continued debate with other places of scripture. So much so, that we might say that the modern writer is never more Job-like

than when he is rejecting the Job model! In Chapter 7 Job recalls
Psalm 8 with its vision of man a little less than the angels, but
rejects it in disgust, saying "Let me alone till I swallow down my
spittle." In an earlier passage he recalls the Creation story in Genesis
but does so in order to turn it upside down: in place of the creation of light, he proposes a dark creation: "Let that day be
darkness . . . neither let the light shine upon it." Job's vision of
the world of Shadday is the dark antithesis of that sunnier world
made by Elohim in six days. The book of Job in this constitutes a
model for all radical revisions of prior texts, including the radical revision of Job itself! When Job becomes hardened into dogma,
its message reified by a too confident interpretation, the true Joban
reading involves a rejection of such dogma and interpretation
and a return to the basic grammar of this book.

The Trial is one such return. Like the book of Job, *The Trial*
consists of a series of unanswered questions. The first is that
addressed by Joseph K. to the unwelcome visitor who has come
to arrest him: "Who are you?" The last are those quoted a little
earlier on in this discussion – "Where was the Judge whom he
had never seen? Where was the high Court to which he had
never penetrated?" If Job achieves, incredibly, a sense of the worth
of his own life through the word addressed to him out of the
storm-wind, we should remember that like his own earlier speeches
that word consists of a series of unanswered and unanswerable
questions. There is dialogue to be sure, but dialogue of a very
special kind, one that consists of questions and of answers which
are themselves questions. Job passes his test because he obstinately perseveres in his questioning.

The Trial becomes a true, almost one might say, an indispensable, translation of Job by virtue of this same importunacy. Joseph
K. is importunate in his search for the strange meaning of his
destiny. It is an importunacy which communicates itself to the
reader who tirelessly seeks to fathom the meaning of the fable –
a meaning which eludes him just as the meaning of what is happening to himself eludes Joseph K. and just as the meaning of
the parable eludes both the priest and his interlocutor. Such
importunacy, such an unremitting intensity of desire for enlightenment is central to the Job paradigm. It seems often that what
matters in the end is not meaning but the search for meaning.
Kafka has, as noted earlier, omitted the "play-without-the play"
– his text has no transcendent point of reference; there is no

affirmed or assumed metaphysical order – but a search so intense itself takes on a transcendent value. Kafka we may say does not hear the word of God but he constantly strains his ears to catch its echo; and even though it tarries he awaits it daily in that same agonized posture of attentiveness as the man from the country or as the Jew awaiting the footsteps of the Messiah.

6

Being Possessed by Job

1

We are used to thinking of poets and novelists as interpreters of prior canonical texts. Milton sets himself in *Paradise Lost* to interpret the first chapters of Genesis; in *Samson Agonistes* he has before him the story of Samson's life and death as set out in Judges 13–16. Thomas Mann deliberately and explicitly develops an extended midrash on the story of Joseph and his brothers, with frequent use of actual midrashic materials from Josephus and the Rabbis. As we saw earlier on, Henry Fielding in *Joseph Andrews* uses both the Joseph story and the model of Cervantes, patterning the figure of Parson Adams on that of Don Quixote. And he tells us on the title page that that is what he is doing. In all these cases the source text is evoked and subjected to an interpretive rereading. In this mode there is always an element of dialogue as the prior text is cunningly echoed; at the same time it is either validated or satirically undermined. The decision as to which of these directions to take belongs to the latter-day artist or exegete; he may even take both directions at once as Fielding does in his handling of the Joseph story. But the mastery belongs to him; he exercises a marked degree of interpretive freedom, often bending the ancient story or poem to his will by means of such interpretive strategies as typology or allegory. This is the way that interpretive fictions normally work.

There is, however, the possibility of a more radical hermeneutic. This may be discerned in some of the examples discussed in the last chapter. Job is present in the writings of Kafka and Dostoevsky with a certain existential immediacy. In this mode the interpretive situation is, so to speak, reversed. The ancient source interprets us, forces itself upon us, disturbing us with its power of addressing our historical situation. As noted earlier, particular locations and episodes in *The Pilgrim's Progress* became a funda-

100

mental presence for the soldiers of the First World War, providing them with a language needed for defining their existence.[1]
Many readers find that Kafka's writings work in this fashion for
them in a latter half of the twentieth century – they provide an
essential system of signs to enable us to relate to the condition
of man in our depersonalized environment.

Such a use of poetic models takes us beyond literary "influence" and "echo" in the narrow sense. Texts are re-enacted,
repossessed in the historical present. The words invade our lives,
seeming to shape the world around us and above all to shape
our literary inventions. The books of the Bible in particular have
exercised this kind of controlling power. We do not escape the
ancient text. It is not a question of men seeking the meaning of
a text, it is more a matter of texts seeking them out, determining
their individual and collective life patterns. Not perhaps surprisingly, Jewish history and the testimony of many Jewish writers
reveal this text-haunted condition in a special degree. The ancient
record of the Exodus governs one's self-perception in the present.
Life is inevitably shaped by the modalities of exile and return.
These modalities have their origin in powerful texts but they are
not discovered by a studious interpretive process. On the contrary, many are embarrassed by the compulsive way in which
the unforgotten word imposes itself on their lives. They would
rather not face Amalek in every generation (Exodus 17:16); they
would rather not find themselves re-enacting the biblical Return
as the Lord roars at them like a lion and they come trembling
out of the west to be restored to their "homes" in Zion (Hosea
11:10–11). Such texts are no light matter; they seem to anticipate
the things that happen and when they have happened those same
texts serve as an indispensable language for understanding them.

It will be evident that what I am saying owes something to
the hermeneutic philosophy of Heidegger who emphasized the
function of the primary text as the site of a fundamental
Sprachereignis – or speech-event. The poem he says names the
gods. We listen reverently, not seeking mastery over the poem,
but waiting for it to disclose its meaning.[2] This meaning is a truth
of Being (*Dasein*) and as such exists prior to the subject/object
dichotomy on which such mastery depends.[3]

Heidegger has had an important influence on New Testament
theology and hermeneutics, as reflected in the writings of his
contemporaries, Rudolf Bultmann, Gerhard Ebeling and Ernst

Fuchs.[4] The speech-event is the Word beyond the Word, the *kerygma* or proclamation which is concealed in the gospel narrative and parables. The new hermeneutic stance involves exposing oneself to, or being seized by that Word.[5] When that happens, like the wedding guest in Coleridge's poem, we cannot choose but hear. Quite simply, as R.W. Funk has said, "the Word of God is not interpreted: it interprets."[6] Or as Fuchs expresses it: "What is therefore exposited is actually the present, exposited with the help of the text."[7]

Whilst acknowledging a debt to these formulations and welcoming the perception of an interpretive stance different from that understood in more traditional hermeneutics, I find myself unable to share the Heideggerian (and more particularly Bultmannite) perception of an original "speech-event" removed from the materiality of history or the circumstances of daily life. What will be rejected in short is the principle of *"Demythologisierung."* According to this, poems are revelational speech-events in the sense that all historical circumstances and allusions are cast aside. The synoptic gospels with their stress on the historical and geographical background of the Christ-narrative achieve meaning only when such "mythological" trappings are abandoned in favor of something more like the purity of the Johannine text which proclaims: "In the beginning was the Word." That is the true *kerygma*.

If we need to remove the husks of historical reference from the gospels in order that they can reveal their kernel of transcendental meaning, there would clearly have to be an even more violent stripping down of the story of the Exodus with its even greater weight of materiality. For it to be experienced as the Word, the new hermeneutic would require it to be radically demythologized, its historical and geographical concreteness set aside. But one wonders what would be left of the specificity of that record, that realism which Auerbach pointed to in his famous essay on the Akedah narrative, if the demythologizing razor were to be applied to it!

Unredeemed readers of the Old Testament will consequently be somewhat selective in regard to the new hermeneutic. There is clearly great value in reversing the direction of our traditional understanding and seeing the biblical paradigms as interpreting us rather than we them. In certain hermeneutic situations we should be concerned with that dynamic rather than with the traditional tasks of exegesis and commentary. Something happens to us in our encounter with the ancient poem, and it happens because that poem is inside us, biding its hour. The encounter of many modern Jewish writers with the story of the "Binding," or the Exodus, or with the book of Job constitutes an event of this kind. But we do not remain on the high ground of Being. Whilst the revelational encounter takes place in words, it points beyond the closed circle of language to concretely realized moments in the past, joining those moments to the gross historicality of the present moment. Here we have a direction different from that proposed by Bultmann. There is a joining of Self and not-Self through the power of language, and there is a joining of past and present through the marvelous power of memory. This is what is meant by speaking of the poem as "witness" – the term used in Deuteronomy 31 to define the hermeneutic encounter. We are seized but we are also challenged. And there should be no mistake about the difficulties involved, the resistance which has to be overcome as the remembered text comes at us charged with new historical urgency. The text is like a revenant not only because it haunts us, but also because we seek to defend ourselves from it. This dialectic seems to mark the reception of the book of Job in the examples which we shall be considering.

2

The Jew in the latter half of the twentieth century is of course possessed by Job to a special degree; he is coerced by that Word. Its connection with his world is not a matter of interpretation; we may speak rather of an existential continuity between Job's questions and silences and the literary responses which Jewish suffering has yielded in our time. Nelly Sachs for instance has a brief poem entitled "Job" in memory of her father:

> Your eyes have sunk deep into your skull
> like cave doves which the hunter
> fetches blindly at night.
> Your voice has gone dumb,
> having too often asked *why*.[8]

It is from this perspective that we should consider the Austrian writer Joseph Roth's remarkable novel, *Job: The Story of a Simple*

Man (1930),[9] the work to which I shall devote the remainder of
this chapter. Roth's hero, Mendel Singer is not trying to rewrite
Job – if anything he is trying to get away from that paradigm.
"Why do you quote the example of Job?" he screams at his friends
who try to speak to him after he has suffered unbearable misfortune (230). Perhaps you are being tested like Job, they suggest to
him. He retorts: "Why do you break my heart . . . why do you
tell me all that was, now, when I have nothing left? My wounds
have not yet scarred, and you tear them open" (229). Job had
said the same to his "comforters."

Job we are told was simple, upright, and godfearing (1:1). Likewise, of Mendel Singer we learn:

> He was pious, godfearing, and ordinary, an entirely common-
> place Jew. He practised the simple profession of a teacher. In
> his house, which was merely a roomy kitchen, he instructed
> children in the knowledge of the Bible. He taught with honour-
> able zeal and without notable success. Hundreds of thousands
> before him had lived and taught as he did.
>
> (1)

But there is a difference. Mendel lives in a Jewish township in
Czarist Russia, not in the legendary land of Uz. His story and
mode of living are all too familar: he is drawn from the life. Poor
and ineffectual, married to a loyal, but occasionally shrewish wife,
Mendel is the Jewish Everyman, the typical shlemiel figure from
the East European *shtetl*. But Mendel and his story acquire singularity through the cruel and unusual suffering to which he is
subjected. This elective suffering is associated in the first instance
with his youngest child, Menuchim. Menuchim is severely retarded
and in his years of infancy and early youth never learns to speak
or to walk independently. More loved than the other children,
he is also his parents' biggest misfortune. The scene depicting
the anguished relationship between father and son back in
Zuchnow is sharply realistic; it is also memorable for its dramatic
economy and force.

> Mendel and Menuchim remained alone. Mendel ate a barley
> soup which he had cooked for himself, and in his earthen-
> ware plate left a bit over for Menuchim. He slid the bolt, that
> the child should not creep through the door as he liked to do.

Then the father went into a corner, lifted the child upon his knee, and began to feed him.

He loved these quiet hours. He was glad to be alone with his son. Yes, he sometimes wondered if it would not be better if they stayed alone altogether, without the mother, without the brothers and sister. After Menuchim had swallowed the soup, spoonful after spoonful, his father would set him upon the table, sit still before him, and stare with tender curiosity into the broad sallow face with its wrinkled brow, netted eyelids, and flaccid double chin. He tried to guess what might be going on in that broad skull, to gaze in through the eyes as through a window in the brain, and by talking to him, sometimes loudly, sometimes softly, to draw from the stolid boy some sort of sign. He would repeat Menuchim's name ten times, moving his lips slowly so that the boy could see him say it if he could not hear. But Menuchim never responded.

Then Mendel would take a spoon, strike it against a teaglass, and immediately Menuchim would turn his head, and a tiny light would flame in his great, grey, liquid eyes. Mendel would ring again, begin to sing a little song and to beat time on the glass with the spoon, and Menuchim would clearly display uneasinesss, turn his great head with a certain effort, and dangle his legs. "Mama, Mama!" he would cry out all the while.

Mendel stood up, fetched the great black Bible, held the first page open before Menuchim's face, and intoned, in the chant in which he was accustomed to instruct his pupils, the first verse: "In the beginning God created the heaven and the earth." He waited a moment in the hope that Menuchim would repeat the words, but Menuchim did not move. Only in his eyes the listening light still stood . . .

Then with a heavy sigh Mendel set Menuchim again upon the floor. He slid back the bolt and stepped before the door to wait for his scholars. Menuchim crept after him and squatted on the doorsill. The tower clock struck seven notes, four deep ones and three high ones. Then Menuchim cried: "Mama, Mama!" And as Mendel turned towards him, he saw that the little one stretched his head in the air as though he breathed in the music of the bells.

"Why am I so afflicted?" thought Mendel, and he explored his conscience for sins but found none that was grave.

(58–61)

This passage gives us the key to the way the Job paradigm works in this very Jewish novel. Mendel's question after verifying how hopeless was the condition of his crippled son, "Why am I so afflicted?" – is the reduction to its simplest form of all Job's questionings. He also expresses Job's most fundamental affirmation – the affirmation of his innocence (cf. 27:5–6, 31:1f). Mendel has searched his conscience but has found no sins to match the weight of his afflictions. The question therefore is, Why? And as in Nelly Sachs's poem, Mendel's voice too eventually becomes silent, "having too often asked why." For in the end he ceases to pray. Of Mendel's three healthy children, only one, Shemariah, who gets to America, is moderately successful. Jonas, the oldest, goes into the Czarist army and adopts the manners of a Russian peasant, whilst the daughter Miriam, rebelling in her fashion too against the norms of the community, gives herself to the handsome Cossack officers quartered in the town; she keeps her love trysts in the cornfields during the hot summer days. When they discover their daughter's shame, Mendel and his wife, Deborah determine that they must leave for America to join Shemariah, taking Miriam with them.

Here is the tragic turning point of the book. Despairing now of ever seeing him grow into a healthy child, they tear themselves away from Menuchim, whom they leave behind with the daughter and son-in-law of a neighbour, Billes. The couple receives the use of the Singer home rent-free in return for caring for the idiot boy. With the parting from Menuchim the light goes out of their lives and the stage is set for the subsequent Job-like afflictions that will follow after Mendel Singer gets to America. For misfortune pursues him to the new land. When America enters the First World War, Shemariah – now calling himself Sam – enlists and is killed; hearing the news, Deborah collapses and dies and Miriam shortly afterwards becomes deranged and has to be hospitalized in a mental institution. Mendel is left bereft and broken. In the extremity of his grief, he exclaims against the God whom he had worshipped unquestioningly for 50 years; he even prepares a fire in which to burn his prayer-shawl and phylacteries.

Here is surely one of the most powerful scenes in twentieth-century Jewish writing. It is also a prevision of the crisis of faith which would visit the Jewish collectivity 12 years later with the Nazi Holocaust. Joseph Roth wrote this novel in 1930. He was dead in 1939 but this work should be reckoned among the great literary testimonies of the Holocaust. The Word we may say anticipates the event – it is a witness sure enough, a witness to what was still to come. Mendel has lit a fire in which to burn his *tallit* and *tefillin*. Stamping his feet and crying out in a terrible song "It is over, all over, it is the end of Mendel Singer," he raises the red velvet sack above the flames, but his hands refuse to obey. "His heart was angry against God, but in his sinews the fear of God still dwelt" (225). "You will be astonished when I tell you what I really intended to burn" he declares later to his four friends, "I want to burn God" (227). In the end he does not burn God; but he ceases to pray. When his friends use his rented backroom as a temporary synagogue on the Day of Atonement he stands "black and silent, in his everyday clothes, near the door, unmoving" (242).

It is easy to see that Mendel's not-praying is itself a dialogic gesture. He is conducting a fierce and unremitting quarrel with his God who is as vividly present to him in his grief as at any other time. Or as the narrator puts it, "in his sinews the fear of God still dwelt." This is in a word covenantal suffering. Mendel is no latter-day atheist. God continues to speak even though "no sound issued from his lips but thunder" (240). In fact he speaks more articulately in thunder than in any other way. In refusing to pray, Mendel is not denying God; he is defiantly confronting him:

> "I shall not pray," thought Mendel. Yet he suffered because he did not pray. His rage hurt him, and the impotence of his rage. Although Mendel was angry with God, God still ruled the world. Hate could move him no more than piety.
>
> (239)

"God still ruled the world." This awareness is created here for the reader precisely in the scenes where Mendel reaches the nadir of his misfortunes. In striking contrast to the metaphysical emptiness glimpsed by Joseph K. in his final questions – "where was the Judge whom he had never seen? where was the high Court, to which he had never penetrated?" – there is here an inexorable presence. Mendel is not shut out from that presence by a doorkeeper standing guard at the entrance to the Law: he is right inside demanding justice of a judge of whose power he is all too vividly conscious. The remarkable achievement of Roth is that, for the space of the novel, the reader too, however skeptical his bent, comes to share this same awareness.

3

It is now possible to suggest what kind of novel we are dealing
with. The literary genre which permits the gods to play their
part in the daily lives of men is of course the epic. Roth's novel,
in spite of focusing on the unassuming commonplaces of Jewish
existence in the ghettos of Eastern Europe and New York at the
beginning of the century, makes a genuinely epic statement. In
Zuchnow, God is always near at hand, invoked in Mendel's prayers
– morning, afternoon and evening. Deborah, uninstructed in the
sacred texts, finds her way to God through the mediation of her
dead parents in the village cemetery. When she is desperate for
a word from on high on the destiny that awaits Menuchim, she
undertakes the arduous journey to the township of Kluczysk
to wait among the suppliants at the court of the hassidic Rabbi
of that place. And there the word is given by which the future
will be governed, as it is to Aeneas on his visit to the halls of
Dis, or to Odysseus at his meeting with Teiresias in the grove of
Persephone. The Rabbi's oracular announcement (18–19) that
Menuchim will be healed and will become strong and wise, coupled
with a strict warning to the parents that they must never leave
him or send him away even if he becomes a great burden to
them – determines the shape of the story. Menuchim will fulfill
the Rabbi's promise. Pain will make him wise, ugliness good,
bitterness mild, and sickness strong. But Mendel and Deborah
who fail to heed the warning, will suffer the tragic consequences
of their dereliction.

There is thus an overarching divine "plot" and, what is more,
as in the genre of the epic, there are channels of communication
bringing the divine order and the human order into relation with
one another. Northrop Frye notes that "in the traditional epic
the gods affect the action from a continuous present."[10] The
difference is that for Roth's characters the "divine society" is a
much more familiar presence than it is for the epic heroes of the
western tradition. There is no need for a Hermes with golden
wings and sandals to descend with pomp and circumstance to
mediate the message of the high gods; there is no such ironic
space to be spanned. Instead we have a ritual of daily conversation and observance. And even the more dramatic encounters –
such as that of Deborah with the hassidic Rabbi – take place in a
setting of familiar piety. Strangely the poor Jewish teacher feels

at home with "the high and lofty one that inhabiteth eternity" of Isaiah's oracles. He is clearly nearer to him than is the larger than life hero of the Greek epic to the deities of the Greek pantheon! What Roth gives us is an epic without epic distance – in some ways, indeed, an anti-epic.

Such a combination of awesomeness and familiarity takes us back of course to biblical models, to the patriarchal narratives, to the book of Ruth as well as to Job itself, all of which have some affinity to the epic. Milton spoke of Job as a "brief epic."[11] But if Job gives us a vision of the primordial world, of the great sea-monsters and of the far-away constellations of Orion and the Pleiades – it also ends on the domestic note, presenting to us a Job who is no longer a figure in a cosmic drama but something of a middle-class *paterfamilias*, counting his livestock and dividing his property among his sons and daughters. This is the inevitable lurch into the quotidian which the biblical narratives seem to achieve. Even Adam and Eve seem to move from legend to middle-class domesticity in Genesis 4. The Bible has from this point of view been extraordinarily serviceable in the history of the novel which has from the beginning tended to hark back to the Epic with a certain nostalgia. Fielding spoke in the preface to *Joseph Andrews* of his project as that of producing a "comic Epic-Poem in Prose." The epic ambition is especially central for the greater nineteenth-century novelists: Dickens, Dostoevsky, Tolstoy, George Eliot, and many others. Each in his different way tried to capture the larger theme – the grand sweep of history, the march of mind – but justice had to be done also to the world of everyday. The Bible pointed to this possibility. Epic sublimity could be achieved without abandoning the "Biedermeier" world to which the novel from its origins remained committed.[12]

But the inevitable problem of mediation remains. How was one to bring the everyday and the "high" regions of romance and epic into a common focus. The biblical "lurch" would not do. There had to be a smoother transition than that. Rarely have novelists succeeded in finding the form and language which would satisfy the twin needs of realism and epic sublimity. Fielding seeks mediation through burlesque – a limited and limiting solution; Dickens's attempts in *The Tale of Two Cities* and elsewhere are flawed by mawkishness; Melville in *Moby Dick* remains in the sphere of cosmic struggle, his characters rarely shedding their symbolic, superhuman status. George Eliot, as we noted earlier, achieves a notable success in *Silas Marner*, where Silas (like Mendel in Roth's novel) is a simple man who also carries on his back the weight of history – the social and religious history of his time. He has in this respect the representative, symbolic function of the epic hero. Moreover, in *Silas Marner*, as in Roth's *Job*, the providential order is apprehended by the characters as a condition of their daily lives. "Our life is wonderful" – is the testimony of Silas. And Godfrey too has a sense of the mystery and miracle involved in those "dealings" to which he too is subject. In all this the novel performs what we have noted as the epic function of communicating between the human and the divine.

But Eliot, as we saw in an earlier chapter, betrays a certain uneasiness in regard to this very enterprise. She wondered whether, instead of aiming at prose fiction, she should not perhaps have cast the story into metrical form.[13] There were weighty reasons for choosing prose, but she was left with the problem of doing justice to the biblical-type epic mode in everyday, domestic English. How was one to bring the sublime down from heaven to inhabit among men, in clubs and assemblies?

This was a major preoccupation in her longer fictions also. Both in *Middlemarch* and *Daniel Deronda*, for instance, the aim was to harmonize the epic vision with domestic realism. *Daniel Deronda* was probably her most ambitious attempt in this kind. Here in a novel of truly epic scope she brings together the heroic, public world of Daniel, who seeks a future for his race in the East, and the "little" world of Gwendolen Harleth, whose tragic history remains essentially personal and private. The conjunction is explicitly foregrounded and made a matter of discussion in the novel:

> Strangely her figure entered into the pictures of his present and his future; strangely . . . their two lots had come into contact, hers narrowly personal, his charged with far-reaching sensibilities, perhaps with durable purposes, which were hardly more present to her than the reasons why men migrate are present to the birds that come as usual for the crumbs and find them no more.[14]

How was one, artistically speaking, to overcome this strangeness, to join together the grand design of history, indeed of prophetic history, and the little facts of everyday? Interestingly enough for our present discussion, she had the feeling that the internal world of Jewish society and the Jewish family might provide a key. She tells us that the main advantage of the Jewish characters for her was that they had the ability to suggest "the presence of poetry in everyday life" (Chap. 32). That is the quality that had attracted Deronda to the *Judengasse* in Frankfurt. (We may add that it had earlier attracted Rembrandt to the Jewish figures in Amsterdam.) The ordinary coexisted with the miraculous and the extraordinary, materialism with idealism, weekday huckstering with Sabbath-day magnificence. Ezra Cohen is an unadmirable pawnbroker who strikes a hard bargain with Deronda over a diamond ring, but Mordecai, the dreamer and saint, occupies a place at his sabbath-table. "It was" says the narrator, "an unaccountable conjunction" (Chap. 34). Some critics have argued that in *Daniel Deronda* the conjunction remains unaccountable; she did not in practice succeed in combining the marvelous and the mundane and as a consequence the reader is left unconvinced of the reality of the Jewish portraits.[15] It would be left to a number of Jewish writers later on, among them Joseph Roth, to give more convincing expression to those epic possibilities to which George Eliot had so remarkably directed our attention.

4

In effect Roth's extraordinary achievement is to introduce into the everyday, realistic pattern of the novel the element of the marvelous, or to use the term which becomes central in the book itself and a key to its understanding – the element of miracle. And in the end he makes the miracle as convincing a part of that everyday world as the suffering. In this he was being faithful to an essential dimension of the book of Job. In that book God acts in the story in two ways. On the one side, he is answerable for Job's intolerable sufferings – in Chapter 31 Job will call him to account for that. But he is also responsible for Job's vindication and the restoration of his fortunes, for God will in the end acknowledge Job's essential innocence and miraculously reinstate him. This is the about-turn which, for the great writers of the western tradition, inevitably destroyed the tragic symmetry; it was also theologically indefensible. A God so inconsistent as to humiliate and crush his servant and then raise

him up was not easy to accommodate in literature or life. But
what one would wish to say is that Jewish history – and that
means Mendel Singer's history also – does not ultimately make
sense without this. Arguably Job was written in order to exhibit
and in some sense interpret this paradox. Thus the phrase used
to denote the happy ending of Job is: "And the Lord restored
the captivity of Job" (42:10). The same phrase is used in numerous places of the Bible for the restoration of Israel to its land (for
example Ezekiel 39:25), restoration being as central to covenantal history as exile. One awaits it attentively day by day without
ever quite giving up one's faith in the miracle of renewal. What
Shakespeare, Dostoevsky and Kafka could not or would not do,
Joseph Roth has done – he has written a Job story in which the
happy ending takes its place as naturally as the suffering. The
note of wonder in fact is already struck in the passage cited earlier
describing Mendel feeding Menuchim with the barley soup. Mendel
himself is only aware that he is smitten of God and afflicted, but
the reader is also struck by the "listening light" in Menuchim's
eyes as his father sings his little song and beats time on the glass
with a teaspoon, or when the bells ring outside. Those details
will be recalled later in the story and will acquire portentous
meaning. If Mendel's afflictions are to be related to the sufferings
of Job, then the wonder and the miracle intimated in this scene
belong also to Job. And for Roth in this novel this becomes just
as real as the suffering.

The miracle for which Mendel and his wife had hoped and
prayed before their departure for America was the miracle of
Menuchim becoming normal and healthy. As the appointed day
for their departure from Zuchnow approaches, they look at their
sick child constantly to see if the miracle has already happened.
But his face becomes even more flabby and sallow, his limbs if
anything more ungainly. Deborah finally gives up her childish
hope. At the hour of parting she stands with the cripple in her
arms. Finally she lays him gently down upon the doorsill "as
one lays a corpse in a coffin."

> Naked tears over her naked face. She had made up her mind.
> Her son was to stay. She would go to America. There had been
> no miracle.
>
> (150)

But the miracle would finally come. Long after the Singer family have moved to New York, Menuchim, left unguarded one day in the Billes home, runs out in terror as a burning faggot accidentally falls out of the stove and threatens to set fire to the house. From that moment of shock he begins to walk and talk. A doctor who had earlier taken an interest in Menuchim's problem, arranges for him to go to Petersburg to a special sanatorium. There he not only becomes well but he begins to show musical talents – to sing and to play the piano. The final stage of the miracle is when he turns up in New York after the War as the conductor of a visiting philharmonic orchestra. They are playing music which he had himself composed. He is in search of his father, now a broken man, alone and without hope, subsisting on charity or doing odd jobs for the friends who had like him come to America from the *shtetl*.

The meeting between father and son takes place on Passover-eve in the home of Skovronnek, one of these friends. Passover-eve commemorates the Exodus, the original "return of the captivity" of Israel. Here once again is the epic dimension in the linking of past history with that of our own time through the symbolism of the Passover celebration. And there is also the linking of the personal life of a simple and commonplace Jew with the greater epic story of the suffering of the collectivity of Israel in our time and their promised deliverance. The moment in the Passover-eve ritual arrives when the door is traditionally opened to admit the prophet Elijah, the harbinger of restoration and return, who is thought to visit all Jewish homes on Passover-eve. Mendel steps out to open the door. Shortly afterwards a knock is heard. "The old melody had brought grown-ups and children to the point where they almost awaited a miracle" (274). When the tall dark stranger is admitted and is invited to join the family and guests at the festive board, he does not immediately identify himself but introduces himself as a relative of Mendel's dead wife. Mendel is struck with wonderment. In the visitor's countenance every-thing was strange except the eyes behind their rimless glasses. "His gaze always strayed back to them, like a homecoming to well-known lights behind windows, in the unfamiliar landscape of the narrow, pale, and youthful face" (277). We are reminded of the scene back in Zuchnow when Mendel had gazed in through Menuchim's eyes "as through a window in the brain." The novel is full of such verbal echoings and recallings. It advances by the poetic technique of incremental repetition – the phrase or image when recalled bringing with it a new turn in the story.[16] Roth makes telling use of this method in other novels. In *The Radetzky March* (1932), on the last years of the Austro-Hungarian Empire, the strains of the famous march are heard (or recalled) at intervals throughout the story. Each reference comes to express a different phase in the changing fortunes of the hero.

When Mendel's visitor finally identifies himself as Menuchim, now cured of his disabilities and a recognized musical genius, Skovronnek runs out to bring together the other three friends who had earlier been Mendel's Job's comforters in his misfortune: "We tried to comfort you, but we knew it was in vain. Now you in the flesh experience a miracle. As we mourned with you then, so we rejoice with you now" (291). The novel ends on a note of hope; perhaps something can be done for Miriam, perhaps Jonas will still be found. "Mendel fell asleep. And he rested from the burden of his happiness, and the greatness of the miracle" (304).

Mendel's good fortune is felt to be part of the "real life" character of the story. It may be a miracle, but miracles are in a way a part of our everyday lives. Behind every Jewish musical genius there is somewhere no doubt a Mendel Singer. Cures of congenital disorders are not unknown and, as for the "miracle" of Menuchim's return to his father, reunions as passionate and as poignant with long-lost relatives, given up for dead, are almost an everyday affair for a people as scattered as the Jews and as much given to wandering around the world. But there is clearly also another side to the miracle. Miracles happen because Mendel's God is an active presence in the story and because the story is powerful enough to cause the reader willingly to suspend his disbelief. Earthbound, drab and commonplace though he is, Mendel also touches the heavens. "His sleep was dreamless, his conscience was pure, his soul was chaste" (2). He is inglorious in appearance but, mysteriously, when he moves we hear the beating of angels' wings. The skirts of his caftan we are told flapped when he hurried through the street and "struck with a hard regular tact like the beat of wings against the shafts of his high leather-boots" (ibid.).

Roth has written an imaginative reconstruction of Job, but this is not in the strict sense an interpretation of that book, not even a midrashic interpretation. It is rather a novel of modern Jewish experience, suffering and exile – about the great migration from Eastern Europe to America at the end of the last century and the beginning of this. Migrations we may remind ourselves have always been central to the epic. Job comes to provide us with an interpretation of that – giving us a key to the understanding of our world and our time. The author allows the text of Job to disclose its meaning, its *kerygma* if you like. And what it yields is its power as witness, a witness to the time in which Roth lived as well as to a time still to come. For when Roth died in misery in Paris in 1939 he could not have foreseen the extent of the coming disaster nor did he foresee – any more than did Mendel Singer – the possibility of a redemptive miracle to follow.[17]

7

Biblical Patterns for Sale: Malamud, *The Fixer*

1

Not all twentieth-century writers surrender to biblical archetypes in the manner of Joseph Roth, Kafka, or Dostoevsky who were in their different ways possessed by the Joban paradigm. Conrad, for instance, strongly responsive though he is to myth-patterns of all kinds, is not seized in this fashion. Marlow in *Heart of Darkness* is a questing hero who, like Aeneas, visits the underworld there to confront Erebus, son of Chaos, and to behold Phlegethon, the river of Death.[1] There are also arguable traces of Dante's *Inferno* in Marlow's journey up-river.[2] Kurtz – who is not only an adventurer but also a poet, painter and musician – re-enacts Orpheus's descent into the region of Hades, there to behold forbidden things and eventually to be torn to pieces by the Thracian women. In "The Secret Sharer," Leggatt's deed and subsequent fate explicitly recall the biblical story of Cain and Abel, whilst the relations between Leggatt and the Captain belong to the archetype of the Double.[3] In these examples, Conrad is clearly exploring the artistic possibilities of these archetypal stories and myth-patterns. Much the same is true of Hardy. The stories of Saul and David from the first book of Samuel are seriously evoked in *The Mayor of Casterbridge*, lending a kind of universality and strength to the story of Henchard and Farfrae.[4] But none of this possesses us like a dybbuk. We experience rather what may be termed a controlled surrender. The patterns are valued as shaping images, savored for their power and resonance. But there is no Jacob-like struggle with the ancient word, no agonized quest for its meaning.

Another change becomes evident if we turn our attention to Hardy and Conrad. With Joseph Roth, Dostoevsky and Kafka,

116

the story of Job had been *sui generis*. It was not just one archetypal scheme out of many which might be tried out. On the
contrary, it seized one against one's will. It exercised a compulsion over the author and his fictional characters unlike that
produced by any other literary source. In Defoe's novel also
Robinson returned obsessively to the same biblical words and to
the same verses in the book of Psalms. With Hardy and Conrad
there is a difference: the biblical patterns, marked though they
are both in the narrative discourse and in the management of
the plot, operate in precisely the same manner as other myth-
patterns. In Conrad's fiction Cain and Jonah occupy the same
kind of aesthetic space as Aeneas and Orpheus. For Hardy, the
background of Roman Britain in the Wessex countryside and the
influence of Greek tragedy are structural elements as important
as the biblical patterns which we may detect in *The Mayor of
Casterbridge* or *The Return of the Native*. The various powerful myths
and legends coming to us from the ancient world, both biblical
and non-biblical, are suggestive in the same way and to much
the same degree and they easily merge together to form a syncretic
landscape.

This trend, bound up no doubt with the new emphasis on
comparative mythology in the writings of anthropologists from
James Frazer on, becomes more marked as we reach the mid-
twentieth century. Writers are often extremely dexterous in the
handling of myths and archetypes of all kinds which they seem
to exhibit for the reader's attention and admiration. In this context, biblical patterns are frequently encountered but rarely privi-
leged; they may be valued, discussed, found to be apt, but they
do not govern the text or compel the reader in a special way.

Writers of our own time (and readers too) tend to be knowledgeable about myth, too knowledgeable for uninhibited surrender. Seemingly, they have all been to graduate school and have
read Jung, Joseph Campbell, Northrop Frye and Leslie Fiedler
for themselves. They are fully aware of the power of the archetypal patterns that they use and discuss but at the same time
they are too sophisticated to submit to that power, even to the
extent of the limited surrender which we noted in Hardy and
Conrad. They will treat them wittily, quizzically, sometimes
deliberately inverting them for comic effect. Thus *Henderson the
Rain King* is Bellow's witty inversion of *Heart of Darkness*. The
imagery playfully equates darkest Africa with the everyday world

of New York City. At one point Henderson performs a ritual dance
to bring on the rain; the authorial comment is typical: "After the
gust of breeze came deeper darkness, like the pungent heat of
the trains when they pass into Grand Central tunnel on a devas-
tated day in August." It is a reductive strategy. We are reminded
of Fielding rewriting the story of Joseph and Potiphar's wife in
terms of a latter-day Joseph defending his "virtue" against the
advances of Mrs Slipslop and Lady B. But there, in spite of the
mock-epic tone, the biblical paradigm had not been seriously
undermined; the Joseph story retained its authority as a model
for Charity if not for Chastity. By contrast, *Henderson the Rain
King* tends to trivialize the myth-patterns inherited from the past.
The continuing viability of the myth itself – that of Faust or the
Wasteland, for instance – is called in question.

Bernard Malamud is peculiarly well versed in the encyclopedia
of mythic motifs and uses them with a deftness and lightness of
touch for which he has few equals. A great part of the critical
work done on Malamud turns out to be, in fact, a matter of identifying these motifs and allusions – quest rituals in *The Natural*,
seasonal myths in *The Assistant*, the archetype of the Double in
"The Last Mohican" with Susskind and Fidelman fantastically
changing roles halfway through. In all these examples we have
irony, distance and a high degree of authorial control. To the
extent that the identifications are correct, we may be fairly sure
that Malamud had thought of them first and had hidden them
in his fictions for us to find. It is that which explains the cunning, enigmatic quality of his text, especially that of the short
stories. If in "The Lady of the Lake" both Levine and Isabella
have their secret to hide – the secret of their Jewishness – then
the narrator too has secrets with which to tease us. There is for
instance the parodic evocation of Peter's thrice-repeated denial
of his Master in Freeman/Levine's repeated denial of his identity
or the comically distorted Jamesian *topos* of the American amid
the relics of European antiquity.[5] We are invited to pick up these
threads of allusion hidden in the texture of the novel or short
story and to enjoy them for their inventiveness and fantasy.

Modern invention in the realm of myth and archetype is also
characterized by virtuosity and multiplicity. Not one or two but
many mythic motifs will often be hidden in the same text; the
reader for his part is invited to exercise a virtuosity similar to
that of the artist in disentangling the varied and infolded motifs

and *topoi.* The master here is Borges, whose brilliant stories often prove to be labyrinths – the name of course of one of his collections. The skilled reader is provided with a number of clues which enable him, not indeed to find the exit, but to get to the heart of the labyrinth. The artist above all *chooses* those myths and patterns of allusion which can be most happily and ingeniously combined or which can be most artfully contrasted with one another.

The Israeli novelist S.Y. Agnon has a novella in which, by a metapoetic device, we see the actual process of choosing a myth or archetype. "In the Heart of the Seas" presents a group of travelers voyaging in the Black Sea on their way to the Holy Land. One day they sight a strange figure riding on the waves. It turns out to be the hero of the story, Hananiah, who had missed the boat and had embarked instead on a kind of magic carpet, using this as his means of transport! In the meantime the travelers make different guesses as to what the strange figure signifies. Some of them suggest that it is the Wandering Jew of Christian legend; another, who is given Agnon's own name, suggests that it is the "Shekhinah" – the female part of the Divine Presence – which according to Jewish folklore is destined one day to return with her people from exile. In addition, we have a reference to the mysterious music of the Sirens which serves to link the episode with the Odysseus legend and we also hear of a strange bird which accompanies the travelers on their voyage.[6] In effect, the voyagers (like the reader and like the author) are choosing the myth or myths which suit them best from a great variety of possibilities.

2

Bernard Malamud's use of myth and archetype in *The Fixer* (1966) exhibits a high degree of such virtuosity. This novel is based on the story of Mendel Beilis, a Ukrainian Jew, who was arrested in 1911 by the Czarist police and charged with the ritual murder of a Christian child. Beilis was finally put on trial and acquitted in 1913, his ordeal being accompanied by violent anti-Semitic propaganda and also by worldwide protests at this revival of the infamous medieval blood-libel. Malamud has reconstructed this chapter of Czarist history with some care, at the same time freely reinventing the character and attitudes of the hero for his own ideological purposes, renaming him Yakov Bok. A project of this kind involving the constraints of a longer fiction and marked by a certain gravity of tone and an attempted fidelity to historical circumstances, necessarily precludes the lightness of touch and fantasy which we noted in the shorter fictions. Nevertheless, the work exhibits in more muted form the same kind of inventiveness, the same trying out of different mythic possibilities. Each critic, like the voyagers on Agnon's ship, picks up one or two strands of allusion, but in fact we are presented with a multiple choice. And we can if we wish have them all. Indeed, criticism in the case of a fiction such as this should properly concern itself not so much with identifying the allusions, overt or hidden, as with determining the manner in which they combine or collide with one another.

The most obvious echo-patterns are those associated with the names he chooses for his hero. "Bok" is, as has often been pointed out, a goat, therefore also, appropriately, a scapegoat which is exactly Yakov's role both in Jewish and Russian society.[7] The name Yakov is even more significant, connecting him rather obviously with Yaakov/Jacob, the third of the patriarchs.[8] The biblical Jacob is the prototypical Man of Troubles, as he himself testifies: "few and evil have the days of the years of my life been" (Genesis 47:9). Midrash often sees him as prefiguring in his life of wandering and trial the tribulations of the exiled Jew of history. He is the archetypal shlemiel figure, meek, non-militant, rarely standing up for himself except when his mother pushes him to act, cheated by his father-in-law into marrying Leah whom he didn't love in place of Rachel whom he did. All this surely defines Yakov Bok's function and personality down to his luckless marriage and his unfortunate encounter with Nikolai Maximovitch Lebedev who is a kind of Laban-figure, only worse.

But of course, Jacob in the Bible makes his covenant with a personal God; Yakov quite explicitly does not.[9] These two options are evoked and beheld in relation to the present time (that is, that of the reader of 1966). On the one hand, there is the world of the Bible narratives with its "huffing-puffing God" always busy talking, appearing, acting in history; and on the other hand, there is a world – the one we inhabit – emptied of justice and mercy alike, in which God has been elevated, as in Spinoza's philosophy, into "an eternal infinite idea" (240). These two opposing views of reality are here wittily juxtaposed, made an object of discussion. We are placed in a position to *choose* between them – between a universe in which we are addressed by a personal God and one in which there is no one to address us. The confrontation becomes the ground of many quizzical reflections, but it does not yield the existential horror of Joseph K. in the final chapter of *The Trial,* when he seeks a saving presence, "a friend, a good man, someone who sympathized" and becomes aware instead that there is no one near, no judge and no saviour. This is the measure of the difference between the two texts. For Kafka the absence of dialogue and the metaphysical void thus created represented a fundamental category; the felt absence counted as testimony. For Malamud, on the other hand, we have two alternative and balancing modes of imagining which may be played off against one another and neither of which needs to be entertained with absolute seriousness.

The figure of Christ and his sufferings provide another major myth-pattern.[10] Yakov takes up this model after Zhitnyak smuggles a "small green paper-covered New Testament" into his cell (231). It is an episode perfectly modulated so as to define what is happening in the poetics of the narrative. The Christian myth is being "smuggled into" a story about a *Jewish* victim of persecution to see if it will serve as a language for expressing his *Jewish* troubles! When he first begins to read it, "the story of Jesus fascinated him" (232). What stays with him chiefly is the human aspect, the account of the suffering of an innocent man, like himself – "there was a man crying out in anguish in the dark" (ibid.). Like himself, he is a man being unjustly punished and persecuted. The analogy he draws between Christ and himself in fact had already begun to shape his own story. It has been plausibly suggested that in saving the life of Lebedev who had collapsed in the snow by the wayside, Bok was acting the part of the Good Samaritan in the parable.[11]

The Christ-role merges, moreover, with that of the "suffering servant" of Isaiah of whom it is said:

He was despised and rejected of men; a man of pains, and acquainted with sickness: and we hid as it were our eyes from him; he was despised and we esteemed him not. But in truth he has borne our sicknesses and endured our pains; yet we did esteem him stricken, smitten of God, and afflicted. But he was wounded because of our transgressions, bruised because of our iniquities.

(Isaiah 53:3–5)

Yakov Bok uses the term explicitly, if ironically, of himself:

The rod of God's anger against the fixer is Nicholas II, the Russian Tsar. He punishes the suffering servant for being godless.

(240–1)

"The suffering servant" would have had no particular Christian connotations for a self-taught Jew living in the Pale of Settlement. But the Christian associations inevitably suggest themselves to a western reader with a college education. And it is this readership and this setting that Malamud has in view when creating the mental world of his hero, much as Arthur Miller in "The Crucible" is really concerned not with the Salem witch trials but with the problems of American intellectuals in the 1950s accused of "un-American activities." Here Malamud's hero Bok (like Morris Bober in *The Assistant*), in seeking to comprehend the nature of his sufferings, uses language and imagery which have an inevitable Christian coloring. But it is part of the novel's intellectual sophistication that Yakov questions and debates this very issue. The author is conscious of his own cultural presuppositions and habits of language and these become the focus of debate in the novel.

Here in regard to the "Suffering Servant" Yakov, whilst showing in his language an awareness of the christological reading of these chapters, also resists this reading. His emphasis instead is on the suffering individual ("nobody suffers for him and he suffers for no-one except himself") but as Yakov matures and changes, his suffering will be seen by others as a vicarious sacrifice. "You suffer for us all" says the lawyer Ostrovsky. This is the Christian note again, and we may be tempted to categorize him as a Christian hero dying for the world. But it should be pointed out that Bibikov seems to feel that Yakov's sufferings have meaning for the political liberation of the Russian people from tyranny. This would make them a prefiguration of the Revolution of 1917 and Yakov would become the hero of a Marxist or quasi-Marxist salvation-myth. Yakov himself has important reservations. He cannot quite see

the point of one man suffering for others either for the purpose
of Christian redemption or for the sake of bringing about a social
revolution. The nearest he can get to vicarious sacrifice is the
notion of suffering for those he loves.

> Suffering I can gladly live without, I hate the taste of it, but if
> I must suffer let it be for something. Let it be for Shmuel.
>
> (273)

As this meditation proceeds, Yakov extends the circle of his love
to include the collectivity of the Jewish people. To suffer for them
and with them and to protect them through his endurance makes
sense:

> Overnight a madman is born who thinks Jewish blood is water.
> Overnight life becomes worthless. . . .Those Jews who escape
> with their lives live in memory's eternal pain.
>
> (274)

Yaakov has here moved away from the Christian reading of the
"suffering servant" chapters and has adopted something more
like the traditional Jewish exegesis which sees the servant as the
persona of the whole Jewish people, suffering the trials of its history.
And of course the last-quoted passage is clearly proleptic; it
associates Yakov's story with the Nazi Holocaust which would
occur 30 years after the events recorded in the novel. A madman
would be born who would shed Jewish blood like water – Yakov's
sufferings would then become symbolic of this larger chapter of
martyrdom, a prefiguration of the Holocaust rather than a
postfiguration of the Passion. Robert Alter sees *The Fixer* very
much as a holocaust novel, remarking aptly that "the Beilis case
gave [Malamud] a way of approaching the European Holocaust
on a scale that is imaginable, susceptible of fictional representation."[12] So that if we see Yakov literally picking up the Christian
salvation-myth at one point and applying it to himself, we also
see him as clearly considering other possibilities.

Actually, the testing and weighing of the Christian against other
systems of imagery and doctrine begin earlier – in a kind of Socratic
dialogue with Kogin, the prison guard, which takes place soon
after Yakov's introduction to the gospels. "All that blood and matzo
business is an old part of your religion," says Kogin. Yakov replies

that the Old Testament forbids the eating of blood; it is the gospel of John that declares that "he who eats my flesh and drinks my blood, abides in me, and I in him." Kogin, even more a novice in theology than Yakov, retorts that blood and flesh are only intended here as metaphor. Trust a Jew to get it wrong! Yakov does not easily give up the disturbing implications of the imagery: "Blood is blood. I said it the way it was written." There must in short be some relation between signifier and signified. He goes on to say that he reads the gospels "to find out what a Christian is." Kogin replies,

> "A Christian is a man who loves Christ."
> "How can anyone love Christ and keep an innocent man suffering in prison?"
> "There is no innocent Christ-killer," Kogin said, shutting the disk over the spy hole.
>
> (233)

Myth, for Yakov, cannot be so completely isolated from the doings of men in history. He reads the words referentially, as having a relation to the world we know; Kogin enjoys them for their own sake – "I like to hear the words of Christ." He complains that when Yakov says the words they sound different from the way he remembers them. Yakov tries another text: "Judge not, that you be not judged." "'That's enough,' said Kogin. 'I've had enough.'"

The final rejection comes in the next chapter. Yakov is visited in his prison cell by a priest of the Orthodox Church who has been told that he "religiously" reads the gospels. If he agrees to forgive his enemies, repent for his sins and embrace the true faith, he will be saved, says the priest. In fact, he may even be released from prison! But Yakov declares that he will forgive no one. Nor does he seek forgiveness for himself – what he seeks is vindication, the recognition of his truth and innocence. On that ground he stands. In rejecting the priest's offer to accept him into the bosom of the Church, he now affirms his loyalty to his own people by demonstratively donning prayer-shawl and phylactery. This gesture is not without absurdity. He grotesquely ties the phylactery for the arm around his head, and makes no pretence at reaffirming the faith of a Jew, the terms of which are inscribed in those phylacteries.

Nevertheless, Yakov will now take up the Old Testament –

some torn portions of which are tossed into his cell – and search it for a different myth and one which may perhaps make better sense than the Passion as a basis for his story. It is like the hermeneutic quest of Robinson Crusoe, only in reverse. Robinson's conversion experience had begun with him casually opening the Bible at Psalm 50 and applying its promise of deliverance to his condition; but a few days later, in true protestant fashion, he embarked on a systematic and serious study of the New Testament (see above, p. 35). This led him to conclude that "deliverance from sin" was a much greater blessing than deliverance from his imprisonment on the island! Defoe was here ironically weighing two different ways of reading: one we said was metonymic, the other, metaphoric. Robinson at this point (like Kogin) chose metaphor; Yakov, we may say, chooses metonymy.

3

It thus comes about that in the next chapter (Part 7, Chapter 3) Yakov, recoiling from the gospels as understood by Kogin and the visiting priest, applies himself (like Robinson) to a serious course of bible-reading. But in his case it will be the Old Testament in Hebrew that he will search for models relevant to his condition and needs:

> Yakov read the Old Testament through the stained and muddied pages, chapter by fragmentary chapter. He read each squat letter with care, although often the words were incomprehensible to him. He had forgotten many he once knew, but in the reading and rereading some came back; some were lost forever.
>
> (239)

His reading, unlike that of Robinson Crusoe, leads Yakov to no firm ground of self-understanding. He is excited by the stories, "gripped by the narrative of the joyous and frenzied Hebrews, doing business, fighting wars, sinning and worshipping" but he cannot accept the central myth which portrays God as entering into a covenant with his people and with each prophet and patriarch in turn. "He covenants, therefore he is" (ibid.). This does not accord with Yakov's experience – his covenant is with himself as he later declares (274), or, at the most, with his people, not

with the Almighty. But sometimes he finds the experience of one
of the bible heroes metonymically contiguous with his own. Thus
he is fascinated by the story of the prophet Hosea and his wife
Gomer, whose behavior reminds him of that of his own wife Raisl:

> He turned often to pages of Hosea and read with fascination
> the story of this man God had commanded to marry a harlot.
> The harlot, he had heard it said, was Israel, but the jealousy
> and anguish Hosea felt was that of a man whose wife had left
> his bed and board and gone whoring after strangers.
>
> (242)

The Old Testament too had its metaphors and parables. "He had
heard it said" that Hosea's domestic crisis is a metaphor for the
troubled course of God's covenant with Israel. But it is not the
metaphoric aspect that interests him; it is rather the anguish of a
man, like himself, betrayed by his wife, but who can give marvelous
voice to his suffering and humiliation. That is the dimension that
grips him.

Later on there is another Socratic-type dialogue on the question
of biblical models and their application to Yakov. It is when
Shmuel, Yakov's father-in-law, comes to visit him in the prison,
after having bribed one of the guards, Zhitnyak, with all his
accumulated capital of 40 roubles. The main controlling pattern
in the dialogue and the scene undoubtedly is that of Job. Shmuel,
like one of Job's friends, comes to pity and condole, to express
his sorrow at Yakov's plight. But like Eliphaz, Bildad and Zophar,
he passes quickly to a note of rebuke. If Job had suffered, they
say, he must have been guilty of some moral or religious
shortcoming (Job 8:3–6, 11:6,14, 22:5–10). Similarly, Shmuel, though
more gently, rebukes the wretched sufferer: "You see, Yakov, what
happens when you shave your beard and forget your God?" In
the conversation which follows we have the precise note of the
dialogue between Job and his comforters:

> "Don't talk to me about God," Yakov said bitterly. "I want no
> part of God. *When you need him most he's farthest away.* Enough
> is enough. My past I don't have to tell you, but if you knew
> what I've lived through since I saw you last." He began to say
> but his voice cracked.
>
> "Yakov," said Shmuel, clasping and unclasping his excitable

hands, "we're not Jews for nothing. Without God we can't live. Without the covenant we would have disappeared out of history. Let that be a lesson to you. He's all we have but who wants more?"

"Me. I'll take misery but not forever."

"For misery don't blame God. He gives the food but we cook it."

"I blame him for not existing. Or if he does it's on the moon or stars but not here. The thing is not to believe or the waiting becomes unbearable. *I can't hear his voice and never have. I don't need him unless he appears.*"

"Who are you, Yakov, Moses himself? *If you don't hear His voice so let Him hear yours.* 'When prayers go up blessings descend.'"

(256–7, emphasis added)

"When you need him most he's farthest away" is what Job had said in somewhat more polished language: "he passes by me and I see him not; he moves on but I do not perceive him" (9:11). Like Job, Yakov has the presumption to demand that God come down and grant him an interview: "I don't need him unless he appears." Job had said the same thing. "In my flesh I would see God; that I might see him for myself, that my eyes might behold and not another" (19:26–7). Shmuel's reaction is to say that Yakov should be content to turn to God without expecting a reply. It is the burden of Eliphaz (5:8) and indeed of all Job's friends.

But what we have just said seems to be contradicted later on in the same conversation when the book of Job itself becomes a topic of discussion between Shmuel and Yakov.

"Yakov," said Shmuel, "He invented light. He created the world. He made us both. The true miracle is belief. *I believe in Him. Job said, 'Though he slay me, yet will I trust in him.'* He said more but that's enough."

"To win a lousy bet with the devil *he killed off all the servants and innocent children of Job.* For that alone I hate him, not to mention ten thousand pogroms. Ach, why do you make me talk fairy-tales? Job is an invention and so is God. Let's let it go at that."

(258, emphasis added)

In this exchange, Shmuel holds up Job as a model but Yakov summarily rejects it. Yet at another level, he is through that very rejection confirming his identity for us as a Job figure![13] When a character such as Shmuel proposes glib, high-sounding solutions to the mystery of human existence and of God's dealings with the just and the unjust – even if he cites Job as his example and Job's words as his proof – he will have Job against him! By the same token, when a character passionately rejects the Job model as an example of divine injustice, he will have Job with him! Shmuel confidently brandishes a prooftext from Job – "Though he slay me, yet will I trust in him" (13:15). Here it would seem is the Kierkegaardian leap. But as we noted earlier (above, p. 83), the Hebrew of that verse can yield an opposite, more despairing sense, "See, he slays me – I have no hope!" That in effect is what Yakov is saying. In short, Yakov in rejecting Shmuel's pious argument is being faithful to another dimension of Job as essential as the Kierkegaardian leap of faith.

The Hebrew writer, Yosef Haim Brenner gives us an analogous instance of the same paradox in his novel, *Breakdown and Bereavement* (1920). There too we have a suffering character, or rather a group of sufferers: Yehezkel Hefetz, Yehezkel's kinsman, Haim and the latter's son, Hanoch. Yehezkel's trouble is partly physical – he suffers from hernia – and partly neurasthenic. But it is acute just the same and explicitly brings to mind the sufferings of Job. Again the Job motif is foregrounded by way of rejection:

> In the book of Job the Leper it is written: "And he took a potsherd to scrape himself with." Only I am not Job: I have no complaints against God. In fact, I have no God. I have nothing to do with God . . . I'm not Job. And I don't sit in ashes, either, but in refuse, in the refuse of my own ugly suffering. Only I don't let go of the potsherd. I can't stop scratching.[14]

Here Brenner seems to reduce the analogy to absurdity when Yehezkel tells us that like Job on his dung-hill, he can't stop scratching! But the humorous and irreverent tone of this passage is not a way of dismissing the Job model as a joke. On the contrary, I would want to argue, the effect is to bring the two figures, Job and the anti-hero Yehezkel Hefetz, startlingly near to one another.[15] For Brenner, Job is a familiar presence; he lives, so to speak, on the same block! For Hebrew writers in general, as we shall see in subsequent chapters, however much they may seek to disassociate themselves from the stories and figures of the Bible,

those figures occupy the same linguistic and cultural space as
they themselves. Such proximity is on the whole lacking in the
more studied and contrived use of the Job analogy in *The Fixer.*

One other, directly Joban aspect of Yakov Bok's situation,
however, which Malamud emphasizes, suggests a more everyday dimension of understanding. What Job had demanded was
justice, his day in court.

> Oh, that I had one to hear me! Here is my signature! Let the
> Almighty answer me! Oh, that I had the indictment written by
> my adversary! Surely, I would carry it on my shoulder; I would
> bind it on me as a crown.
>
> (31:35–6)

This passage, cited here from the Revised Standard Version, echoes
in *The Fixer.* Yakov Bok's constant plea is that they serve him his
indictment; he too would treasure it as his most precious possession. His moment of maximum frustration is when Grubeshov
withholds the promised indictment and demands instead that
he sign a confession (224). Yakov refuses. He will not become a
party to a monstrous lie. He endures only for the sake of his
hoped-for trial. "I'll live, I'll wait, I'll come to my trial," he shouts
from his cell to anyone who cares to hear him (275). What he
too desires is his day in court. This is the basis of his moral stand.
We might say that from this point of view the lesson which Yakov
learns from Job is the duty the innocent owe themselves not to
allow themselves to be brainwashed into accepting the notion of
their own corruption. In today's world it sometimes seems that
liberalism itself requires us to believe that if all men are equal,
then they are all equally bad; nations likewise. It requires a good
deal of moral courage to maintain, with Job, a contrary thesis.

Here *The Fixer* shows a genuine affinity to Kafka's *The Trial.*[16]
The unknown nature of the charges against Joseph K., the agony
of waiting for the trial, the stubborn avowals of innocence – all
these features link *The Trial* to *The Fixer.* And they connect both
to the book of Job. In both novels the issue of suicide is raised.
In Part 8, Chapter 1 of *The Fixer,* Yakov, tortured now beyond
endurance, takes secret pleasure in the thought of his death and
the knowledge that he has it in his power to bring it about. In
the next chapter he rejects this option, not because he is afraid
to die, but because he would be betraying Shmuel and indeed

all his fellow-Jews. He determines to survive and await his trial. At the end of *The Trial*, the two executioners first offer the knife to Joseph K. so that he might "plunge it into his own breast." It is only after he refuses to do so that they kill him "like a dog." Both novels are here arguably indebted to Job who had refused to curse God and die.

But having said all this, we must not ignore the essential difference between the way that the Job pattern operates for a mid-century writer such as Malamud and for an earlier writer, even one so aware and sophisticated as Kafka. If Kafka, as Frye maintains, is writing a kind of commentary on Job, it is because that powerful archetype has him in thrall. Though he does not refer to Job explicitly, it is for Kafka, as we have seen, an inescapable presence. With Malamud it is different. He does refer explicitly to Job and indeed discusses the relevance of that book to his hero's situation, but there is a far greater degree of contrivance, of irony and distance in the handling of the Job analogy. And there are also, as we noted earlier, the elements of virtuosity and multiple choice. The author in writing his novel is looking around for appropriate models in a supermarket of mythic patterns; he is even inviting the reader to see how he makes his choices. The pleasure of the reader is very much bound up with such inventiveness. A more total and single-minded submission is perhaps not to be expected from the contemporary writer in the West. Nor would it necessarily be welcomed by the contemporary reader for whom the Bible has become, at the most, a fruitful source of ideas and images rather than – what it had been for earlier generations – an inescapable presence.

Part IV
Isaac Unbound

8

Saul Bellow and
Philip Roth

1

Virtuosity and self-consciousness also characterize other contemporary American Jewish writers in their handling of biblical archetypes. Saul Bellow achieves even richer combinations than Malamud. In *Mr Sammler's Planet* the ironical reflections on the Holocaust which Sammler shares with his Indian visitor Dr Lal, centre on a passage he quotes from Job Chapter 7. "What is man, that thou shouldst magnify him?" Job asks; why does God expect so much of wretched human beings? The Nazis succeeded in crushing the very humanity of their victims. What was left, Sammler remarks, was "the imaginary grandeur of insects." His example is the case of Rumkowski, a former actor, whom the Nazis appointed as "the mad Jewish King of the Jewish ghetto of Lodz." Having done so they then sat back to enjoy his grotesque antics before finally putting him to death along with the others.[1] Here, as in *The Fixer*, is Job operating as a fundamental paradigm for our dreadful twentieth-century experience but the linkage is made with greater subtlety and a lighter touch.

Another biblical paradigm even more crucial for the structure of the book as well as for the understanding of its central character is that of Ecclesiastes. Like Kohelet, Sammler has in his long years beheld much wisdom, madness and folly and has come to the conclusion that all is vanity. There is no new thing under the sun. The feverish search for novelty, for new worlds and fresh beginnings, reveals its emptiness (136). Space ships and moon flights are already well established in the writings of Jules Verne and H.G. Wells (whom Sammler had known personally). Musing on the specimens of moon-rock that the astronauts had collected, Sammler ironically reverses a text from Ecclesiastes: "A time to gather stones together, a time to cast away stones" (51). Sammler like Kohelet keeps his feet on the ground – on this planet. Solomon's wisdom here blends with Sammler's life-experience; it is a wisdom of one who has reconciled himself to his human limitations and who no longer harbors Utopian dreams of world-betterment. A survivor from a Nazi "Aktion" and without illusions about human goodness ("I saw all the oppressions that are practiced under the sun" – Kohelet had remarked) he will nevertheless strive to maintain his integrity. Like Kohelet he ends his book with grave thoughts on dying; the occasion is the passing of Elya Gruner, his kinsman and benefactor. Sammler sums up Elya's life much in the way that Kohelet had summed up the "whole duty of man." "Fear God and keep his commandments," Kohelet had said. Sammler says the same as he calls upon God to remember the soul of Elya Gruner as one who had always been "eager, even childishly perhaps . . . to do what was required of him."

> He was aware that he must meet, and he did meet – through all the confusion and degraded clowning of this life through which we are speeding – he did meet the terms of his contract.
>
> (313)

But Bellow with greater intellectual clarity than the other authors we have so far considered not only sets the biblical paradigms to work in his fictions; he also sets up their antithesis. The result is an *agon* conducted between opposing patterns and archetypes. Here in *Mr Sammler's Planet* we find, juxtaposed to the Ecclesiastes-pattern with its worldly wisdom, its gravity, its disenchantments, and its final vote for rightdoing and justice, also a pattern of vivid depravity. Sammler is drawn to scenes of violence either as witness or participant; he is sensitive to modes of corruption and excess, the *fleurs du mal* of a world which has been shaped by a "dark romanticism." Bellow traces this back for us to its nineteenth-century origins in Baudelaire, Nietzsche and Wagner. The modern city, here exemplified by New York, testifies, especially in the sexual mores of its inhabitants, to that dark region. Neither Bellow nor his protagonist adopts a judgmental stand. "Sammler felt no prejudice about perversion, about sexual matters. Nothing. It was too late in the day for that," we are told (296). He is powerfully aware of the uncurbed sensuality of his daughter Shula and of Elya's daughter Angela (31–5).

He is a perplexed but fascinated observer of this scene of corruption. His job is to register it. Like the prophet Tiresias in Eliot's poem he has seemingly "foresuffered all/ Enacted on this same divan or bed" and the result is a certain Shakespearian impartiality towards the Dionysiac streak in modern culture – what in *Herzog* Bellow terms in a telling phrase, "the creative depth of modern degeneracy." This creative depth is matched in the novel against the biblical resonances which we have noted and Bellow tries to do justice to both.

In *Mr Sammler's Planet* the central symbol of the Dionysiac mode is the Negro pickpocket who is introduced at the very beginning of the novel and who accompanies the action to the end, where he makes a final entry just before the death of Elya. He clearly represents not only violence but also sexual power. In a central episode, his phallus, like that of the god Dionysus himself, is exhibited in almost ritual fashion before Sammler's fascinated gaze (49–50). The black man's startling power and magnificence are clearly beheld as the antithesis to Sammler's intellectual bent, his Jewish sensibilities and inhibitions. There is a pointed reference to the Negro's uncircumcised state.

But Bellow's sense of the mythic conjunctions which govern our age is much more dialectical than that. It is not a matter of simple antithesis. In the final episode involving the Negro, Eisen, Sammler's Israeli son-in-law, injures the black man by striking him violently in the face with a bag of heavy, metal artifacts. Sammler is horrified; Eisen must be crazy. But Eisen, projecting the less pacific image of the new Israeli, laughingly reminds Sammler that in his younger days as a partisan in the Zamosht forest he had himself carried a gun and had not hesitated to use it (291). In short Bellow is interested in representing archetypal patterns from many sources and in the subtle and complex dialogue enacted between them. Where Conrad and Hardy give us a syncretic blend of mythic motifs drawn from both Pagan and biblical antiquity and Malamud allows us a multiple choice, Bellow develops and illustrates their mutual tensions as well as their convergences. Moreover he not only shows the different patterns in action in plot and character, but as a student of romanticism and its aftermath, he also analyzes the cultural situation that they yield in abstract terms. Again, we have conscious control, that of the artist who fashions images of the world for our delight but is also detached enough to be able to define the different forces at work and their interaction. We have in short a seminar rather than a supermarket. But it is a seminar which also remains close to the lived reality of the times and places which it surveys. That is Bellow's strength.

2

I would like to turn to one other important biblical pattern used, or rather hinted at, by Bellow to great effect. It is that of the Binding of Isaac (the Akedah) which is evoked towards the end of *Herzog*. The "Last Trial" of Abraham as recounted in Genesis 22 had attracted renewed attention among American intellectuals generally and Jewish writers in particular with the appearance of Willard Trask's English translation of Erich Auerbach's *Mimesis* in 1953. But Chapter 1 with its analysis of the Akedah story in contrast with a famous episode in the *Odyssey* had appeared earlier in the *Partisan Review* for May, 1950.[2] Bellow was at that time closely associated with the *Partisan Review* and so it is not surprising that the text of the Akedah which Auerbach by his seminal essay had placed at the forefront of critical attention should have stirred Bellow's imagination in the writing of *Herzog* a few years later.

   In the final section of Bellow's novel, Moses Herzog arrives at his country home in Ludeyville in the Berkshires feeling, as he tells us, joyful and contented. He has emerged from a nervous crisis, having gained a kind of moral victory over his divorced wife Madeleine in their confrontation at the Chicago police precinct. His servitude is ended, he says. Here is a scene in which the outer world with its pastoral imagery harmonizes with an inner zone of tranquillity. Herzog's spirit rejoices at the marvelous beauty of the summer afternoon and he signals his arrival in Ludeyville with the Hebrew word Hinneni, "Here I am!"

> Here I am. *Hineni* [sic]! How marvelously beautiful it is today. He stopped in the overgrown yard, shut his eyes in the sun, against flashes of crimson, and drew in the odors of catalpa-bells, soil, honeysuckle, wild onions, and herbs.[3]

Hinneni, as Auerbach points out, is a key term, occurring three times in the Akedah pericope. When Abraham is commanded to

go to Mount Moriah, God calls him by name "Abraham, Abraham"
and he answers: "Here I am!"; he answers Isaac in the same fashion
as they climb the mountain; and finally when the angel calls out
from heaven to prevent the sacrifice, we have the same formula:
the angel cries out to him, "Abraham, Abraham" and he answers
"Hinneni!" "This opening startles us," says Auerbach. It seems to
speak of a location but in fact we are not told where the two
speakers are.

> He says indeed: Here I am – but the Hebrew word means only
> something like "behold me," and in any case is not meant to
> indicate the actual place where Abraham is, but a moral posi-
> tion in respect to God, who has called to him – Here am I
> awaiting thy command.[4]

It would seem to follow from this that Bellow is using the Hebrew
word in a contrary sense to that of the Akedah text itself as
understood by Auerbach. His hero is decidedly speaking of a
location and is saying: Here I am in Ludeyville; I have arrived
here, *in this place*, to find a cure for my spirit in this tranquil
setting with its wonderful sights and smells. In other words there
is a naturalistic, secularized transformation of the pattern. If any
more transcendental meaning is implied in Moses Herzog's
"Hinneni," then Bellow would seem to show no recognition of it
at this point. Moses Herzog is no Abraham and the pastoral abun-
dance of Ludeyville is an image far removed from the rocky slopes
of Moriah. The pronounced emphasis on soil and the smells of
the earth in the quotation from *Herzog* might even seem to mark
this passage as a parodic version of Auerbach's reading of the
text. The biblical stories do not flatter the senses, he tells us more
than once in his essay. But Bellow is doing just that. From this
point of view the Ludeyville episode (both the rich outer scene
and the detailed inner response of the protagonist to that scene)
would seem to represent a mode of realism quite different from
the Akedah – indeed its antithesis. The Hebrew prophets abhor
the pastoral with its languor and nostalgia; theirs is a more strenuous doctrine, a harsher vision. Bellow, in situating his hero at
the close of the novel in a kind of Forest of Arden where he will
be rejuvenated under the benign influence of Nature, is thus again
making a Shakespearian gesture of open-mindedness. Even as
he utters the word which seems to express the very nature of

biblical man, he shows himself entirely receptive to the potency of those other non-Hebraic patterns which have likewise and to an equal degree shaped our western culture.[5] Here we may note again the acknowledgment, if not acceptance, of the Dionysiac inheritance, with its celebration of Nature, of the gods of the earth. Herzog adapts himself to this rhythm, passively "satisfied to be, just as it is willed" (414).

But there is the other, contrary rhythm also, for Bellow is nothing if not subtle and his sense of history nothing if not dialectical. In his stream of consciousness following his arrival at Ludeyville Herzog reflects on this very phenomenon of the Dionysiac inheritance in a letter that he writes to "Dear Herr Nietzsche." He wonders whether Herr Nietzsche had really considered where his ideas would lead. Some of his expressions he says, like "the luxury of Destruction" have a "very Germanic ring." We have seen enough destruction in our time to test to the full the Dionysian spirit which according to Nietzsche "has the same power of recovery as Nature itself" (388). The conclusion clearly is that we cannot rest satisfied with that kind of naturalistic philosophy as an answer to our troubles. He writes other letters, as his thoughts meander through earlier passages of his life. He is troubled in case his brother Will tries to place him under psychiatric care. He knows that he is in an abnormal state of excitement but he is determined not to let go of his new-found self-possession. He feels now that he is, above all things, *responsible*. The word is repeated three times. And now as the word "responsible" still resonates, Herzog writes his final letter – to God. In it he discovers (without quoting the term) the other meaning of *Hinneni*. Auerbach had said that what it signified was "a moral position in respect to God, who has called to him – Here am I awaiting thy command." Herzog uses almost the same language in his letter to God:

> To God he jotted several lines.
> *How my mind has struggled to make coherent sense. I have not been too good at it. But have desired to do your unknowable will, taking it, and you, without symbols. Everything of intensest significance. Especially if divested of me.*
>
> (396–7)

These words have the same weight as Mr Sammler's summarizing tribute to Elya Gruner. At this point in his reflections, Herzog is like Abraham, not passively awaiting events as they might come, but responding to a call, "desir[ing] to do your unknowable will." That is the extra meaning that the word responsibility seems to acquire in this context.

One other word stands out in the passage just quoted. It is the word "intense" – "everything of intensest significance." This is an important term in Bellow's characterization of Herzog and, as here, in defining Herzog's apprehension of a divine order. It is also, as we shall see, an important term in Auerbach's discussion. Let us be clear about what Auerbach does not do. He scarcely touches on the meaning of the Akedah as doctrine; he does not follow Kierkegaard in an attempt to determine the philosophical and theological implications of the story. To the extent that he approaches these matters he does so obliquely by way of an examination of language and style. Above all he examines the story as an example of realism of a certain kind, in particular, psychological realism. In this it is typical of the Genesis narratives in general. The characters come to us he says, in a phrase several times repeated, "fraught with background" or "fraught with their own development." They carry the burden of the past and the promise of the future. It is this which gives suspense and tension to the narration. The characters have an inwardness which is lacking in the more externalized scene of the Homeric narratives. They are more profoundly tested than are Homer's characters. "Humiliation and elevation go far deeper and higher than in Homer." And then he goes on to say;

> The reader clearly feels how the extent of the pendulum's swing is connected with *the intensity of the personal history* – precisely the most extreme circumstances, in which we are immeasurably forsaken and in despair, or immeasurably joyous and exalted, give us, if we survive them, a personal stamp which we recognize as the product of a rich existence, a rich development.
>
> (15, emphasis added)

It is precisely this intensity of his personal history which Bellow's hero exhibits here and elsewhere in the book. He has endowed him with a rich inner life marked by extreme states, a capacity for suffering but also a capacity for joy and vision. Moses, fraught with his past development – the phrase is exactly right – is being healed of his sore affliction. In short he has passed his test; in his case this means coming out of the neurotic condition which has plagued him throughout the period covered by the book, expressing itself in a compulsive writing of letters to all manner of people, dead or living. Now in his final letter to God he defines himself and the meaning of his life in terms very reminiscent of Auerbach's chapter. If the biblical characters were marked by the richness of their inner lives and by the intensity which conditioned their existence, then Herzog recognizes that same intensity and richness in himself as he surveys his past struggles and his future hopes. "Everything of intensest significance" – is a phrase he throws out (397) and later, at the conclusion of these final meditations, he wonders what this intensity of his inner life might portend:

> Something produces intensity, a holy feeling, as oranges produce orange, as grass green, as birds heat. Some hearts put out more love and some less of it, presumably . . . But this intensity, doesn't it mean anything?
>
> (414)

Is the intensity he feels within merely a gesture, a reflex of the organism, or does it mean something? Is it the effect of being addressed, summoned – which would make it a holy feeling, akin to love? Bellow does not give a single answer to this question; he leaves the ambiguities in place.

There is no way that a modern American intellectual who has endured the crisis of modernity can wholly affirm the life of dialogue to which the Akedah bears witness and which the term *Hinneni* fundamentally implies. What we have instead in Bellow's case is an aesthetic achievement, the willing suspension of disbelief for the moment. This may constitute poetic faith, but it need be no more than that. What Bellow offers is a kind of *trompe-d'oeil*, a trick of language. The cunning artist joins the pastoral and the anti-pastoral, monologue and dialogue, without ever really deciding between them; he adopts the stand of skeptic and believer at one and the same time. But this does not answer the questions that Job or the Akedah narrative raises. Kierkegaard had remarked that with his single-minded faith Abraham "does not lie within the circumference of aesthetics." And he goes on to say that his task of sacrificing Isaac for God's sake (the first *Hinneni*) "is an offense to aesthetics."[6] We might add that the third *Hinneni*, marking the aborted sacrifice, is an even greater offence! Here is the denial of closure. Instead of an ending, a "dying fall," we have the imperative of survival, the necessity laid upon the reader to continue retelling and reliving the story. Bellow avoids these sharp extremes; he gives us an ending which, without being quite terminal, provides a kind of sunset glow. He remains within "the circumference of aesthetics."

Shakespeare is more his model here than the Bible and I suspect that the fifth act of *Hamlet* with its rich ambiguities was in the author's mind as he penned this closing section of his novel.[7] He seems to say with Hamlet – "the readiness all" meaning both a readiness for death and a readiness to act. These meanings contradict one another but the artist can get away with such contradictions. Similarly, Herzog often seems to be saying with Hamlet that "there's a divinity that shapes our ends" where ends can mean purposes, aims still to be achieved, or it can mean the end of life to which we resign ourselves with a wise passivity. The artist need not decide; his saying is a play of opposites which does not obligate him or us in the business of living. Bellow is the playful artist. Auerbach had said that the Akedah seeks to overcome our reality; it challenges us "to fit our own life into its world" (12). Bellow does not take up this challenge. He does not take the strenuous path of existential interpretation. Instead he chooses play, the play of words and the play of ideas. As an intellectual historian of the modern period, Bellow likewise offers us the Hebraic inheritance and the Paganism of Nietzsche. He offers us the Dionysiac and the biblical in playful combination and, with seeming impartiality (another word for which might be irresponsibility), he watches the puppets dallying.

It may be objected that this is art; the writer is supremely *homo ludens* and nothing more should be demanded of him. He is not expected to be a prophet or a saviour. But the times we live in have created new exigencies and have imposed new constraints on the serious artist. Is aesthetic closure any longer viable? Can the golden world of the pastoral still function as a sustaining myth? The failure of the Enlightenment – evidence for which Bellow himself clearly spells out through the words and thoughts of Artur Sammler and Moses Herzog – obligates us as readers and writers in radically new ways.[8] A new kind of honesty is now called for – the sort of searing honesty that we noted in Kafka – and it may be questioned whether Bellow for all his high intelligence has proved capable of it.

3

It will be obvious that the notion of "trial" in the sense of God's "trying" of Abraham has undergone a radical change in *Herzog*. Herzog is not called upon to sacrifice his child, though this threat momentarily suggests itself when his daughter Junie narrowly misses injury in an automobile accident for which he was responsible. This episode indeed provides the background for the final meeting with Madeleine in the police station. But Moses' basic problem is not child-sacrifice but mental disorder, neurosis – partly brought about through the emotional battering he has suffered from a number of overpowering female characters. (In this he is not unlike Joseph in *Dangling Man*, an earlier Bellow story.) His basic need is to become adjusted and achieve mental stability; and it is to satisfy this need that the Akedah is invoked in the final pages of the novel. He will be saved in the sense of finding a cure for his typically modern sickness – that of alienation, involving the loss of a secure identity, which afflicts so many inhabitants of the urban Wasteland in our time. The recognized and recommended modes of treatment are clinical, involving sessions with the psychiatrist – the modern secular substitute for prayer and meditation. But the individual sufferer has a great deal to do for himself by way of self-examination and self-control. Moses is on the way to such self-adjustment as the novel ends; he has secured a perilous foothold on sanity. In this regard his "Hinneni" signifies the overcoming of a crisis of identity. He now knows who he is – "Here I am!" he says. Personal integration or reintegration is here the basic issue rather than readiness to do the will of God.

This focusing on mental pathology would seem to represent a certain trivializing of the Akedah, but it might also be claimed as the universalizing of the biblical pattern which now has reference to the *Angst* suffered by Man-in-general in our depersonalized environment. Bellow makes these grand gestures of inclusiveness. Moses, more than he is a Jew, is a representative of the human condition. Herzog is being cast as both Leopold Bloom and Stephen Dedalus in Joyce's novel – aspiring hero and *schlemiel* at the same time.[9] He is the average sensual man but he is also the intellectual, engaged in the high quest for Truth, seeking some principle of order and wholeness in a fragmented universe.

A less grandiose attempt to link the Binding of Isaac with the modern search for identity is Philip Roth's extravagantly comic masterpiece, "Eli the Fanatic" (1957), a short story witnessing, like *Herzog*, to the impact of Auerbach's famous essay. But here the treatment of the Akedah is frankly reductive, at least on the surface. Again the hero, Eli Peck has a history of nervous disorder and, again his neurotic tendencies are related to the suffocating presence of a dominating wife. As his name implies he is the henpecked husband. Miriam, who keeps reminding him that he needs therapy, is more than anyone else the cause of his disturbance. Like Vala in Blake's poem, "The Mental Traveller", "her fingers number every Nerve,/ Just as a miser counts his gold." Moreover she is about to bear his child; this gives her extra bounce and confidence, thus making Eli's thraldom the more exacting. At the same time, it opens up the possibility of his achieving a new independent identity as a father.

Eli's need to escape and liberate himself takes the form of another Akedah trial, this time done in comic fantasy. As a lawyer, Eli is charged by the modern, thoroughly Americanized Jewish community of Woodenton, New Jersey, with the task of ridding them of the embarrassing presence of a group of immigrants from Europe – Holocaust survivors, who bring to the town their ancient superstitions. The most notorious of these, according to Eli's friend Ted, is represented by the story of the sacrifice of Isaac:

> "Sundays I drive my oldest kid all the way to Scarsdale to learn Bible stories ... and you know what she comes up with? This Abraham in the Bible was going to kill his own kid for a sacrifice. She gets nightmares from it, for God's sake! You call that religion? Today a guy like that they'd lock him up. This is an age of science, Eli. I size people's feet with an X-ray machine, for God's sake. They've disproved all that stuff, Eli, and I refuse to sit by and watch it happening on my own front lawn."[10]

"You're dealing with fanatics," he adds. Eli tries his best to brush Ted's fears aside, "Nothing's happening on your front lawn, Teddie. You're exaggerating, nobody's sacrificing their kid" – but the thought lingers in his own mind. Later that evening, seeing a light from a window of the building occupied by the aliens and the 18 orphan schoolboys in their charge, he wonders what Tzuref, the headmaster and the leader of the group, was doing in his office at that hour. Perhaps he was killing babies, he mused!

Strangely, Eli's unborn son is menaced by the strangers in their dark dress. At an earlier meeting Tzuref had wished him peace and good luck on his approaching fatherhood, of which he had mysterious intelligence. Fantastically, the candles go out as he pronounces his wish. "But the instant before, the flames leaped into Tzuref's eyes, and Eli saw it was not luck Tzuref wished him at all" (194). Tzuref it would seem has paced an evil eye on the child. Will the child be safely born and, more particularly, will Eli, now succumbing to a nervous breakdown, achieve his identity by becoming a true father? That is the trial he must undergo in the three days that follow.

The identity crisis is symbolically resolved when Eli performs an exchange of dress (and personalities) with one of the strangers – "the one in the black hat" – never named in the story but only referred to as "the greenie" or "the fanatic." He was the one most often seen in Woodenton where he did the shopping on behalf of the "Yeshivah." After the birth of his son, we see Eli dressed in the black garb of this stranger, which he has appropriated. "But he knew who he was down to his marrow" (212). He has made his peace with Tzuref, the archetypal father-figure from the past ("Tzuref, father to eighteen" "I know what it is to have children" [191, 194]) and with himself. Ted meets Eli arriving in his strange dress at the maternity ward and comically supposes that in his mental crisis he has come to re-enact the Akedah sacrifice:

> Ted tapped Eli's arm. "You're not thinking of doing something you'll be sorry for . . . are you Eli? Eli – I mean you know you're still Eli, don't you?"
> In the enclosure, Eli saw a bassinet had been wheeled before the square window.
> "Oh, Christ . . ." Ted said. "You don't have this Bible stuff on the brain –"
>
> (215)

Here in the repeated "Eli" we have the call, "Abraham, Abraham" done in low mimetic. Eli has "flipped" but he has understood the Akedah event better than Ted. Isaac will be saved and so will the father. Before they plunge the hypodermic syringe into his arm to drown his consciousness, Eli "rose suddenly, as though up out of a dream, and flailing his arms, screamed: *'I'm the father!'*"

All this seems to be nothing more than excellent fooling, the Akedah being subjected to a merely comic or reductive treatment. The reader feels with Ted the ridiculous incongruity of the Bible story of Abraham sacrificing his son when transposed into the world of American middle-class suburbia. ("Today a guy like that they'd lock him up.") In that sense Roth has given us no more than an elaborate joke. But at another level, he is pointing to a more universal crisis of identity than that which afflicts Eli Peck.[11] Here in this whimsical restoration of the father it may be argued that Roth has not only correctly read the Akedah myth but has also correctly understood its meaning in the spiritual and literary history of the West from the Enlightenment onwards. There is in this story no universalistic posing, no high discourse in the history of ideas – it seems to operate at the personal level only, with Eli, a wife-ridden American bourgeois, having a nervous breakdown. But it may be argued nevertheless that Roth's story has reference to a larger crisis, one that may be described in terms of a family narrative beginning in the aftermath of the Enlightenment and continuing to the present day.

The first stage of this narrative occurs with the late eighteenth-century and nineteenth-century rebellion against the Father who incarnates the authority of the Past, an authority now become too oppressive to be borne. If we do not cast him off, he will destroy us. In Melville's *Billy Budd*, Ibsen's *Brand* and Samuel Butler's *The Way of All Flesh*, the younger and more hopeful generation is threatened by a murdering father or father figure. The son may be literally done to death or he may be only threatened with a kind of psychological extinction. Either way, the Binding of Isaac is regularly invoked as a means of defining this situation. Captain Vere catches Billy to his breast before sending him to be executed "even as Abraham may have caught young Isaac on the brink of resolutely offering him up in obedience to the exacting behest."[12] Christina Pontifex imagines herself taking her first-born, Ernest, to Pigbury beacon to plunge the knife into him. The intended victims naturally rebel; they rebel in the name of Freedom, Nature and the Rights of Man. ("Rights-of-Man," we may remember, was the name of the ship from which Billy Budd had been press-ganged.) Elizabeth Barrett Browning makes good her escape from a domineering Victorian father. With Matthew Arnold, whose very strong-minded father was also his headmaster, escape must have been more difficult. He achieves a kind of exorcism through his poetry, often poems like "The Forsaken Merman" or "Sohrab and Rustum" which reflect the very theme of child-sacrifice or child abandonment through an emotional mist.

The net outcome of this phase is that by the time the century is over the father has been all but eliminated from the household. Ernest Pontifex in *The Way of All Flesh* will strike out for Freedom, whilst his father Theobald will be reduced to insignificance. In D.H. Lawrence's *Sons and Lovers* (1912) Walter Morel no longer functions as the head of the family – he has become a beer-drinking helpless creature. The mother, Mrs Morel, will now rule. In *Call It Sleep* (1934) by the American writer, Henry Roth, David, the boy hero, runs from the house to escape his father's violence and in the course of his flight barely escapes death through electrocution. It is a typical Akedah episode. The father, Albert is seen at the end thoroughly chastised and humiliated; authority now belongs exclusively to the mother.

But now begins the third phase of the narrative. The exclusive authority of the mother proves to be no more tolerable in the end than that of the father had been earlier on. Lawrence powerfully expressed the suffering of the child in the fatherless household exposed to unbridled mother-love. "The mother-child relationship" he declared, "is today the viciousest of circles."[13] And speaking of the Morel family in *Sons and Lovers*, he noted that "these sons are urged into life by their reciprocal love of their mother – urged on and on. But when they come to manhood they can't love, because their mother is the strongest power in their lives and holds them."[14] This oedipal crisis beomes a commonplace in the mid-century. It receives its extreme (and I would add its most scabrous) formulation in Philip Roth's *Portnoy's Complaint* (1967). With his usual clarity and comic extravagance Roth not only represents the situation but analyzes it for us:

> If my father had only been my mother! and my mother my father! But what a mix-up of sexes in our house! Who should by rights be advancing on me, retreating – and who should be retreating, advancing! Who should be scolding, collapsing in helplessness, enfeebled totally by a tender heart! And who should be collapsing, instead scolding, correcting, reproving, criticizing, faultfinding without end! Filling the patriarchal vacuum.[15]

Alex's father, a sufferer from chronic constipation, has been reduced to helplessness and his mother Sophie is to all intents and purposes the head of the family. She "fills the patriarchal vacuum" (42). It is against the suffocating warmth of his mother's love that Alex rebels. The rebellion against her is as characteristic of the literary imagination in our time as the rebellion against the father had been in the nineteenth century, and as universal.

Here then is the obverse side of the Akedah where the issue is not a murderous father but a castrating or otherwise threatening female figure. It is thus not altogether surprising that in both Bellow's *Herzog* and Philip Roth's "Eli, the Fanatic" the Akedah-pattern is again invoked or hinted at as in *Brand* or *Billy Budd*. We are dealing with a parallel situation. In the opening episode in Proust's great novel, Marcel, one of the first heroes in modern literature with a decided mother fixation, is sent to bed by his father without his mother's kiss. Hours later, still violently disturbed and unable to sleep, he waylays his parents on their way to their bedroom. The scene calls up in his mind the image of Abraham in an engraving after Bonozzo Gozzoli telling Sarah she must tear herself away from Isaac.[16] In the two texts that we have been discussing, namely, *Herzog* and "Eli, the Fanatic," the element of sacrifice is less prominent and the akedah references focus on the moment of liberation or self-liberation. The subject or victim, pictured here in the role of Abraham rather than Isaac, overcomes a crisis of identity; this is the "test" and at first sight he seems to pass it successfully. When Eli declares "I'm the father," we might perhaps see him as symbolically gaining his independence and at the same time restoring the father to his place in the family after an estrangement of two hundred years. And this might lead us to conclude that the Akedah is here being read as a salvation-myth, holding within it, as in the biblical source, a promise for the future (Genesis 22:17–18). But can the story as a whole and, in particular, its ending truly support such a conclusion?

4

In attempting to answer this question we might usefully glance once again at the device which Roth uses to precipitate Eli's crisis and also to point the way to its resolution, namely, the exchange of personalities between Eli and the dark stranger. Here, neatly

interlocking with the Akedah, Roth introduces the archetype of
the Double, a device which he has used to great effect in a number
of subsequent fictions, notably *The Counterlife* (1986). His model
is evidently Conrad's "The Secret Sharer." The Captain who narrates
that story finds himself to be a stranger on board his new ship
"and if all the truth must be told, I was somewhat of a stranger
to myself."[17] Leggatt, a fugitive from justice, is the Captain's double
whom the Captain hides on board until such time as he can make
good his escape. When he does so he will, like a scapegoat, take
this burden of strangeness upon himself, symbolically ridding the
Captain of the shadow which had come between him and his
new command. Something like this happens in "Eli, the Fanatic."
There is also a verbal conceit at work. Eli's problem is alienation.
The way therefore to highlight, and also to exorcise it is to introduce an actual group of aliens into the story. They are referred
to regularly as fanatics (that is, crazy people). But the reader is
constantly prompted to ask himself: who are the real aliens, the
Woodentonians with their anxieties and phobias, or the strangers? And who is the real "fanatic," Eli or the dark stranger? The
two groups, the settled Woodenton community and the strangers, lend themselves to a schematic comparison. The Woodenton
group is bourgeois, "normal," superficial, and subject to matriar-
chy. The aliens are patriarchal (they are in fact all male), attached
to the past, and unimpressed by the necessity to conform to the
"normal" pattern. Ironically, our first introduction to the word
"normal" is in reference to Miriam's anxiety-ridden probing of
Eli's psyche. Her constant exhortations are aimed at "get[ting]
things back to Normal." But as the narrator adds,

> The difficulty with Miriam's efforts was they only upset him
> more; not only did they explain little to him about himself or
> his predicament, but they convinced him of *her* weakness.
>
> (183–4)

Her pressing desire for normality and conformity is a sign of her
basic insecurity. The same applies by extension to the Woodenton
group as a whole. It is their insecurity which makes it necessary
for them to demonstrate their likeness to everyone else – this is
what prompted their move to get rid of the aliens in the first
place. This obsession with conformity is given a Jewish coloring,
but it is less a Jewish phenomenon than it is an aspect of middle-

class rootlessness. They have moved up the social scale from the ghettos and the lower-class neighborhoods but have not yet made it to the patrician world with its wealth and self-assurance. No such ambiguities beset the strangers. Ironically, the strangers are less alienated because less concerned with their surroundings than the Jews of Woodenton. Eli tries to press his argument that the townspeople in requiring conformity are seeking to protect their property, their well-being and their happiness. Tzuref sees through this and retorts, "Happiness? They hide their shame."

> "We do it," Eli said, wearily, "for our children. This is the twentieth century."
> "For the Goyim maybe. For me the Fifty-eighth." He pointed at Eli.
> "That is too old for shame."
>
> (192)

Although he is sick and alienated from his surroundings (or rather, because he is thus alienated) Eli can empathize with the strangers. His identity is in a manner adrift and the very question of where he stands existentially as between the two groups becomes the focus of his dialogue with Tzuref. In this dialogue the first, second, and third person pronouns are wittily juggled between the two speakers. Eli tells him that the residents won't give up their legal action:

> "But you, Mr. Peck, how about you?"
> "I am them, they are me, Mr. Tzuref."
> "Aach! You are us, we are you!"
>
> (192)

and later:

> "It's not me, Mr. Tzuref, it's them."
> "They are you."
> "No," Eli intoned. "I am me. They are them. You are you."
>
> (193)

But Eli does not succeed in keeping identities as separate as that. From their first meeting his identity merges with that of the tall man with the hat. "His face," we are told, "was no older

than Eli's." When, on the final day of Eli's "trial," the day that
Ted had said would be the Day of Judgment, the dark stranger
appears in the town wearing the green suit that Eli had left for
him – his own best tweed suit – the identification is complete.
"Those eyes were the eyes in his head. They were his" (205).
This motif is again taken from "The Secret Sharer" where the
sleeping-suit which the Captain gives Leggatt to wear becomes
the sign of a profound identity of experience. They have a silent
understanding of one another – "I needed no more," says the
Captain, "I saw it all going on as though I were myself inside
that other sleeping suit" (658). Finally, Eli clothes himself in the
stranger's worn black suit and black hat, and "zooms off towards
the hill" (209) – Eli's Mount Moriah. Here he encounters his double
once again for the last time:

> "Sholom," Eli whispered and the fellow turned. The recogni-
> tion took some time. He looked at what Eli wore. Up close, Eli
> looked at what he wore. And then Eli had the strange notion
> that he was two people. Or that he was one person wearing
> two suits.
>
> (209)

The "greenie" in spite of his strange behavior and his silence (he
never utters a word in all their meetings) is the saner of the two.
When in his delusion Eli puts out his hands to the fellow's throat
merely with the idea of buttoning down the collar of his shirt
(which is of course Eli's shirt), he runs from him in terror. He
has reason to be afraid of him, Eli being obviously the crazy one,
the fanatic. Eli thereupon appeals to him – "Tell me, what can I
do for you, I'll do it . . ." (210). But in fact it is the stranger who
does something for Eli. The black suit which he has given him is
we are told "all he's got" (190). Tzuref explains what he means
by that: having lost his parents, his wife and their ten-month-
old baby, he has nothing in the world except his suit. "And a
medical experiment they performed on him yet." He is the man
of sorrows. But he has been a father. Like Tzuref he knows what
it is to have children. That knowledge will be transmitted to Eli
along with the suit. His loss – for he will have no more children
– becomes Eli's gain. Eli receives that of which the stranger has
been robbed – namely, his fatherhood. "I'm the father," he screams
at the end.

This is as we noted earlier a whimsical triumph, but it is not quite the end of the story. The father figure displaced in the nineteenth century, is not going to be actually restored. Eli, unlike the Captain in Conrad's tale, will not be cured of his alienation by means of an exchange of identities. Nor is he headed like Moses Herzog for calm of mind all passion spent. The final sentences of Roth's short story do not speak of such consolations; they point rather in the opposite direction.

> But the window disappeared. In a moment they tore off his jacket – it gave so easily, in one yank. Then a needle slid under his skin. The drug calmed his soul, but did not touch it down where the blackness had reached.
>
> (216)

After the deployment of these two myths of salvation or restoration, we are left with something of an anticlimax. The black suit is ripped off Eli in one yank and he is left mentally worse off than he was before. How are we to read such an ending? One way would be to conclude that neither the Akedah nor the Secret Sharer can any longer be taken seriously by the writer of fiction. It is too late in the day for such patterns: when they are set to work in the New Jersey setting of 1957 what stands out is their absurdity. The exchange of dress, a seriously imagined event full of mysterious force in "The Secret Sharer," is here seemingly exploded. It is no more than a good joke. Likewise, no one is going to sacrifice his kid on Ted's front lawn. Nor is anyone going to be cured of a nervous breakdown by learning to say "Here I am!" These remain amusing and witty literary constructions, tricks that we learn about in graduate school. But nothing more.

There is another rather different way of reading the ending. In this reading the alienation of which the story speaks and which both mythic patterns are designed to resolve is ultimately too grave for literary make-believe. The wound in the collective psyche is both too deep and too long-standing for us to deceive ourselves that it can be wished away by a mere story. In this reading the last line is not in the least funny. It is where Roth puts off the motley. The author, however lacking in solemnity throughout this witty fable, exhibits in the end something of Kafka's honesty, something like Kafka's denial of the aesthetic. We are not flattered with a pleasing moment of closure as the hero saves himself and the human image as well; instead he is swallowed ever more deeply in the darkness of his psychotic state. There is here just a hint of the ending of *The Trial* as the baby in the window disappears before Eli's failing vision and the "executioners," playing their part in this final "act," plunge their steel into Eli's flesh. "The shame of it," we feel like adding, "must outlive him."

Whichever way we read it, the ending does not fulfill the promise of the Akedah as salvation-myth. There is not even the ambiguous hope that supports the happy ending of *Herzog*. Roth does not accept facile consolations. If this is a sign of honesty, it can also be defined as a sign of failure – the failure to imagine and to reinvent for our own time the potent language of dialogue. Job's triumph is that God finally addresses his word to him. What he says matters less than the fact that he speaks, that he "answers" Job out of the storm-wind.[18] The Akedah also functions as salvation-myth by virtue of the dialogic force of Hinneni. This does not signify a turning to the Self as if to say: "Here I am, this is me!". It is not a matter of self-acceptance. It is rather, as Auerbach renders it, a turning away from the self as if to say, "Here am I, awaiting thy command." Herzog makes such a gesture, however ambiguously, in his final meditations. Eli in Roth's story does not. More than that, through his choice of the Double as the prime device for defining and resolving the problem of Eli's alienation, Roth – deliberately it would seem – inhibits that gesture. The archetype of the Double does not permit dialogue. It is much rather a substitute for dialogue. One seems to encounter another person but it turns out to be not another person at all. The Double is rather a way of avoiding the other, removing from him the aspect of *difference*, ridding him of his true alterity. The Doppelgänger who visits Ivan Karamazov on the eve of his brother Dmitri's trial is a fragment of himself, temporarily broken off and given autonomy. As Ivan himself recognizes, he is Ivan's darker side, all that was mean and contemptible in him. But he could equally well have been his brighter self. Either way, the Double is merely a shadow of the self which must be reintegrated or cast out. But these are clearly achievements of monologue, not dialogue.

Roth seems to understand this limitation and to have accepted it. Significantly, as I have already noted, the dark stranger in Roth's story never speaks. The absence of dialogue is here sharply foregrounded. Like the patient undergoing psychotherapy, Eli is seeking personal integration. And he seems to achieve just that, so much so that we are told that as a result of the encounter with his other self "he knew who we was down to his marrow" (212). But that is precisely what is not enough. It is the wisdom of the Delphic oracle which says – "Know thyself." But as Emmanuel Levinas tells us, the biblical *hinneni* – a crucial term in his whole ethical system – is something else entirely. It is, "a sign given to the other . . . quite the opposite of return upon oneself, self-consciousness. It is sincerity, effusion of the self, 'extradit-ing' of the self to the neighbor." It is finally: "to respond with responsibility . . . *here I am for the others.*"[19] Roth, though innocent of the concepts and language of phenomenology, nevertheless seems to have perceived in his own fashion that knowing oneself is not enough, not even knowing oneself down to the marrow. Without something more than that neither Eli's sickness nor ours can be cured. The unspeaking other self whom Eli encounters cannot it seems touch the soul down where the blackness has reached.

9

The Akedah in
A.B. Yehoshua

1

Some years before his death in 1986, Bernard Malamud gave an interview to Daniel Stern in which he spoke of how the idea of *The Fixer* came to him. He made it clear that he had first thought of a novel based on the trial and execution of Sacco and Vanzetti, heroes of American radicalism, but when he found that he was not able to reshape that story in the way he wished, he remembered that when he was a child his father had told him of the ordeal of Mendel Beilis. "So I invented Yakov Bok, with perhaps the thought of him as a potential Vanzetti." In the continuation he speaks of the prison as a universal symbol:

> *Interviewer*: Some critics have commented on this prison motif in your work.
> *Malamud*: Perhaps I use it as a metaphor for *the dilemma of all men*: necessity whose bars we look through and try not to see. Social injustice, apathy, ignorance. The personal prison of entrapment in past experience, guilt, obsession – the somewhat blind or blinded self . . .
> *Interviewer*: Does this idea or theme, as you call it, come out of your experience as a Jew?
> *Malamud*: That's probably in it – a heightened sense of prisoner of history. . . . I conceive this as the major battle in life, to transcend the self – extend one's realm of freedom.
> *Interviewer*: Are you a Jewish writer? . . . There are qualifications by Bellow, Roth, others.
> *Malamud*: I'm an American, I'm a Jew, and *I write for all men*. A novelist has to or he's built himself into a cage . . . Like many writers I'm influenced by the Bible, both Testaments . . . as

154

a writer, I've been influenced more by Hawthorne, James, Mark Twain, Hemingway, more than I have been by Sholem Aleichem and I.L. Peretz, whom I read with pleasure . . . the point I'm making is that I was born in America and respond, in American life, to more than Jewish experience. *I wrote for those who read.*[1]

(emphasis added)

It will be seen that there is a certain ambivalence here in the use of the metaphor of the prison or the cage. In his first answer to the interviewer he speaks of the prison as a necessary condition of human existence – "necessity whose bars we look through and try not to see." It is due to our "entrapment in past experience." This is "the dilemma of all men." As Freudians would tell us, it is not to be avoided; we are what we are as a result of personal, individual experiences going back to earliest infancy, if not beyond. That is what selfhood means. In answering the second question, however, he sees the "entrapment" as much more negative and this is because Jews are more imprisoned than others, more singular, more isolated by their history. And so a Jew needs to make a major effort to "transcend the self" so created; and to transcend it becomes, he says, "the major battle in life." In the third passage cited, responding to the question "Are you a Jewish writer?" he shifts to the metaphor of the cage. This has now become wholly negative. To be just a Jewish writer is to build oneself into a cage. He finds it necessary to insist that he is first an American and then a Jew and that he "writes for all men . . . for those who read." Thus whilst the "entrapment in past experience" is a necessary condition of existence for all men, one needs demonstratively to liberate oneself from it so as to avoid the reproach of being merely a Jewish writer confined to the Bible and other Jewish sources. He assures us that he has read the Bible but feels it necessary to insist that as an American he has been influenced by much else besides.

Malamud betrays a certain anxiety here about the necessity to affirm a universal standard. There is a need to portray Yakov Bok, the Jew as the "prisoner of history," the scapegoat, his destiny prefigured in the trials and sorrows of the biblical Jacob. But there is also the necessity to escape from that "prison" and attach oneself to a more "universal" standard. One invents Yakov Bok but "with the thought of him as a potential Vanzetti." In this way one writes "for all men." In the story as told, Yakov Bok seeks freedom from a Czarist prison; but in the meta-narrative, author and reader need to escape from the prison, the cage, that would confine them to such models as Yakov Bok. We may see in this commitment which is simultaneously affirmed and denied a certain lack of authenticity.

Not all the powerful texts we have considered so far have been produced by those who see themselves as "writing for all men." There were those who responded rather to particularity and uniqueness, who sought to define a reality, even a biblical reality, not necessarily shared by "all men." George Eliot in *Silas Marner* or Joseph Roth in *Job: The Story of a Simple Man* seem to draw an opposite conclusion from that of Malamud. For both writers the singularity of the hero's fate determined both his suffering and the manner of his liberation from that suffering. Paradoxically, the emphasis on particularity, on a mode of existence felt to be distinctive, was what finally gave such novels their epic range, indeed their universal interest! This is true also of Robinson Crusoe who constantly communicates to us the terror of his unique situation. "Why were you singled out?" he asks himself. It is the question of Moses, of Jeremiah and of course, of Job. Indeed it is a question that runs through the Bible as a whole. The Children of Israel in the wilderness found the burden of election too heavy for them; they wanted to know why they were singled out, why they were not left in Egypt to enjoy regular rations along with all the other slaves. But we are persuaded by the narrative that the scandal of such aloneness has to be borne. They are seized by it against their will, just as the writer is possessed by the text in which this strange destiny is encoded.

Chosenness and the existential terror that goes with it is of course also at the heart of the Puritan experience in America. The American settlers too were embarked on an Errand in the Wilderness, chosen, like the Israelites of old, for elective suffering as well as elective blessings. But this sense of a special destiny with all its epic and dramatic potential now seems to have been cast aside. It would seem that even in the American-Jewish experience much of this biblical imperative, this condition of being possessed by the Word, has disappeared. Robert Alter, writing about *The Fixer* and evidently responding to its universalizing tendency, remarks that "all people are in their way chosen, Jews only more transparently than others."[2] Indeed, for latter-day liberals and universalists – as children of the Enlightenment – it is axiomatic that everyone is chosen. Which is the same as saying that no one is chosen. In this, the Enlightenment explicitly opposes itself to what it perceives as the fanatical narrowness of the biblical ethic. It declares in effect: *nihil humani mihi alienum*. But however high minded such an ethic may claim to be, the literary result will necessarily be a certain impoverishment, a loss of intensity.

Not only does the Enlightenment call for a universal standard, it all but abolishes the past. We recall Tom Paine repudiating the authority of institutions derived from the past as "the most ridiculous and insolent of all tyrannies."[3] In such works as *Silas Marner* and Joseph Roth's *Job*, however, the characters are, as we noted, fraught with their background. The past reveals the hiding places of its power. The pastness of the past is never in doubt, but neither is the power of its connection with the present. It is still with us. We are constrained by memory, our doings subject to an order long ago imposed upon time. Such diachrony is only whimsically evoked in Philip Roth's story. Ted's fear of a latter-day Abraham come to carry out the Akedah on his front lawn is an amusing fantasy. These patterns no longer obligate in the way that they once did. The Enlightenment has won. There is no existential continuity between the sacrifice of Isaac and the world inhabited by the Anglo-Jewish or American-Jewish writer and his reading public; nor does the book of Job any longer address itself to their exiled status. For very simply they are not in exile. No more so, at any rate, than other cultivated Americans and Europeans – readers of Kafka or Camus – who see themselves as suffering alienation and exile. But they are not sitting by the waters of Babylon, nor are they remembering Zion.

To define this loss a little more sharply, we would do well to return to our primary category, that of testimony. The biblical paradigms search us out, point a finger at us. They link past and present, historical memory and the realities (whether harsh or wonderful) of the present or the fictive present, witnessing both for and against us. Job witnesses against Mendel Singer in his time of tribulation. But in the final episode of Menuchim's return, taking place significantly on the Passover-eve, Mendel relives the redemption from Egyptian exile. The present occasion testifies to the continuing force of a saving paradigm. In both cases, the ancient writing, like a revenant, returns to haunt us in the present. We cannot choose but hear. It has a message for us personally and it demands that we attend to it. There is something profoundly disconcerting but also exalting about such particular attention.

For the contemporary Jewish writer in the West – and the non-Jewish writer too – the all-embracing reality of the present moment admits the biblical paradigm as myth, excludes it as memory. Bellow makes his pilgrimage "To Jerusalem and Back." Jerusalem is where memory and hope intersect, it is the goal of historical striving. But the emphasis is on the last two words of the title of Bellow's travelogue.[4] After observing the Israeli scene with its agonies and debates in the second winter after the disastrous Yom Kippur War, it is back to a continuous present, a synchronic order unburdened by elective promises or warnings or obligations. For America (or England) is where we are now. It is possible to enjoy Levy's rye-bread but to opt out of Jewish history. The biblical patterns continue to make a strong appeal; they enrich our perceptions. But they no longer fundamentally structure our existence, nor do they threaten us.

There is, however, a group of modern writers who are in this regard sharply different from their fellows in the West. I refer to the Hebrew writers of our time and earlier, both those born in Israel and those coming to Israel from Eastern Europe and elsewhere. They have not necessarily desired to inherit the singularity of Jewish biblical experience. But no matter how hard they try, they cannot easily cast it off. As a result they have helped through their writings to articulate the biblical subtext which would seem to govern Israeli existence. That they have also rebelled against this subtext only serves to confirm its seemingly inescapable force. Malamud might say that they have built themselves into a cage, but, as he himself acknowledges, there is a sense in which all writers are in a cage. Malamud and Bellow are in an American cage. For there are no unmediated literary works; writers live in geographical space and in historical time; they both read and write the world in language. And that language is given, determined by its context. But in the case of the Israeli writer it turns out to be a biblical cage: the language that he uses is inevitably loaded with biblical meanings, just as the space he inhabits is biblical space and the history he endures strangely forms itself into biblical patterns. That is the difference.

2

Let us take up the Akedah-pattern again, this time as it is found in two leading Israeli novelists, S.Y. Agnon and A.B. Yehoshua. If the Akedah – as the story of the Binding of Isaac is known in Hebrew – was an important *topos* for so many writers in the West (especially in the nineteenth century), then it has been a virtual obsession in Israeli fiction and poetry from its beginnings to the present day. It would be impossible to do justice to this subject in a single chapter or even in a whole book. From Yitzhak Lamdan to Hayyim Hazaz and Amir Gilboa in the mid-century and down to Aharon Megged, Hayyim Guri and Amos Oz in our own day, it is hard to think of a major writer who has not at some time found this pattern indispensable.[5] But the results have been strangely varied, even contradictory – which is what we might expect from inventions founded on this strangest and most troubling of all biblical narratives.

Nowadays, we are accustomed to the idea that myths have a dialectical character. The "savage mind" attempts by their means to resolve such basic contradictions as endogamy versus exogamy; nature versus culture; rituals of death versus those of marriage.[6] But the Akedah story exhibits and seeks to overcome an even sharper and more disturbing antithesis. What is involved is no less than the opposed fascinations of life and death, of sacrifice and survival. On the face of it, the Akedah is a salvation-myth. In being commanded to offer up his child as a burnt-offering Abraham is "merely" being tested; Isaac is saved and the announcement of this gift of life culminates in a blessing to be mediated by the seed of Abraham "to all the nations of the earth" (22:18). From this point of view it might be argued that the Akedah is not about death and sacrifice – it is rather about the opposite; it resists and denies such an implication ("lay not thy hand on the lad, neither do anything to him"). But the resistance is what we are talking about; through this explicit denial, the story bears witness to a still active temptation and horror – that of human sacrifice. For the reader does not only respond to the rescue and the words of blessing and promise at the end; he responds to the radical menace expressed in the second verse of the chapter. Here each word renders the command more absolute as the sentence rises incrementally to its unthinkable climax:

> Take now thy son, thy one-and-only, whom thou lovest: Isaac!
> And get thee into the land of Moriah, and offer him up there
> for a burnt-offering on one of the mountains which I shall tell
> thee of.

There are in fact two voices in the text: one calls for the sacrifice
of Isaac as the saving event, the ultimate expression of faith. It is
Abraham's readiness for this which is rewarded (v. 16). The other
voice rejects such ferocities; it is that of the angel who, so to
speak, snatches the deadly knife out of Abraham's hand just in
time (v. 12a). This ambivalence[7] gives rise to two opposite interpretive tracks. One track would emphasize the parallels with those
other patriarchal narratives involving survival and rescue – Jacob
fleeing from his brother Esau and then becoming the recipient
of a divine promise at Bet-El, and Jacob too, returning later from
his long exile to survive the night-long struggle with the angel
at Peniel; Joseph in the pit, saved from death through the inter-
vention of his oldest brother, Reuben.[8] All the patriarchs are in a
deep sense survivors and Isaac is surely a survivor also, like the
others.

But, surprisingly, this is not how the story has been read. In
one well-established tradition of interpretation, based on the ethic
of sacrifice, Isaac is not a survivor at all. Again there is a kind of
swerve as a result of which the sacrifice is seen to be actually
carried out by the Father or at the behest of the Father! In Christian typology, Isaac, bearing the wood for the altar pile (22:6),
becomes the prototype of Jesus carrying his own Cross. And of
course that is the preliminary to the Crucifixion – that is, a sacrifice
actually performed. Of this we are told in the gospel: "For God
so loved the world, that he gave his only begotten Son" (John
3:16) – a formula in which we hear the distinct echo of the words
quoted above: "Take now thy son, thy only one, whom thou
lovest." The Crucifixion thus becomes a kind of midrash on the
Akedah, but it amplifies only one of its two voices, developing
one of its interpretive options at the expense of the other. The
rescue is ignored.[9] The story was read in this way in much
nineteenth-century literature. In *Billy Budd*, as mentioned earlier,
and in Ibsen's *Brand* the Binding of Isaac is explicitly recalled
but these stories lead up to the death of the "son," not to his
survival.

This compulsion or swerve also occurs in Jewish writings totally

uninfluenced by Christian thinking. Some early midrashim speak
of a wound that Abraham makes on Isaac's neck; he loses the
measure of blood needed to sustain life. Other medieval Jewish
sources speak of the actual death and resurrection of Isaac.[10] Later
on, the notion of the completed sacrifice gained support from
the exigencies of contemporary history. In the Rhineland during
the period of the Crusades there were many attested cases of
people taking their own lives (after first slaying their children)
rather than submit to forced apostasy or death at the hands of
the crusaders. The Akedah was regularly recalled. In a twelfth-
century liturgical poem by Rabbi Ephraim of Bonn, who had
himself witnessed such horrors, Isaac dies at his father's hand,
but is resurrected; after his resurrection Abraham makes a second
attempt to carry out the command; it is only then, on the second
time round (see v. 15), that the angel successfully intervenes to
save Isaac's life![11]

The most serious modern Israeli writers feel the need to do
justice to what I have termed the two voices in this biblical pericope
and at the same time to overcome the opposition between them;
and, corresponding to this, there is the existential need to make
sense of one's everyday historical experience with its strange
combination of triumph and tragedy. From this point of view,
the modern texts which I shall be discussing contain readings of
unusual depth and richness. To this richness many factors have
contributed, not the least among them being the return to biblical seasons and spaces as well as the renewal of the actual language
of the biblical poets and narrators in the living speech of the
modern writers and their audiences.

A.B. Yehoshua's brilliant short novel *Three Days and a Child*
(*Shelosha Yamim Veyeled*, 1965) is a model of precise construction.
It could almost have been written to demonstrate the structural-
ist method. Dov, the first-person narrator, is a young mathematician, who is left in charge of a child, Yaali, for three days, in
Jerusalem. Dov is in love with the child's mother, Hayya, and
consequently takes a deep, passionate interest in the child. The
characters represent opposite and balancing qualities held in a
kind of mathematical relation to one another. Thus Hayya (whose
name signifies "living creature") is associated with water and
fertility, whilst Yael, the girl that Dov is living with, is associated
with thistles and cacti (dry plants). Zvi, a friend of Dov, collects
snakes (dryness); he is attracted to Yael but is separated from

her by Dov, just as Hayya is separated from Dov by her husband, Zeev. It is not by chance that Dov, a mathematician, is at the center of this pattern of mutual attractions and oppositions. He is, so to say, seeking a solution for a mathematical problem. In fact, we are told early in the story that he is hung up in the writing of his thesis for the University by a "logical contradiction."

> I have been stuck ever since the spring, within a self-made labyrinth, laid open to a suddenly discovered logical contradiction. I need inspiration, a special kind of light. As though I were writing a novel.[12]

Of course the narrator, insofar as he speaks for the author, *is* writing a novel! And it is a novel built on an antithetical pattern of relationships between the characters. This is the "self-made labyrinth" which is seen to be founded on a contradiction. This contradiction could be expressed in almost algebraic form. Thus the antithesis of fertility and harshness, vines and thorns, wetness and dryness, all reduce to a single code, namely: life and death. The same code determines not only the pattern of relationships between the characters but also the physical geography of the country which belongs likewise to the symbolic core of the novel. Thus Jerusalem, "a harsh town" (66, 71), in the fierce heat of the end of summer, with its stony landscape and its many tombs is contrasted throughout with the Galilean kibbutz where Hayya and her husband live with their child and where we are made aware of the rank fertility of the wet earth with its sprouting fields and abundant vineyards (63). The violent contrasts in the human and physical landscape are matched by the sudden transitions of the seasons. The story begins in the torrid heat of the late summer; as it ends three days later a chill morning breeze can be felt, and there are tufts of cloud visible high up in the sky, an omen of the coming autumn rains.

Hayya and Zeev have come to Jerusalem to take their entrance examinations to the University, and they have asked Dov to take care of their young son, Yaali for the three days of the examination. The parents are going to be examined (tested) but Dov mentions that he has the sense of being tested also (97). This more mysterious test is clearly related to the myth of the Akedah and the three-day journey of Abraham and Isaac to the place of sacrifice (Genesis 22). It is as though Dov feels himself to be re-enacting the sacrifice of Isaac, now symbolized by this child who has come from his home to Jerusalem (that is, Mt. Moriah) and has been given over to his care, making him a kind of surrogate father. He may even be the real father. We are told towards the end of the novel that Dov had once slept with Hayya when visiting her kibbutz during his army training (121); this turns out to have been exactly four years previously and Yaali is over three years old. The question of his paternity is thus left open as an unspoken possibility.[13]

It not altogether certain that Yehoshua was aware of the Akedah-pattern during the writing of this novel. Mordechai Shalev, in a masterly and detailed analysis of this story, suggests that the pattern forces itself on the writer from unconscious depths.[14] As with other powerful literary archetypes, the story in a sense is writing him rather than he it. The question of what was in the author's mind at the time of writing does not much concern us here; he may have been partly aware of its link to the Akedah and partly unaware. But as far as the reader is concerned, once Shalev has given him the key to the interpretation of this novel, it becomes impossible for him to read it in any other way. The Akedah-pattern determines the story in its totality.

The narrator finds himself consumed with an overpowering love of the child in whom he sees the image of the mother. He is "her son, her one-and-only" (71), also perhaps *his* son, *his* one-and-only, whom *he* loves, the Hebrew form of words from Genesis 22:2 inevitably invading the discourse. But his jealousy and his frustrated yearnings for Hayya bring the sacrificial connotations of this verse to the fore. He fantasizes about her death and that of Yaali (101, 110–11). But this is not only a matter of fantasy as in Philip Roth's more playful "Eli the Fanatic." We are made to feel the still active quality of menace in the Akedah-pattern. Thus the narrator, Dov, is drawn, grotesquely, to seek the death of Yaali, Hayya's son, her one-and-only. In no other way can he express his love (111). But there will also have to be survival and rescue. That compulsion is just as powerful as the other. How is justice to be done to both? This is an artistic problem no less than it is a psychological or theological problem. Here is the ultimate "logical contradiction" on which the writing of the narrator's "thesis" (but in fact this very story) is hung up.

Yaali begins to run a fever; Dov takes him out into the intense Jerusalem midday heat exposing him to a variety of risks. Everything in Jerusalem, he tells us, is symbolic. He even considers himself a symbol (68). Instead of water which he needs, he gives him milk and feeds him on chocolate. The text tellingly echoes what was said of Yael and Sisera in the Song of Deborah (Judges 5:25): "He asked for water and she gave him milk" (88). Yael we remember would in the next verse assassinate Sisera, smashing his head with a tent peg! Ignoring his fever and the searing heat out of doors, Dov drags the child on a three-hour visit to the zoo. He himself settles down to doze on a bench in the shade of some pine trees and deliberately lets Yaali wander around alone. When he wakes he sees that the infant, following some older children, has climbed up onto an insecure fence which connects with a high wall. He is in imminent danger of falling, with possibly fatal consequences. The child, suddenly realizing his danger, screams with terror. Dov, who has covered his face with a newspaper, takes no notice. But someone else hears him and rushes to save him. Only then does Dov stir himself to take charge of the child. When he reflects on the incident later, the word that stands out is "balance." The older children had "carefully balanced themselves" (70); Yaali had no such skill. Instead "his life had been in the balance" (72). Like the "logical contradiction," this foregrounding of the notion of balance has a metapoetic function – it suggests the "balance" that needs to be struck between extinction and survival. The figure of Yaali, suspended on the fence, graphically defines this narrative requirement.

Another image for this precarious line of division between life and death is the border which passes through the city a few hundred yards from the zoo amid olive trees, rocks and thistles – "a belt of menace encircling Jerusalem" (81). (It is the period before the Six Day War when Jerusalem was still divided between Israel and Jordan with a dangerous stretch of no-man's-land in the middle of the city.) Dov feels a strange compulsion to take Yaali to this border and leave him in no-man's-land. The child is also in danger from a snake which Dov's friend Zvi accidentally lets loose in their apartment. In the end, it is Zvi and not Yaali who will be bitten by the snake. He will reach the hospital only just in time to be saved from death. Zvi, as Shalev notes, functions as "the ram caught in the thicket" in the Akedah story (Genesis 22:13). He and not Yaali will suffer near-death.

For two days Jerusalem is a place of death, dryness, heat and danger. But on the final day of the story, the city discloses its secret fertility (121). Like the prophet Zechariah (14:8), Dov has a dream of a river flowing through Jerusalem, its muddy banks thick with lush vegetation (116). Later on that day he suddenly becomes aware that the logical contradiction on which he was hung up is probably not so logical after all (124). At the same time Yaali's fever drops to normal and there is a return to life-affirming values. The child survives and is returned to his parents. This, we may say, is the Akedah the right way up – a story of escape from death. But Dov's own reaction contradicts this "happy ending." He has the feeling of having failed the test, as though the death of the child is what he had desired but this has not been achieved! "I was shattered. The child was in their hands now. I had failed" (126).

The relation to the akedah archetype is complex. We have the feeling that not only is the narrator compulsively seized with the necessity of acting out the Akedah, but he is also seeking to escape from those very compulsions. It is part of the recoil against the grim imperatives of Jewish history – a history which involves us in wars and the threat of wars, unease and abnormality. Yehoshua in his writings on public questions frequently inveighs against the abnormality of Jewish existence.[15] Why can't we be like everyone else? The Jewish myth, the Scriptures, have us in thrall. If only we could be free of that thraldom. Perhaps we can throw off these mythic structures altogether and live in a kind of neutral history. There is an intimation of this desire in the somewhat hysterical final episode in Yaali's three-day sojourn in Dov's apartment. It appears that Yaali has brought with him some story books which Dov has promised to read to him. But the stories turn out to be stupid and to have many hard words. Moreover, the child is used to having them read to him in a particular sing-song, he himself joining in at the end of each sentence "as though we were praying" (124). Dov tries to read one of them to him, but gives up. "This book is not for us," he declares and promptly throws it out of the window. Yaali decides that this is a great game, so laughing with pleasure, he gets up on a chair and he and Dov together toss all the books out of the window to the autumn winds.[16]

Instead of reading these Dov proceeds to tell Yaali a marvelous story of his own invention about the battles and adventures of all the beasts of the forest – a bear, together with foxes, wolves and a long-legged deer – and their wives and children. The majority die fearful deaths. Yaali is enthralled. "Never has he heard such a long and wonderful story." He puts his hand on Dov's shoulder and strokes his hair; it is an hour of perfect accord like the walking together of father and son, twice repeated, in the Akedah story itself (Genesis 22:6, 8). Dov decides to include the vegetable world also and finally "I make up my mind to exterminate every living creature and plant, save one little wolf-cub" (125). The child himself is evidently the "wolf-cub" who survives, Hayya's husband being Zeev (=wolf), just as the name Dov signifies a bear, Zvi signifies a deer, and Yael, the wild goat or ibex, often seen in the Judean hills. In fact the characters in the novel itself all return in this story-within-the-story, the tale that Dov spins for Yaali, as do the thorns and the river plants of the vegetable kingdom which likewise had served as paradigms within the semiotic pattern of the novel itself.

At the same time, the tale of the forest that the narrator invents for Yaali may be read as a wildly fantastic parody of the "story-outside-the-story" that is, the sacred writings from the past which they have just tossed out of the window! For what are the narratives which make up the substance of Genesis and Exodus – the Flood, the overthrow of the Cities of the Plain, the Akedah, the Crossing of the Red Sea – if not tales of destruction on a vast (even universal) scale with, incredibly and capriciously, one surviving individual, or family, or tribe left to continue the line? This we might say is Israel's fundamental myth, not extinction, but extinction averted, missed by a hair's breadth. This is not death and resurrection in the world to come, as in the New Testament (cf. I Cor. 15:42–55), but captivity restored, amazingly, in this world – that is, survival, *but only just*! That qualification is of the essence. Yitzhak is saved but over the story of his rescue falls the shadow of the "Akedah" of the Jews of York, of Mainz, of Speyer, of Cologne, of Worms. Conversely, Job, the man who has reached the outer limits of despair – "see, he slays me, I have no hope!" – will survive, his fortunes restored.

By representing all this as a wild fable of the beasts of the forest whom he exterminates or saves at will, he is dismissing as absurd all the promises and disasters which make up Israel's covenant history. But if the beast fable lights up the logical absurdity of Israel's story, it nevertheless enables us to come to terms with it as a metaphysical paradox. The story that Dov tells to Yaali has a serious, interpretive function. Dov is the author and is thus free to create worlds and to destroy them as he pleases. If that is the privilege of the maker of stories, it is no less the privilege of the creator of the universe. There is no "why" about it. Kingdoms and empires all come and go; nations disappear without a trace. It is the way of story-tellers and of world history alike and it is also that which captivates Dov's auditor. Death is what we expect to happen; it is simple, natural, obvious. The question Why arises in regard to survival, that, for instance, of the little wolf-cub whom Dov leaves alive. What is the meaning of this survival, this act of grace? Yehoshua is, it seems, committed – however reluctantly – to this aspect of the Akedah. The sacrifice is aborted and the victim survives. In this Yehoshua reverses the dominant trend among poets and story-tellers, both Jew and gentile, for the past hundred and fifty years, according to which the murderous father almost invariably sends the son to his death.[17] Astonishingly, Yehoshua gives us instead the story of Isaac Unbound.

We may be sure that this reversal is not owing to any new-found sympathy for fathers. As we shall see, the doctrinaire father-teacher in Yehoshua's story "Early in the Summer of 1970," his Bible ever at the ready, is a basically unsympathetic portrait, a kind of Victorian father. But Yehoshua has responded to the ambiguities of the biblical text with more understanding than others. We may begin to arrive at Yehoshua's understanding of this archetype, if we note that Yaali, the Yitzhak of this Akedah tale from the stem *tzahak*="to laugh" – hence Yaali's frequent gales of laughter (71, 124)[18] – is the only character in the novel who is not given an animal name. True Yaali might, by metathesis, be Ayil (=ram) or Ayyal (=stag) but as it stands he just misses being either of these. In fact he is not given a name at all! "Yaali" is it seems a term of endearment, not his true given name which the narrator never discovers (64, 128). He is thus the one character who is unnamed. This reflects his problematical identity – but more than that it refects his ambiguous status, his hovering between life and death. The victim of the three-day trial, the Binding, is felt to be in a kind of limbo, lacking the firm existence of the rest of the figures in the story with their animal names. He represents a gap in the semiotic code, an absence.

Significantly, the question of names and their absence is a feature of the biblical pericope also. The Rabbis in the midrash draw attention to the fact that, after he is placed on the wood-pile,

Yitzhak seemingly disappears from the narrative. He is not named again after verse 9 and he is not referred to again after verse 16. They offer a dialectical explanation:

> And so where was Yitzhak? Said Rabbi Elazar ben Perat: Even though Yitzhak did not die, Scripture accounts it to his credit as if he had died, his ashes strewn upon the altar. And therefore it is said, "And Abraham returned [to Beer-sheba] with the young men."[19]

He is "as if he had died." This "as if" formula is subtly different from the *en parabole* of the Epistle to the Hebrews 11:19. According to this epistle Abraham's faith was demonstrated by his belief that after the slaying of Isaac God would restore him miraculously to life and thus would the promise be fulfilled:

> Accounting that God was able to raise him even from the dead, and from the dead he did in a figure (*en parabole*) receive him back.
>
> (Hebrews 11: 17–19)

The Akedah, seen here as the type or figure of the Crucifixion and the Resurrection, is predicated on the death of Isaac. The midrash quoted above, by contrast, affirms as its basic premise that "Isaac did not die." It is the story of Isaac Unbound but he and his descendants are nevertheless so scarred by the ordeal that they carry the wound of it to the end of the day. It is "as if" he had died. As a sign of this his name is withheld. He has survived, but only just. We might term this the notion of the near miss. It is Israel's basic myth, its ritual equivalent, as I have argued elsewhere, being circumcision.[20] Akedah, as understood in the above midrash, is to the Crucifixion as circumcision is to castration (– "If thy right hand offend thee, cut it off"). Both Akedah and circumcision are examples of the near miss. There is a mini-Akedah in Exodus 4:24–6 where YHWH is said to waylay Moses and Zipporah on their way to Egypt seeking the death of their unnamed child (or it might be of Moses himself – the text is unclear). We experience the same kind of shock as with the command to offer up Isaac as a burnt offering.[21] Zipporah saves the situation by taking a flint with which she tears off the child's

foreskin. Again he will carry the sign on his flesh to the end of
the day, as wound and promise.

Here then Yehoshua's tale witnesses to the singularity of Jewish
existence as represented in the akedah archetype. It is an existence marked permanently by radical anxiety, radical menace, by
the mindset, indeed the historical experience, associated with the
near miss. As with the action of providence in George Eliot's
Silas Marner, we have here a pattern which seems to govern the
author's artistic invention without being held by him as a belief.
Balaam spoke of Israel as "a people that dwells alone" (Numbers
23:9). Some read this as a blessing, others read it as a curse. It
has proved to be both – which perhaps befits the occasion of its
utterance. After all, Balaam came to curse and found himself
pronouncing blessings instead! But either way, Yehoshua himself
wants nothing of such singularity. It is somehow imposed on
the story and its author as a charge that he accepts wearily,
reluctantly. It is a case of the Bible pattern testifying against us,
as we are told in Deuteronomy 31 that it would. This phenomenon of a narrative modeled on an adversary text is reflected in
the story itself by Dov's very ambiguous response to the charge
placed on him. When Zeev and Hayya say they want to bring
him their child, his emotions are stirred but, at the same time,
he asks himself: "What have they to do with me anyway?" (57).
Here is the narrator balking at the responsibility of taking care
of the child; we may also suggest that it is the author balking at
the need to get into this kind of story in the first place. What
has the myth of Jewish singularity to do with him? When Yaali
survives the three-day trial in obedience to that myth and is
returned to his parents, the same weariness is expressed and also
a sense of failure – "The child was in their hands now. I had
failed" (126).

And as we saw, the enclosed tale of the beasts of the forest
whom Dov decides to exterminate gives a further deconstructive
turn to the narration. If (among other things) it serves to define
the covenantal myth governing Israel's existence, then it also
overthrows that myth by presenting it as a wild nursery-tale made
up as one goes along. Thus Dov's bedtime story articulates the
story of Yitzhak/Yaali and his singular and ever problematical
survival. At the same time it dismisses it as a mere whim, a fantasy
on the part of the inventor. Or rather, it makes the gesture of

dismissal, for these Bible stories remain to haunt and obsess Yehoshua and his characters in every new novel. Nor can they so easily be flung out of the window. Or if we try to get rid of them in this way they come in again through the back door.

3

In "Three Days and a Child" the scheme or trope of the beast fable is superimposed on what is in other respects a realistically developed story of the Israeli scene in the 1960s. The visit to the zoo is entirely convincing as is the account of the kibbutz dining-hall at 5 o'clock in the afternoon (61). Nevertheless the slight oddity of giving all the *dramatis personae* (with exception of Yaali) the names of animals subverts this realism, giving to the story what George Eliot had termed a "legendary" character. It is easy to see that this was needed in order to make the action of the novel more credible, in particular to bridge the gap between the strangeness of the fable and the everyday world in which it is enacted. Once the story is accepted as having something of the legendary quality of a beast fable, we do not have the same problem of explicating Dov's strange behaviour towards Yaali. Like the Big Bad Wolf, the bachelor bear in this story need not conform to ordinary human behavior. And deviations from normal psychology will be tolerated in the other characters also.

As a result this fable element becomes one of the strengths of "Three Days and a Child." Such symbolic schemes are, however, by no means the only strategy that Yehoshua employs. Another Akedah story by Yehoshua written a few years later, namely "Early in the Summer of 1970," exhibits the same basic ambiguities, including the father's disappointment and frustration at the aborting of the sacrifice, which we noted in the case of Dov and Yaali but these are now presented in a credibly realistic fashion.

In this story we are told of the reported death of a soldier in the course of the desultory fighting on Israel's borders during the years that followed the Six Day War of 1967. The father – significantly, a teacher of the Bible – has to identify the body, but when he arrives at the hospital mortuary he discovers that the body is not that of his son! It is a case of mistaken identity. This then is a story of escape – the son is still alive. But in a mythological sense, it is a story of failed expectations – the tragic ending with its aesthetic closure, as in the Passion narrative,[22] has been denied:

"It isn't him . . ." I whisper at last with infinite astonishment, with growing despair, with the murmur of the water in this cursed room.[23]

Gradually, in the course of the story in which the father is the first-person narrator, his strange mindset is made clearer. As a teacher of the Bible he tyrannizes over his pupils, setting them difficult "tests" and expecting them to adhere to its stories and patterns as the key to all reality (70). When war broke out in June 1967 he had insisted on remaining with his class although he had reached retirement age. When the younger teachers are being called up, he declared, and we are sending our sons to be killed, we must remain at our posts to give encouragement to our pupils and prepare them for their coming trials (11–12). The result is an absurd situation – for three years he has continued to teach without any official recognition and in defiance of the school Principal. They no longer speak to one another. Bible-teaching is for him thus more than an occupation; it is a private obsession. Moreover, it demands to be related to Israel's continuing history with its wars and threats of war. In reference to this he feels that he has special responsibilities.

The climax, and with it the beginning of the story proper, is reached with the return from America of his 31-year-old son. He, too, had embarked on a career in the area of religious history – he has a work in progress on "Prophecy and Politics" (32). But it is clear at once that there is a wide cultural gap between father and son. The son does not share his father's intensities; his notions are broader and newer, and the father has the same difficulty in adjusting to these notions as he has with those of his younger pupils. They give him the uncomfortable feeling that their world is less mythologically determined than the world of the Bible with its laws, proverbs, and prophecy, all of which they bring to the test of "some other reality." But how can that be? "What other reality? Lord of Hosts, Lord God – *What* other reality for Heaven's sake? Does anything really change?" (70).

For the first-person narrator the world is unchanging, the biblical narratives continuing to play themselves out, while his pupils look at him as though they had "brought some new gospel, tidings

of a revolution, of some other reality, wonderful and unknown"
(71). Symbolically, they tend to drop their copies of the Bible on
the floor, whilst the narrator, walking around the classroom,
continually stoops to pick them up, one here and one there (ibid.).

How, in this situation, is he going to convince the younger
generation that his is the correct reading of reality? It is against
this background that the report of his son's death whilst on reserve
duty on the Jordanian front comes literally as a "God-send." He
has now the opportunity of playing out the role, probably his
favorite, of Abraham in the story of the Akedah, with his son as
the sacrificial victim. Thus, before he arrives at the hospital in
order to identify his son's body he has already fantasized about
the glorious privilege that this might give him of addressing the
pupils and their parents at the annual school graduation exercises.
He would tell them that he speaks to them as a bereaved father.
"Dear parents, students," he imagines himself saying,

> I do not want to burden you with my grief, but I ask you to
> look at me and guard yourself against surprise, because I was
> prepared for his death, in a manner, and that was my strength
> in that fearful moment.
>
> (38)

He is clearly bidding them to prepare themselves for a like moment
of sacrifice, urging them also to consider the need and inevita-
bility of all this. Thus even before the news is confirmed he is
already savoring the honor and lustre that this "fulfillment" would
bring him. In a sense, his ultimate ambition would thereby be
realized; it would even seem as though he himself is requiring
his son's death! As Shalev perceptively notes,[24] there are not only
clear indications here of the Akedah-pattern, but overtones also
of the gospel narrative of the death and resurrection of Jesus.
After they have discovered the son is still alive with his unit in
the Jordan valley, his daughter-in-law, who meets him, looks at him
"in fascination, in wonder . . . as though by my power I had killed
him, as though by my power brought him back to life" (68).

The old man is thus acting out a fantasy in which he plays the
part of Abraham with the element of rescue omitted and the
sacrifice of Isaac a real sacrifice, even a kind of crucifixion. This
impression is confirmed when the narrator picks up the imagined
speech to the assembled pupils and their parents once again

towards the end of the story, in spite of the fact that his son has already been found to be alive and well! In this continuation of his fantasy he shows us that his mind is virtually unhinged. He continues to see himself as a bereaved father, addressing the assembly on the subject of "your disappearance". "On the face of it," he says, "your disappearance is nothing, is meaningless, because historically speaking, however stubborn you are, your death will again be but a weary repetition in a slightly different setting." Here is the supposed message of the Bible, perverted of course by his obsession, and by the suppression of the notion of rescue and the possibility of change. He warns against any attempt to find an ongoing meaning in history. "To glue oneself to the radio again and again, or seek salvation in the newspapers is," he says, "utter madness." But of course it is his message that is seen as madness (60).

Apart from the return to the narrator's imagined discourse at the graduation exercise, there is another main structural feature of the story, involving a pattern of repetition which holds the narrative together in a kind of *inclusio* and at the same time provides a final disclosure. I refer to the thrice-repeated return to the moment when the news of his son's supposed death reaches the father. This is the subject of the opening section; it is also the subject of another section[25] a little more than half-way through the story; and finally it is the subject of the last section of the story. All three versions begin with almost exactly the same phrase: "I believe I ought to go over the moment I learned of his death once more; (9) or "I believe I must go over the moment when I learned of his death again;"(45) and finally – "I must still go over the moment when I learned of his death" (69). All these accounts in spite of variations in detail seem to tell the same story, namely that it is the school Principal who had first been informed of the supposed death and that it is he who had communicated that intelligence to the narrator. It was given him, he tells us, when he arrived in school one morning and to his surprise found that the Principal had been waiting for him. As he went into his classroom, the Principal, who had not spoken to him during these three years, followed him and gave him the information of his son's death in the presence of the class. When we reach the last account and then compare the three versions, however, we discover that this is not necessarily the way it happened.

As we look back from the end of the story we note some oddities.

First of all, in all three repeated accounts of this moment we have the phrase "somewhat stunned." He says in the first: "I rise late, faintly stunned" (9) – he has lost his sense of time. This did not perhaps draw attention to itself very sharply at that stage, but we recall this phrase later on in the second account, when he also speaks of himself as being "faintly stunned, unaware of time" (45) and then going up the school steps. What we wonder had disturbed him? Finally, in the third and last account of the announcement, he notes: "I rise late, stunned, as after an illness, straight into the sun" (69). Then we begin to wonder seriously what it was that had "stunned" him and why he had left the house so late. Moreover, when we read the final account, we notice some significant differences: he is disturbed here much more than in the earlier two accounts. He is disturbed by the sense of his ideological distance from these pupils and the need to do something which would fix him in their memories. "All of a sudden I long for a different parting, one that will be scored on their memory." This expressed desire for "a different parting" makes us wonder whether he is not already aware of the coming disclosure! As though to confirm this impression he asks himself: "Am I setting them a trap? Am I here, or am I not?" (71). This mention of a "trap" could mean that the whole scene with the Principal had been deliberately planned as a performance! For in this third discourse he sees the headmaster coming "from afar," as though it was he, the narrator, who had been lying in wait for the headmaster. We have the clear sense that the initiative is in the hands of the narrator. It is he who opens the door and awaits the headmaster as though he knows what the headmaster is coming to tell him; or perhaps he himself is going to do the telling! (He would then simply be waylaying the headmaster on his rounds.) All this is not stated, but it is a legitimate inference, a suggestion hovering about the text.

> And then I see the Head from afar, striding sadly and pensively along the empty corridor. Approaches slowly and heavily, like an obsolete tank.

> (71)

In contrast to the previous two accounts he deliberately places himself at a point where he can see the headmaster coming down to the classroom. The narrator is standing in the open doorway, and is also facing a corridor window in which the seated pupils of his class are reflected against the background of the hills of Judea and of Moab. He has thus set up his performance, with his audience in place and the antagonist about to enter the stage on his cue. And then we have the final words of the text, which seem to confirm this reading.

> And the Head stops beside me. For the first time in three years. Very pale. And must break the silence at once.

As the punctuation shows, it is not clear who must break the silence at once. The Hebrew is equally ambiguous; it might mean: "And I must break the silence." The final words are:

> Five or six hours ago –
> In the Jordan Valley –
> Killed on the spot.

> (72)

This could well be the narrator speaking to the Principal.

What are we to make of this different presentation of the event? Simply this: that we now suspect that if the father is feeling "stunned," if he is delayed at home and arrives late at school, it is because he has already been informed of his son's death, having received the news before leaving home that morning. And he comes to the school determined to give the greatest effect to his role of bereaved parent, announcing it to the Principal in the presence of the whole class! In other words he exploits the opportunity given him in order to further his ideological aims in respect to his pupils, whom he thereby traps. He also exploits it in his ongoing battle with the school Principal.[26]

This is the surprise ending: we had regarded him as a bereaved parent, as a tragic figure after his son's death, then as a parent who had to adjust himself to the fact that this report was false. Instead of this we see him now as self-deceived and out of touch with reality. More than that, we see him as both cunning and repellent in his single-minded obsession with the teaching of the Bible. Yehoshua has here given us not so much an Akedah story as an anti-Akedah. I would want to argue that it is this develop-

ment, this final intimation we receive of the moral and psychological twist in the make-up of the narrator, which makes the
story credible. Here the source of the narrator's strange compulsions
is discovered. We have moved from myth to paranoia.

It would be instructive to compare Yehoshua's story with
Rudyard Kipling's "The Gardener",[27] a brilliant short story based
on a biblical myth-pattern where likewise the truth of the situation
is only revealed at the end. We are told of an upper middle-class
spinster, Helen Turrel, living in an English village with her adopted
nephew, Michael, in the period before the First World War:

> Every one in the village knew that Helen Turrel did her duty
> by all her world, and by none more honourably than by her
> only brother's unfortunate child.

Her brother George, it seems, had joined the Indian police and
had had an affair with the daughter of another policeman. A
few weeks before their baby was due to be born, George had
unfortunately died from a fall whilst out horse-riding. Helen had
thereupon gone to Europe to arrange for the child to be transferred to her care. Michael was duly christened by the village
rector, and after receiving a gentleman's education, had, like so
many of his generation at the outbreak of war in 1914, volunteered and taken a commission in an infantry regiment. One day
in 1916, whilst his battalion was serving in the Ypres sector, "a
shell-splinter dropping out of a wet dawn killed him at once." In
the course of the years Helen slowly emerged from the fearful
shock of her bereavement. Eventually she received the documents
enabling her to visit Michael's grave in a military cemetery. Arriving
in Belgium she discovered that Hagenzeele Third, counting 21,000
dead, was a "merciless sea of black crosses . . . she could distinguish no order or arrangement in their mass." Finally, in despair,
she approached the only person in sight, a gardener, who was
firming a young plant in the earth. As she produced her paper
he arose and asked who she was looking for:

> "Lieutenant Michael Turrel – my nephew," said Helen slowly and
> word for word, as she had many thousands of times in her life.
>   The man lifted his eyes and looked at her with infinite
> compassion before he turned from the fresh-sown grass toward
> the naked black crosses.

"Come with me," he said, "and I will show you where your son lies."

When Helen left the Cemetery she turned for a last look. In the distance she saw the man bending over his young plants; and she went away, supposing him to be the gardener.

Helen is in fact Michael's mother and she has been living a lie until this moment. The reference in these closing sentences is of course to two passages from the gospels relating the discovery of the empty tomb. Retrospectively, every detail of Kipling's short story takes on new significance in the light of these gospel narratives. In Matthew 28 the two Marys visit the sepulchre to find that an angel has rolled away the stone from the door and sat upon it. The angel tells them: "He is risen . . . Come, see the place where the Lord lay." The stone becomes the guilty secret which the "gardener" through his disclosure removes from Helen's heart, thus enabling her to achieve truthfulness at last. In John 20, it is Mary Magdalene who comes and is startled and shocked to find the tomb empty. She sees a man standing outside, not realizing that it was Jesus himself.

He said unto her "whom seekest thou?" and she, supposing him to be the gardener, says unto him, "Sir, if thou have borne him hence, tell me where thou hast laid him."

Helen of course is both the mother of Jesus and Mary Magdalene in this story of illicit motherhood. Michael, if we conflate the two sources, likewise is an angel of mercy and also a saviour figure. Through his death, he rolls away the stone which had blocked his relationship with his mother, thus taking away her sin as Jesus is said to take away the sins of the world.

Now, the surprise ending introduces the element of mystery which Kipling's stories so often exhibit. The gardener who says to Helen, "Come with me and I will show you where your son lies" represents the swerve into mythology which transforms a story of everyday English middle-class life into a tale touched by mystery – that of the Crucifixion and the Resurrection. This change of direction is achieved through the *frisson* of the supernatural conveyed with marvellous economy in the last lines of the story – indeed the last six words. Something similar, I would suggest, though more hesitantly and only by hint and ambiguity, occurs towards the end of Yehoshua's tale "Early in the Summer of 1970." There too the truth regarding the father and the way in which the report of his son's death reaches him is brought out in the last lines of the text. We may want to add that "The Gardener" has reference to a parallel archetype – Crucifixion and Resurrection being in some sense (*en parabole*) a Christian revision of the Akedah.

But when that has been said, one must add that the two stories follow opposite directions. In Kipling's plot a quotidian, normal order is transformed into something else by the introduction of the mysterious gardener in the last sentence of the story. Then and only then is the everyday world invaded by mystery. With Yehoshua by contrast, it is precisely in the final episode of the story that the element of mystification is dispelled; it is then that we are made fully aware of the true state of mind of the protagonist. From being a tragic figure moved to testify to a biblical myth, he becomes a crazy old man, his delusion taking the form of seeing himself called upon to re-enact a biblical role. The situation is felt to be absurd; myth has given way to anti-myth.

Whilst both have a surprise ending, it should also be noted that Kipling's story has the neater closure. The *consummatum est* of the Easter event seems to lend itself to the wonder of the surprise ending. We have here the aesthetics of miracle. By comparison the ending of Yehoshua's tale is markedly untidy; it leaves us with the incompleteness of unfulfilled expectations, of a survival, of an ongoing responsibility, of lives still to be lived in a future as yet undetermined. It is the deluded father narrator in the story by Yehoshua who seems to desire the perfected pattern of a myth governed by the modalities of death and resurrection. Yehoshua, in denying him this consummation, is also denying himself and the reader the roundedness of artistic closure.

Many readers would claim that in this Yehoshua is taking a modernist stand, expressing a modernist (or post-modernist) suspicion of myth as a whole. But on this point other readers would disagree. I would wish to argue that in the last analysis, Yehoshua is haunted and possessed by the Akedah, no less than is his protagonist, the deluded schoolmaster. But he has seized, or been seized by, the Akedah in its more authentic biblical form. If the schoolmaster is fixated on the biblical myths and paradigms as unchanging patterns, as decrees rigidly controlling our destiny, then Yehoshua would seem to read them rather as testimonies inviting new understanding and new responses from each generation. The story, from this point of view, does not in fact end – hence the lack of roundedness and closure. Yehoshua is also focused, at least as far as this story is concerned, on the Akedah as a saving event. But what is at stake is the survival of the children of Abraham and Isaac, newly restored to their land, for a still uncertain future. The ending leaves nothing solved or, to put the case more positively, it leaves all the possibilities open.

From this point of view, it is also evident that the Akedah is, in the last analysis, a more serious business for Yehoshua than the message of Easter is for Kipling. The introduction of that paradigm is little more than a skilful device, providing us with the mystery of the surprise ending. He is essentially no more committed to it than he is to the legend of the Angel of Mons referred to in another war story ("A Madonna of the Trenches") published in the same collection. Yehoshua rejects the mystery but he is seized, and above all threatened (as Kipling is not) by the biblical archetype. It will not go away but will remain to be passionately opposed as a delusion or to be alternately embraced and resisted as historical testimony. Either way it is ultimately beyond the reach of literary exorcism or the magic of closure.

4

Yehoshua's final, and it would appear, summarizing treatment of the Akedah-pattern, is to be found in his full-length epic novel *Mr Mani*, published in 1990. It has deservedly attracted wide attention both in its original language and in the English translation by Hillel Halkin (1992).[28] This novel is remarkable for its extraordinary range and detail. It takes in two hundred years of Jewish history, focusing on the successive generations of the Manis, a family stemming from Salonika, until we arrive at Roni, the child of Hagar Shiloh, whom she bears to Efrayim (Efi) Mani in 1983. He represents the hopeful new generation of the Mani family and will be brought up in a kibbutz in southern Israel. Although he is a Mani, his father does not in fact marry his mother and his relationship to his father is tenuous. The range of the novel in geographical and social historical terms is impressive. It is not merely a family that Yehoshua depicts but rather the interface between the family and the Jewries of Turkey, Greece, Poland

and Palestine at different periods. Their wanderings take them to many other places including Beirut in the Middle East and Basle for the second Zionist Congress in 1898. The generation of the Second World War even find themselves on the island of Crete where the story is picked up by a German soldier who is strangely torn between his almost instinctive anti-semitism and his wonder and curiosity at these Jews whom he encounters in Crete. The period of the First World War is recounted in the monologue of a young Jewish officer from Manchester who is acting as a military advocate charged with investigating the suspected espionage activities of the current member of the Mani clan, namely Joseph Mani the Third. All these stages of the family history are actually recounted in dialogue form, but we only hear one side of this dialogue, the speaker varying from chapter to chapter.

As noted, the last generation is that of the son of Hagar, Roni Mani, the hopeful child of the last person to record her side of the dialogue. But this is not, as one might expect, the last chapter of the book. Instead of that, it is the first. The book is told backwards; we start with the present day, with the youngest Mani and we work back until the revelation of the origins of the story are the subject of the final section which takes us back to the end of the eighteenth century and the beginning of the nineteenth. Like "Early in the Summer of 1970," here too there is a surprise ending with the full shock only coming on the last page of the final monologue. Yehoshua here converts the strategy of the surprise ending into a primary instrument for organizing his vast canvas.

The main portrait given in the first section is that of Efi's father, Judge Gavriel Mani whom Hagar meets and whose behavior and whose background and life she describes in her conversation with her mother, Yael. The impression is gradually built up that Gavriel is a disturbed and abnormal person. The abnormality consists in repeated suicide attempts which Hagar discovers by chance when she goes to visit him in his Jerusalem apartment at the request of her lover Efi, who is serving in Lebanon. (It is the winter of 1982–3.) In the course of these visits she succeeds in diverting his attention from suicide, or at least preparations for suicide, on two occasions. This kind of insanity, or at least weird behavior, seems to run in the family. His great-grandfather, Moshe Mani, had committed suicide in Beirut in 1899 whilst his grandfather had died in Crete, in 1941 (either from suicide or, less probably, from natural causes) while being held hostage by a German soldier who had bound him in army bandages like a veritable akedah victim. Each other major figure of the Mani family is marked by some strangeness of behavior, if not a suicidal tendency then a tendency to seek out eccentric solutions to the Arab-Jewish equation. One ancestor, Joseph Mani the Second had pursued a wild scheme for convincing the Arabs that they were really Jews who had forgotten they were Jews – thereby endangering his own life.

We are continually in search of a clue to the mysterious abnormalities marking the Mani clan and this becomes, as in a detective story, the reader's dominant problem. What is the secret which lurks behind the strange behavior of this family, the madness which already fascinates and horrifies Hagar Shiloh in the first, opening section? The image which the novel itself offers us for this search and this complexity is that of the labyrinth or maze. The labyrinth is explicitly referred to in the account of the events in Crete. After having been parachuted into Crete in the German attack on that island, Egon Bruner, a corporal in the *Wehrmacht*, makes his way to the ruins of the ancient palace at Knossos thought to be modelled on the legend of the labyrinth. As Haya Shaham cogently notes in her study of this book [29], the labyrinth becomes a major image for the structure of the novel itself. We are seeking our way through a labyrinth, constantly in danger of making a false turn, or of coming up against a path which leads nowhere. Basle at the time of the Zionist Congress becomes a labyrinth; so does Constantinople and so, above all, does Jerusalem, where we are told that it is possible to traverse the whole of the Old City using the rooftops only and without stepping into the street (340). We always seem to be seeking for the mysterious horror which lurks in the labyrinth, at the end of the trail. This is one way of speaking of the secret or mystery of the Mani family. But this mystery has a broader significance; it points to the Jewish people as a whole. This is an epic novel, intended to portray the insanity which haunts the history of this family as symbolic of a kind of collective Jewish insanity. We are not only mad but we drive the rest of the world mad. This it seems is what Yehoshua is saying.

The nature of this monster or minotaur, the guilty secret hidden within the labyrinth, is what we shall discover in the last episode. Here Abraham Mani the First is speaking to his teacher and guide, the aged and sick Rabbi Shabbetai Haddaya who is dying in an inn in Athens where Abraham goes to make his final confession. This confession relates to the circumstances surrounding the death of Abraham Mani's son, Joseph Mani, in Jerusalem a little earlier. This is the surprise ending of the book which has been much discussed, not least by Yehoshua himself. Joseph had married Tamara, a niece of Flora, the wife of the Rabbi Haddaya, but he had failed to consummate this marriage. His father, Abraham Mani, becomes aware of the fact that his line will not be continued by his son and so he takes action, rather as in the biblical story of Judah and Tamar (Genesis 38), where Judah impregnates his daughter-in-law when his two sons fail to do so, and thus perpetuates his line. In the same way, after his son's death, Abraham Mani, determined to guarantee a future for his family, lies with his daughter-in-law and produces from her the child who will carry on the family history, namely, Moshe Mani who will be born in 1848 in Jerusalem.

But that is not the only confession he has to make to Rabbi Haddaya. His son Joseph Mani has an idée fixe. It is that the Ishmaelites, especially those of Jerusalem, are actually Jews who had forgotten that they were Jews and would yet remember it, while the Jews themselves are unable to forget their Jewish identity. He aims to bring them together as one people, even at the risk of having them turn against him (313, 325, 334). This notion, which he shares with the British Consul in Jerusalem (evidently a reference to a historical figure, the eccentric James Finn), drives him into the labyrinth of the streets of Jerusalem at nighttime until the fatal occasion – it seems to be Christmas eve – when we find him in flight from the Church of the Holy Sepulchre, where he has angered the worshippers and pilgrims. Pursued by the pilgrims, and still following his idée fixe, he runs, not to the quarter of the Jews, but to the Muslim quarter where he enters the Temple Mount and is overcome by the guards. They laugh at him, recognizing that he is insane, but at the same time they are roused to anger by the provocation which they see in his strange ideas. Abraham Mani relates what happened next to the dying Rabbi in Athens. He hedges his report in ambiguities and indirections so as not to overpower the old man's senses and perhaps shock him into a fatal heart attack. But in the last sentences he comes near to making a terrifyingly clear statement as to what had happened.

And I, my master and teacher, was outside the gate, I was
watching from afar while listening to the distant bell of a lost
flock, silently wretchedly waiting for the worst of the night to
wear itself out and the morning star to appear in the east, faint
and longed for so that I might go to him to the far pole of his
terror and sorrow, whether as his slaughterer or whether as the
slaughterer's inspector, and release him from his earthly bonds
because I was certain that he had already deposited his seed.
(362)

He has suggested earlier that the Mohammedan guards who crowd
around the wild and crazy figure of Joseph have a half-concealed
knife that is passed around from hand to hand and that it is
they perhaps who executed him (ibid). In an earlier passage he
had also suggested that his son's friend, the son of a Moslem
sheikh from Silwan was the real murderer (350). But in the above
passage, Abraham Mani is now alone – the shadowy figure of
the sheikh's son, who was perhaps only imagined, has disappeared and so have the Mohammedan guards. The father is seeking
to destroy his son whose ideas threaten everyone; he appears
"as his slaughterer or . . . as the slaughterer's inspector." The
"*shochet*" is the man who kills the animal for food and the "*bodek*"
is the religious authority who inspects the knife used for the killing.

This is the monstrous deed, the minotaur, so to speak, that is
hidden at the last turn of the labyrinth. Abraham has taken it
upon himself "to release him from his earthly bonds." Behind
Abraham Mani is of course the patriarch Abraham of old carrying out the Akedah, not *en parabole* but in horrifying fact. He
was able to do so, he tells us, because he was certain that he
"had already deposited his seed." This again is ambiguous. It could
mean that his wife had already conceived, and Joseph himself
would become a father, or it might mean that he had transferred
the responsibility for the future of the tribe to someone else. This
someone else could be his own father, Abraham Mani. In either
case, the requirement to produce an offspring (which is Abraham
Mani's own idée fixe) has been taken care of, that is, "deposited."

And so he has come to Rabbi Haddaya in order to know what
his punishment should be. His question to the Rabbi is: can I
permit myself to go on living? Or must it be self murder? In the
afternote to this chapter, we are told that there was no reply
from the Rabbi, who had died apparently of shock, some time

before these final words and final questions were uttered. "Abraham Mani received no answer to his questions nor was there the least movement of the Rabbi's head to interpret as a yes or a no." The reason being that "Rabbi Shabbetai Haddaya whose judgement he had sought was dead" (364). It is thus the memory of this monstrous deed and the punishment that must be exacted for it which give rise to the suicidal tendencies of the later generations of the Manis.

Here then, is a monstrous ending which involves a certain overthrowing of narrative credibility. Yehoshua has written a masterpiece, but it is a flawed masterpiece. It is flawed because it is mythologically overdetermined. In this it is a little like a play by Auden and Isherwood which aroused some attention in the 1930s, namely "The Ascent of F6." It will be remembered that when Michael Ransom, the hero of that play, achieves glory for himself and his country by reaching the top of the mountain, he finds there a veiled figure which turns out to be his mother! This gave literal expression to the notion of the Oedipus complex which Freud had elaborated a few years earlier. If this play were ever to be revived, we would be struck by this denouement as a flattening out of imaginative possibilities by the imposing of a psychological theory on the play at the expense of its poetic richness. In Yehoshua's novel, the father is Abraham; the son, we are told, is "bound with long strips of cloth" (361) and laid down on the ground of Mount Moriah itself, that is, the Temple Mount, to meet his death.[30] This is the paradigm of the Akedah with a vengeance.

In Abraham Mani's monodialogue taken as a whole, the slaying of the son by the father is by no means so factually clear. As we noted, there are other shadowy presences involved. But this nuancing is swept aside by Yehoshua himself in a later statement. Speaking at a conference in Haifa University in April 1992, devoted entirely to the interpretation of this novel, Yehoshua, in an extraordinary presentation of fewer than three thousand words proclaimed the true meaning of the disclosure we have been discussing.

> The Akedah, a subject which has exercised me for many years in different works of fiction, here reaches, or so I hope, its final working out. I feel at this time that in truth I have liberated myself from it. But not only is this a matter of the personal 'I' of the author. What I was in fact trying to do through

this novel (an awful presumption, perhaps, on my part) was also to liberate the collective 'I' [of the nation] from this powerful and terrifying myth which bears down so forcibly upon our history and culture. For make no mistake; we built the Temple and the Holy of Holies on the place associated with this horrific story. I wanted to be free of it, precisely by fulfilling it literally – that is to say, by bringing the threat, the menace which it contains from mere potentiality into actuality. Thus the myth would no longer function merely as a metaphor, would no longer work as a mere hint, a disguise, but would figure as a real-life situation in a credible psychological context and at the very place with which it was traditionally associated.

The title of this essay in which he makes his statement is "Cancelling the Akedah by Carrying it Out." And he maintains that this is what happens in the novel itself:

By killing the son, the father was able to usurp his place and thereby continue the line of the family history. It might seem from his words that Abraham had merely stood on one side whilst Joseph was being killed by others because he knew that he had "deposited his seed". That is to say that he was prepared to let him go to his death so as to spare himself and the community the political consequences of his son's wild ideas. He was also sure that there would be a continuation of the family, Tamara having already conceived.

But the word *hifkid* ("he had deposited") gives away Abraham's real intention, for he very well knows that despite all his efforts to bring about cohabitation between Joseph and his wife he is not successful in this and therefore the word "deposited" in relation to the seed of Joseph, should not mislead us; it does not have a metaphorical sense. Its meaning is not that Tamara has conceived (by her husband) but that the seed has been deposited with a third party, that is to say with father Mani himself. . . .

All these reasons for the act of the father in murdering his son which is the true and terrible crime lying at the base of the Mani dynasty and for which Abraham Mani wishes to pay by taking his own life – all these reasons are in the book only so that the story of the Akedah should not be simply dropped into the novel as a disconnected myth or metaphor, but should have a realistic, psychological and credible basis. What was simply a threat in the Bible story becomes here terrible actuality. And perhaps precisely by the murderous actualizing of this threat, I will succeed in dispelling the fascination of this foundation legend and perhaps also its very soul. It is this which I call "Cancelling the Akedah by Carrying it Out".... For the Akedah is the foundation of the religious covenant, the "merit" inherited from the patriarchs. It hovers ominously over our history like a great black bird".[31]

It is hard to imagine any author so savagely attacking the archetype which forms the basis of his own work. The Akedah had been the inspiration for some of his most important writings and here he is directing all his force against it, terming it a "moral outrage" as if it was the source of everything evil or negative in the life of his people! There is surely a double injustice here. First of all, Yehoshua is prejudiced in his refusal to recognize the positive force of the Akedah as a salvation-myth; secondly, he is far from doing justice to his own complex treatment of the Akedah in this very book.

Nitza Ben-Dov, the editor of the important volume of studies in which Yehoshua's essay appears, forcefully makes this point in her introduction where she says, referring to the passage we have just quoted,

According to the author's claim, Abraham Mani is responsible for the death of his son Joseph. In this the Akedah threat is translated from the potential to the actual. Unlike the patriarch Abraham who merely waved the knife to slaughter his son and then withdrew it, Abraham Mani actually performed the act of slaughter. The ambiguous text of the Bible is here transformed into a univocal text which the author declares to be that which he intended in his story.

In this Yehoshua reveals his ideological purpose. He himself, just as much as his characters, has an idée fixe. He is prepared to give up the rich multilayeredness which he has succeeded in imparting to the text, a multivocal and hesitant quality which is the sign of a complex aesthetic achievement and which testifies to his greatness as a writer. He is prepared to give all that up in order to state his position and convey his message to us; he has sought here to make the Akedah real with the aim of annulling it. The Akedah myth, which signifies the menace of near-death, but also carries within it the message of a last-minute redemption, is probably the most powerful myth which the collective consciousness of the Jewish people has known. But for Yehoshua it is fundamentally misguided, giving rise to a dangerous gamble with fate, history, and [our co-existence with] other nations, based on the assumption that "a lamb for the burnt offering" will always show up at the last moment. But if we are not careful, we are liable to find the Akedah carried out literally. Here he shows this happening. According to its author's own interpretation, Abraham Mani in this most difficult of confessions, after which a normal life will become impossible, now in the final monodialogue of the story, relates to his Rabbi and teacher that it was he who had actually slain his only son.[32]

An even subtler response to Yehoshua's amazingly reductive self-interpretation is that of Mordechai Shalev. "This literal carrying-out of the Akedah," says Shalev, "is inauthentic, artificial and rationalizing." It would have the effect of diminishing the literary work at its close. But in fact the biblical paradigm forcefully re-asserts itself at the unconscious level, so that in spite of Yehoshua's declared intention, what he writes becomes a story of rescue:

> Not only is the Akedah as a salvation-narrative not overthrown as Yehoshua wished it to be, but instead his fictional reading comes essentially to confirm the Akedah as a myth of salvation and to become totally integrated into it. What we have here of course is the model of the replacement or substitute sacrifice, namely the ram "caught in the thicket by its horns" which will be offered up instead of Isaac (Gen. 22:13). Just as the real victim of the Akedah is to be saved, so the substitute, namely the ram, is to be literally offered as a sacrifice. . . . Without that actual sacrifice there can be no valid rescue.[33]

According to the logic of the myth, therefore, the killing of the ram is necessary for the saving of Isaac. There is an exchange. Shalev is here arguing, that through the power of the biblical paradigm itself Joseph Mani becomes "the ram in the thicket" whilst Moshe Mani, the child whom Abraham and Tamara bring into the world, becomes the Isaac figure, the survivor in the story.

Thus the salvation-pattern is itself rescued and the original myth reasserted, as in the other Akedah stories of Yehoshua, "Three Days and a Child" and "Early in the Summer of 1970."[34] Similarly, here in *Mr Mani* in spite of suicides and other disasters, there is a survivor in each generation and the story continues until our own day when we meet the surviving Mani who is going to go on and become the father of a succession of further survivors in the same family history.

This is not the emphasis that Yehoshua evidently intended, for the weight of his polemic focuses rather on the monstrous conclusion and the secret guilt which oppresses the succession of the Manis down to our own time. But one might equally argue from Yehoshua's own testimony that, far from giving rise to murder and madness, the Akedah with its promise of redemption has, over the centuries, inspired a faith in the future. It could rightly be seen as the very key to Jewish survival. It would seem, therefore, that Yehoshua's interpretive judgment has not been equal to the richness of the tale he has actually told. This achieves more in terms of epic depth, scope and range than Yehoshua the polemicist is aware of. It also more truly reflects the continuing force of the myth.

This is the position taken both by Nitza Ben-Dov and Mordechai Shalev. There is, they would say, a conflict between Yehoshua's ideology and the actual thrust of his novel. And creativity wins. According to Ben-Dov, Yehoshua has his "idée fixe" just as Joseph and Abraham Mani have theirs, and his obsession is as much out of touch with reality as theirs. Just as the Arabs will not turn themselves into Jews, so Yehoshua will not succeed in cancelling the Akedah by putting it into practice. It will stay alive and retain its power, not least in Yehoshua's own novel, which was meant to abolish it.

5

I would wish to offer a somewhat different account from that of the critics mentioned above. It does not seem to me as if the ideology is confined to Yehoshua's interpretive essay, and that it is wholly contradicted by the book he wrote. Whilst Shalev undoubtedly has a point when he maintains that Joseph Mani becomes the "ram in the thicket" who has to be sacrificed, whilst

Moshe Mani takes over the role of survivor and becomes the "Isaac" of the Akedah, this seems to me a little too neat and simple. The Akedah as salvation-myth may be working underground in this chapter itself in spite of the author's conscious resistance to it, but the powerful thrust of the polemics is felt nevertheless. In other words, I would want to argue for an unresolved tension within the texture of the novel – a tension between Akedah and anti-Akedah, between witnessing and denouncing, and between the conscious and the unconscious sources of the novel's authority. It is doubtful whether this novelist (or indeed any other great writer) ever works without some degree of conscious control. In spite of Bakhtin's sense of the autonomy achieved by Dostoevsky's characters, novels do not in fact write themselves. If, as Shalev argues, the power of the Akedah as a myth of rescue is working unconsciously within Yehoshua's text, then I would wish to argue that his conscious aims are working no less powerfully against it. The effect of the affirmation of Yehoshua's polemical and ideological aims at this conscious level of the novel's composition is an overdetermination of the Akedah-pattern comparable to the effect of the mother's appearance at the end of Auden and Isherwood's play. In this respect, the novel exhibits signs of a profound unevenness; it is far from being unified either in characterization or plot. Abraham Mani, for example, has resolved that the line of the Manis should continue, and he is prepared to go to all lengths to ensure that. At the same time, and in order to achieve that very same end, he is prepared to extinguish the life of his only child! There are thus two obsessions, not one, and they defeat one another. His author, Abraham Yehoshua, reveals a similar contradiction; he is seen to be driven by the undiminished power of the biblical archetype and at the same time he is engaged in violently attacking it! One thrust represents the conscious aim of the work, whilst the other represents its unconscious driving force.

Compounding this duality is the contrast which Yehoshua insists upon between realism on the one hand and fantasy or delusion on the other. Those who see in the Akedah a valid and continuing witness, a means of understanding "the ways of God to man," are in effect submitting themselves to the absurdity of a blind religious faith which defies both logic and morality. By contrast he declares himself to have "rid the story of its mythical and metaphorical fascination by bestowing on it a realistic grounding in credible psychology."[35] Here is a remarkable claim indeed and it surely betrays a remarkable lapse in self-understanding on the part of a great author. For there could scarcely be a more fantastic notion – using that term in its precise literary sense – than that of the inherited guilt of the Manis mysteriously transferred from one generation to the next. They are shown to be compulsively drawn to suicide again and again in order to expiate the guilt of "father" Abraham Mani and to carry out the death-sentence he had pronounced on himself some two hundred years ago! This notion could suit a legendary tale, or a Gothic romance, or serve as a mysterious ending for a story by Kipling or Edgar Allan Poe. One is reminded of Kenneth Branagh's psychological thriller "Dead Again," where the crime of one generation is fantastically re-enacted by a second and the penalty for the crime is finally visited on the doer. This made a successful motion picture but surely no one – neither Branagh nor his scriptwriter (Scott Frank) – expected it to be taken seriously as "credible psychology." As a basis for Yehoshua's plot, this "transmigration of guilt," as we might call it, also marks the abandonment of common ethical norms which would seem to require personal (rather than inherited) responsibility. His realistic-literalist reading of the Akedah here seems to endorse precisely that "suspension of the ethical" which he vigorously condemns in his essay! These anomalies characterize the "unresolved tension" that I have referred to in Yehoshua's text. There are both realism and fantasy in the novel but these are often distributed in a manner opposite to that intended by the author; so that we get the realism of myth and the fantasy of a literal re-enactment of myth in real time. Such confusions point not to a unified conception and execution but rather to a deep rift in the imaginative structure of this novel.

This rift expresses itself in many forms; it is the power still excercised over the modern writer by the biblical paradigm and, set against that, the equally powerful resistance which it provokes in him. It is the unresolved tension between menace and blessing, the former revealed in the strange aberrations of the Manis, the latter still affirmed in the continuing life of the family, (and by extension, of the Jewish people) who evidently still have some work to do in the world. It is the sense of being in prison, in a confining space and, set off against that, the need to affirm one's freedom. The term that stands out in Yehoshua's discussion of his book is *lehishtahrer* – "to set oneself free". He seeks freedom from an overpowering burden of election, of exclusivity, as implied by the Akedah narrative. But at the same time he has a strong sense of responsibility and cannot put the burden down. He is like the young man in an early story of his, "Facing the Forests" (1968) about a student who is given the task of guarding a tract of forest against arsonists. He constantly puts his binoculars to his eyes to look for fires, unable to free himself from his obsessive burden. It is finally, therefore, the contradiction between the exclusive charge placed by the Akedah trial upon those to whom it is addressed and a more universal message to which the imagination aspires as in the statements of Bernard Malamud with which this chapter began. Thus, Joseph Mani, the Second and Third, give themselves up to an idea of universal fellowship, bringing Jews and non-Jews together in a search for peace and brotherhood. Similarly we have Dr Moshe Mani in the middle of the nineteenth century establishing a maternity hospital open to all inhabitants of Jerusalem regardless of faith or nationality (256).

It could be argued of course that these very anomalies are part of the Akedah paradigm itself. The Akedah after all, as we have argued, is both threat and promise; the two coexist. Similarly in Genesis 22:18 the redemptive program seen as the outcome of the Akedah broadens into a blessing which Abraham would mediate to the whole world. So that if the Akedah is announced as an exclusive burden, it equally proclaims a universal promise. Such contradictions are surely typical of a divinely-ordained mythological system. After all, the demonic and the angelic coexist in the Godhead itself. That is in the nature of theological paradoxes. God is frequently represented as a shepherd; his sheep shall not want. But in Hosea Chapter 13 the shepherd turns round to attack the flock. He has become a ravenous beast, a lion, a leopard, a bear bereaved of her whelps. Likewise the universal and the particular coexist as a major theological paradox throughout the Hebrew scriptures. Thus, Israel is called "to be to me a peculiar people, because all the world is mine" (Exodus 19:5). The connective *ki* ("because," "yet," "but," "though") carries the weight of that immense paradox. But when the metaphysical ground is abolished, as in Yehoshua's writing, then instead of paradox we find unresolved tension. Exclusive aims and universal promises are no longer compatible; sacrifice and rescue can no longer inhabit the same space. Instead they spin off in different directions, no longer controlled by the metaphysic of redemption.

The result of evacuating the divine presence from the myth is thus to render it logically inexplicable even though its power remains. This is the price we must pay for receiving the benefits and freedoms of secularization. The more honest the writer is, the higher is the price. Yehoshua is a very honest writer indeed. So that if he has given us a flawed masterpiece, it is a masterpiece nevertheless.

10
The Day before Yesterday

1

S.Y. Agnon is a major writer by any standard and the central figure in the history of modern Hebrew fiction. He is above all Israel's classic novelist, representing the fullness of the Hebraic tradition with the Bible at its center. "In my writing I have been influenced first and foremost by the Bible, Mishnah, Talmud, Midrash and Rashi's commentary on the Bible," he declared in his acceptance speech on being awarded the Nobel Prize for Literature in 1966. This may suggest a certain scholarly remoteness – as of a Miltonian figure (Milton's poetry carried a like weight of theological and other learning). But in fact Agnon was not the least bit remote; his playfulness, his witty control of so many varied sources, his rich allusiveness and stylistic virtuosity helped him to gain popularity with all ranks and classes of the new reading public in the early part of the century. But what fascinated his readers above all was the amazing fertility of his invention, a kind of midrashic excess. There was always another story, and a story within that story, and another story suggested by that one in a seemingly infinite series. This may suggest something like the wealth of invention of the great nineteenth-century novelists. But Agnon, as his more discerning critics have noted, is also a truly contemporary figure. If his sources are traditional, the tone of his narration is often ironical and the personality of the narrator, quizzical and arcane. With a reflexive subtlety which is thoroughly modern he will share with his readers this very problem of narrative excess. Thus in a short story entitled "Knots Upon Knots" the narrator imagines himself vainly tying up his papers into bundles in order to get them home from a bookbinder's shop where they have been stored:

but the rope was old and had many knots in it, and as I undid them, I cut my fingers and broke my nails, and when I finally managed to get the knots undone, the rope itself came apart and unravelled.[1]

The combination here of symbolism with realistic description is remarkable. It is clearly an allegory of writing and yet at the same time it portrays a firmly localized Jerusalem setting on an autumn afternoon with the narrator waiting for a bus just as the first rains come splashing down. In his masterly full-length novel *A Guest For the Night* (1935),[2] based on a visit he made to his place of birth in Eastern Europe in 1930, the problem of narrative control (as well as ideological direction) is projected through the symbolism of a key – the great brass key to the *Bet Midrash* (House of Study) in the narrator's home town of "Shibush" (itself an allegorical name suggesting "confusion"). The key, found and lost and then found again at the end of the story, when it is discovered in the lining of his suitcase on the narrator's return to Jerusalem, is a powerful unifying symbol calling out rather obviously for interpretation. And yet it belongs also to an everyday world, that of the *shtetl* in decline, which is presented faithfully and in striking detail throughout this novel. This yoking together of the symbolic and the everyday reminds us not a little of Kafka, though Agnon claimed not to have read a line of Kafka at the time of writing these fictions. But whether that is to be believed or not, the analogy with Kafka has become a commonplace of Agnon-criticism.

All this has caused Agnon to be perceived as a modern figure. He is in fact a writers' writer and has been a major force in shaping the novel and short story for a whole generation of younger writers, including David Shachar, Amos Oz and A.B. Yehoshua. These writers and many others have found Agnon to be an exciting and liberating contemporary model, helping them to escape from the narrower modes of social realism coming from Eastern Europe and still widely practiced in Israel in the mid-century. And though they do not acknowledge anything like Agnon's debt to traditional Jewish sources, there can be no doubt that his influence has gone beyond mere technique and narrative method. If he taught them the use of dream symbols, then we should remember that, as he told his audience in Stockholm, his dreams have been above all biblical dreams. The younger writers too, as we saw in the case of Yehoshua, have a copy of the Bible in their baggage even if the key to the old *Bet Midrash* is for them still missing. And one of the biblical dreams (or in this case perhaps, nightmares) which they all share is that of the Akedah.

Agnon's feeling for the biblical patterns is, as we might suppose, more reverent than that of most of the writers we have considered so far. During the greater part of his life he observed the commandments and occupied himself (in addition to his fictional writings) with the collecting and editing of rabbinic sayings and anecdotes. Practically all his major works and collections have biblical titles. The last volume of short stories published in his lifetime is entitled "The Wood and the Fire" (1962).[3] The phrase is of course from the Akedah (Genesis 22:7) and the Akedah is also the subject of the first story in that collection – "According to the Pain is the Reward." It tells of a certain Rabbi Zidkiyyah, noted equally for his inspired liturgical poems and his works of charity. A due note of piety is sounded early on. The Rabbi is contemplating the unending history of Jewish suffering and martyrdom. "Whence" he asks himself, "do we draw this strength, for every day we are slain and butchered and every day we are bound down [*ne'ekadim*]?"

> His thoughts settled on our father Isaac, God's own burnt-offering, the first of those who were bound, who indeed bound himself on the altar in order that he might perform the will of his father in heaven.
>
> (9)

He determines forthwith to compose a hymn on the Akedah to be sung in the synagogue during the coming Days of Awe. He seems to see the ashes of Isaac himself spread out on the altar and is duly inspired.

> And thus he wove his rhymes, as do the sacred poets who "bind" up [*okedim*] their very hearts to their poems out of devotion to God, until he had versified the whole Akedah in wonderful and awesome verses.
>
> (ibid.)

It will be noted that Agnon speaks of the poem which R. Zidkiyyah composes as itself an "Akedah." In fact the many poems on the

Binding of Isaac, regularly inserted in the blessing for the resurrection of the dead during the High Holy Day services, are technically known as "Akedot." He has *"bound up* his heart in his poem" and thus the fate of the poem becomes a symbol for the survival or death of the poet and, by extension, of the community of worshippers.

Agnon's story is conducted at this symbolic level. The question is whether the poem deserves to survive or not. Zidkiyyah has formed the habit of testing the value of his liturgical compositions by the quality of the poor folk who turn to him for alms. If the current applicant is God-fearing and grounded in the Torah he will take that as a sign that his verses are accepted on high; if he is not, then he draws the opposite conclusion. On the present occasion he is visited by a beggar uncouth and defiant in manner; from God, he declares that he expects neither blessing nor salvation. He is clothed in rags and strips of paper, his body covered with filth and running sores. Zidkiyyah gives him all the money he has – a gold coin in fact – which the man takes with a bad grace, complaining the whole time. And so Zidkiyyah sadly determines, in accordance with his principle, to burn his poem. After so clear a sign of divine displeasure, he takes a flint, raises a fire in the hearth, and reduces his "Akedah" to ashes. Not only that. From then on he will write no more poems.

But this is not quite the last word. The years go by and R. Zidkiyyah is now near death, his wife and children having all predeceased him. Too weak to stand or walk and lying on his bed, he is brought to the synagogue with the assistance of a surviving grandson – there to attend the services of the Day of Atonement. It is then, in the interval before the afternoon prayer (the day and hour when, according to tradition, the Binding of Isaac took place), that Zidkiyyah has his hour of grace. He finds new strength, rises from his bed, and approaches the reading-desk to lead the congregation in prayer, as the *seraphim* from Isaiah's vision surround him with wings outspread. But most wonderful of all, the words and the melody of the Akedah which he had burnt are restored to him, echoed in the beating of the angels' wings. They have, it seems, been accepted "above." This is where a simple and pious story-teller might have ended his tale. But Agnon though pious is by no means simple. Having uttered his swan song, R. Zidkiyya falls to the ground and appears to be dead. But the narrator corrects this like the author of the midrash quoted earlier (p. 168) on the disappearance of Isaac at the end of the Akedah chapter. Zidkiyyah, the narrator tells us, did not die. He managed to go home on his own two feet and spent the hours of the following night with quill, ink and paper before him, vainly seeking to recapture the verses of his lost Akedah "which lay on his tongue like Isaac's ashes spread on the altar" (18). But all he can recall is a scattered word here and there. The poem will not consent to return to earth. "Once the 'Akedah' has been accepted above, it is not required here below" (ibid.).

Agnon is here exploring the same ambivalence that we considered in the previous chapter. Abraham Mani is committed to life, to survival – the survival of his seed – and yet he pronounces his own death sentence and that of his son. Likewise Zidkiyyah in Agnon's tale is dead and yet he is not dead; his poem exists and yet does not exist. It is at one and the same time a failure and a success. It does not make it into the festival prayer-book; it fails on earth but it succeeds in heaven! There is here a sharp division between transcendental and earthbound values. This is pointed out by the Israeli critic Baruch Kurzweil who relates this to the near despair, the basic questioning of all historical rewards and promises in the years following the Holocaust and the Second World War.[4] The outer world with its disenchantment, ruin and disaster no longer coincides with the world of the spirit. What would it now mean to speak of God "testing" Abraham? Where in such a dehumanized environment can the dialogue recorded in Genesis 22 be imagined as taking place? In particular, it would seem that the call of the angel in Genesis 22:12 is no longer so confidently awaited or so clearly heard.

From this point of view the key figure in the story is the old man in rags with his running sores, his mouth empty of teeth, who comes begging to Zidkiyyah's door. We have here crossed the threshold of the human in a downward direction; we have reached a point where all faith in man and all hope in God as the ruler of this world – are reduced to seeming absurdity. There is no space left in which the Akedah with its inbuilt concept of the near miss, the rescue, the hope of futurity, can still function. And so Zidkiyyah condemns his "Akedah" to oblivion. He has beheld the ultimate antithesis to its message of salvation – that is, unaccommodated man himself, despised and without honor or dignity, the suffering servant of Isaiah 53 reduced to a subhuman state of wretchedness. It is only when R. Zidkiyyah, on his

death-bed, finds himself reduced to a like condition that the image
of his visitor returns to him (14). And at that same moment his
"Akedah" is marvelously restored to his memory and he finds
himself able to recite the poem in the original words and melody.
But only for that moment. There has been a general declension
of the human, in the light of which devotional poetry, especially
that inspired by the Akedah, is it would seem, no longer possible.
Or else we may say that it only becomes possible by a crossing
of thresholds in the opposite direction, an upward transcendence,
and with that a like eclipsing of human possibilities and hopes.

   And yet this will not quite do as a summary of Agnon's sense
of the Akedah in relation to the events of our own time. He does
not in the end adopt so despairing a conclusion. His sense of the
grand sweep of Jewish history in the twentieth century is not
confined to the horrors of 1942–5. These take their place in a
larger scene of witness which he displays and to which he invites
our attention. And corresponding with that larger vision, he shows
a uniquely informed awareness of the wider literary and theological context of the Akedah narrative itself. The result is one of
the great epic novels of our time.

2

We turn to Agnon's novel *Temol Shilshom* ("*The Day before Yesterday*" 1945)[5] which has been rightly described as "the most successfully realized . . ., the richest in connotation, and the most universal
in import" of his full-length works.[6] Completed, like Thomas Mann's
Doktor Faustus in the immediate aftermath of the Second World
War, its implicit claims are similar to those of Mann's great work.
It sums up the modern history of a nation, focusing for this purpose on a single individual – in Agnon's case it is Yitzhak Kummer
– in whose life that history in its aspirations and its tragic range
is encapsulated. Like Mann's masterpiece, Agnon's novel uses ex-
pressionist devices which break sharply with the traditional realism of the *Bildungsroman*. And there is a similar crossing of time
boundaries. Mann takes us back and forth between the nineteenth
century of Nietzsche, the present day of Leverkühn and the sixteenth century of Luther. But he never strays far from the fearful catastrophe of 1933–45 as the ultimate point of reference.
Agnon's novel, written likewise from the perspective of the War

years and their immediate aftermath,[7] is set in the early part of
this century, the time of the Second "Aliyah" (or "wave of immi-
gration" – approximately 1907–13) which marked the beginning
of the modern renewal of Jewish national existence. And there is
a backward perspective also, an ever present awareness of the
Diaspora world of "the day before yesterday" with its pieties and
continuities. Those pieties were shared also by the "Old Yishuv,"
that is, the Jews who had lived in the holy cities of the Holy
Land for many decades, indeed many generations, prior to the
arrival of the "pioneers" of the Second Aliyah. In that context
we are frequently reminded that Yitzhak Kummer is the great-
grandson of Reb Yudel, representing the world of eighteenth-
century hasidic piety. He had been the hero of Agnon's first
full-length novel, *Hakhnasat Kallah* (*A Bridal Canopy*) published in
1931. Both Yitzhak and Reb Yudel are enchanted seekers, making their way to the Holy Land (Reb Yudel at the end of his tale,
Yitzhak at the beginning of his) there to find the Sleeping Beauty
of Jewish history and to awaken her to new life with a lover's
kiss. But the contrast between them is even more marked. Yitzhak
with his doubts and confusions, is very much a child of our time.
He knows the bitter taste of guilt, frustration and disillusionment,
whilst Reb Yudel, like some Jewish Don Quixote, is blissfully
unaware of discordances. The world without reflects the world
within and the soon-to-be-awaited coming of the Messiah will
set to rights any troubling questions that we may still have. One
is left to wonder whether in the end Reb Yudel's world was not
the saner of the two. We are told, ironically, that what they will
both have in common to enjoy for all future time is a burial place
in the Land of Israel (607).

Yitzhak, obeying an age-old imperative, makes his way from
Galicia in Eastern Europe to the Holy Land (as Agnon had done)
around the year 1907, arriving, like Reb Yudel before him, in a
state of exaltation. But the harsh realities of Jaffa in 1907 lead to
a certain disenchantment. There is the heat, the dust and squalor
and we also note the selfishness and avarice of the existing population. Yitzhak in short becomes aware of the non-ideal character of the land of promise as he makes his way to Petah-Tikvah,
one of the new "colonies." There Yitzhak, who has come to
Palestine to "build and to be himself rebuilt" finds that the idealism
of the new pioneers finds no encouragement from the Jewish
farmers and landowners already established in the country. They

prefer to hire local Arab labor in their farms and orchards. The *halutzim*, or pioneers, actually go hungry from lack of work.

In this gloom Yitzhak is consoled by the comradeship felt among the young workers. Among his friends are Rabinowitz and Yohanan Leichtfuss. With the help of Leichtfuss Yitzhak trains himself to be a house painter. The mode of narration is here above all things realistic, the novel giving us a marvelously informed account of the life of the Yishuv in the early part of the century. The impression of near total realism is well founded; Agnon on arriving in Jaffa in 1907 had become secretary of the local Jewish court and subsequently of the Land of Israel Council. In these capacities he seems to have got to know just about everyone in the Jewish population of the country, the so-called *Yishuv*.

Yitzhak, who has now abandoned the traditional pieties of his ancestors, enters into a friendship with Sonia, Rabinowitz's girl-friend, Rabinowitz having in the meantime gone abroad. After a few months Sonia tires of the rather bashful young man from Galicia and their intimacy cools off, leaving Yitzhak both desolate and also ridden with guilt at the thought of having betrayed his best friend. In this state of mind, he decides to leave for Jerusalem which in all the months since his arrival in the country he has never visited.

Here he encounters a different atmosphere – a religious tone in contrast with the secular tone of Jaffa society. There is much piety but also much suffering – more than in Jaffa. He strikes up a friendship with the artist and fellow Galician Shimshon Blaukopf who is dying of consumption (211). Another tragic figure is Reb Alter, a man of learning from Yitzhak's home town, and also a circumciser (who had in fact circumcised the infant Yitzhak). He is now living, or rather dying, in poverty in a one-room hovel within the walls of the Old City close to the temple-mount – Mount Moriah, of course. But he has never managed to go to the Western Wall. On arrival in the country he had broken his leg and he is still immobilized, his injured leg wrapped in rags (348); in addition he had lost his money after having been per-suaded by the treasurer of a yeshivah to invest it in a lottery fund (346) and he cannot afford medical attention.

Such a figure of extreme poverty and sickness, like the tooth-less beggar in his rags in the short story that we looked at earlier, marks the introduction into the narrative of what may be termed the semiotics of the Akedah. Reb Alter becomes a paradigm for human suffering *in extremis*. Yitzhak – his name is a give-away – had, we are told, never before beheld such poverty (345). He, like Rabbi Zidkiyyahu, is being tested, for he too, at the novel's end will be subjected to the kind of suffering which marks the outer limits of the human. How can Yitzhak sustain the faith which had brought him back to his ancestral land in the light of such misery? In his joy at seeing the young arrival from his old township, Reb Alter presses his visitor to drink tea with him, only to discover that there is no tea in the house. They will have to do with water which Reb Alter heats for him on a kerosene stove, adding to it a tiny piece of sugar, at the same time urging Yitzhak to say the blessing for his refreshment to him "by whose word all things come into being." He has something like the simple faith of Yitzhak's ancestor Reb Yudel. Others in this city he tells Yitzhak are not as fortunate as he is, for he has a water cistern beside his door and enjoys a plentiful supply of that commodity (347). And in general he declares that we who dwell in the Land are given many more opportunities for gratitude and praise to the Almighty than we enjoyed in the Dispersion for there we had all things in plenty but here we are verily become God's favorite child for whom every drop of water has become a precious gift from heaven! The reader is also in a manner being tested; for sharply refracted through Reb Alter's simple expressions of piety, there is the narrator's fierce and ironical questioning. The reader is being forced to ask himself whether it was for this that Yitzhak (along with the hopeful generation of pioneers whom he represents) had ventured on the epic journey, announced, as in the *Aeneid*, in the first sentence of the book. There we are told that he "left his land and his place of birth and went up to the Land of Israel in order to rebuild it from its ruins and to be himself rebuilt." Is this scene of Reb Alter the promised end?

But not everything is black. Yitzhak establishes himself as a house painter in Jerusalem and is much in demand. Before he dies Blaukopf teaches him an additional skill, that of painting signboards for shops and businesses (241–2). In fact he prospers and achieves a "state of tranquillity" (*midat haHishtavut*) (240). Something of the spiritual calm of Jerusalem enters his life, and he also finds himself in love with a new girl, Shifra – devout, modest and beautiful, the antitype of the worldly and emancipated Sonia in Jaffa. Shifra is the daughter of the ugly and unlovable

Reb Faish, one of a group of satirically drawn figures of narrow-
minded bigotry of whom the most colorful is Rabbi Gronam
Yekum Purkan, a popular preacher. Yitzhak plans to marry Shifra
but before doing so, he feels he has to settle things with Sonia in
Jaffa, to assure himself and her that their relationship is over.

Once back in Jaffa he does not easily move away again. Moreover, his friend Leichtfuss goes on a trip and gives him the key
of his home – a lonely hut near the sea (433–6) – where all his
needs are supplied and he enjoys the comfort of perfect idleness.
It is an idyllic interval. This second visit to Jaffa is also marked
by a change in the economic and social situation of the "com-
rades" of the Second Aliyah, indeed of the new *yishuv* as a whole.
There is an atmosphere of promise and eagerness; it is 1909 and
the newest suburbs of Jaffa are going up – the beginning of what
will become Tel-Aviv. The problems of "Jewish labor" have been
overcome. There is work to be had and all around a sense of
hope and a bustle of activity. The Zionist enterprise has been
truly launched and the promise of the future can already be felt
in the present. Nevertheless, when Leichtfuss returns and he has
to move out of his hut, Yitzhak resolves to take the train back to
Jerusalem. Ominously the porter who carries his things to the
railway station turns out to be the porter of a burial society (458).

Returning to Jerusalem is to return to a world lacking the hope-
fulness of Jaffa. Shifra, living in Mea Shearim, tends to her father
who has been struck down by a paralytic stroke. But there are
still idyllic phases and moments. In Shifra it would seem that he
has found his soul's mate. He also returns to his ancestral faith
and practices. He takes up lodging in the home of another artist,
a craftsman who makes souvenirs and religious articles out of
olive wood. There, for the first time since his arrival in Palestine,
Yitzhak enjoys a home setting, becoming almost one of the family and, what is more, he makes a satisfactory living. But Yitzhak
is doomed. He marries Shifra but a week after their marriage he
is bitten by a mad dog, Balak, who is actually – as we shall see
later – a major character in the novel! The novel here lurches
into a wild surrealist mode, not unlike the writings of Kafka.
Yitzhak now infected with rabies, dies in agony, strapped to his
bed on the doctor's advice and kept in isolation in a locked room.
Like his biblical namesake, Yitzhak Kummer is thus bound on a
kind of altar for sacrifice. But unlike his biblical namesake, he is
not going to be saved by a voice from heaven.

Although the Akedah is not explicitly invoked here nor at any other point in the novel, the motif of the Binding of Isaac is surely as powerfully present in *The Day before Yesterday* as in any of the other examples we have noted. Arnold Band did well to point out the parallels in an important article which appeared in 1967.[8] He has returned to the same topic more recently, tracing a similar pattern in Kafka's short story "In the Penal Colony."[9] Other critics have taken up the notion.[10] The Binding of Isaac, it is claimed, provides a key to the understanding of the novel. The fate of Yizhak Kummer belongs to the same region of absurdity, or, put in theological terms, to the inscrutable will of a God who does not have to explain his reasons to anyone. Professor Band sees the novel as focused on this. The fate of Yitzhak becomes a microcosm of the terrible, undeserved, and unaccountable sufferings of European Jewry during the years of the Holocaust.

Apparent confirmation for this view of the centrality of the Akedah in Agnon's novel comes from the publication in 1978 of a passage found in the manuscript of a preliminary draft of the first part of the novel to which Agnon gave the name *Eretz Hefetz* ("Land of Delight") – from Malachi 3:12. In this passage, omitted from the novel in its final form, the Akedah is specifically alluded to in the context of a discourse on the glories of Jerusalem:

> Many events are associated with Jerusalem, the city that God desired for his dwelling. From afar he called to Abraham his beloved to offer up his son. Abraham wondered which place it was where God desired to be thus honoured. God answered, Where you see my glory, there I will await you. Abraham knew at once that that place must be Jerusalem. He saddled his ass and he and his son Isaac went forth with great joy, the one to bind, the other to be bound. Abraham lifted up his eyes and saw the place and said of it: "This is my resting place forever: here will I dwell because I have desired it" (Ps. 132).[11]

Now whilst Sarah Hager has performed a service in recovering this passage from the Agnon archives and pointing out its relevance to the novel, the main critical issue that should be faced is that it was in fact cancelled and does not appear in the novel as finally published by Agnon in 1945! Certainly he had good reason for omitting the rather sermon-like discourse on the spiritual meaning of the history of Jerusalem from the Creation of the world onwards to which this passage belongs and for starting straight into the story of Yitzhak Kummer's arrival in the Land, but in view of the crucial importance of the topic, one might have expected him to reinstate the Akedah passage at some other appropriate point in the narrative. This he did not do.

There are I think two reasons for this. One is that the "Binding" as finally enacted in Jerusalem when Yitzhak Kummer is struck down by rabies to die a violent and horrible death is out of tune with the above-quoted passage which speaks of the "great joy" with which Abraham and his son went up to Jerusalem, "the one to bind, the other to be bound." Such an account is perfectly in tune with the traditional understanding of the Akedah as salvation-myth but could not have served Agnon's purpose as that purpose finally took shape. The early draft was, we may surmise, written either before the outbreak of the Second World War or, at any rate, before the full horror of the Holocaust had become known. It was then still possible to speak of the Akedah as an act of love and devotion in accord with the "spirit of tranquillity" exemplified by Jerusalem. In 1945 we are confronted with a darker Akedah and inevitably with a different kind of interpretive problem, one which tests both reader and narrator in new ways.

Another somewhat different, if not contrary, reason for omitting this passage is that the novel as a whole, as it took shape, does not quite accord with the parameters of an "Akedah." It has a broader range and is also more upbeat than the other examples we have discussed. True, we witness the bitterness and horror of the ending and the troubles and sufferings of so many of the characters – Reb Faish, Blaukopf, Reb Alter. But the novel has also, as a central theme, the trials undergone by the *halutzim* of the Second Aliyah, their overcoming of obstacles, the building up of the *Yishuv*, with its colonies and towns. There are light and hope and creativity as well darkness and despair in this novel, especially in those parts of it which survey the world of Jaffa and the new colonies. It would be to distort the novel not to see the grandeur of the achievements which it celebrates. Indeed, in Book 3 we sense that everything is throbbing with new life. Little by little, Jewish history is being forged anew (388, 448–9). Here is an essential part of the epic structure of the novel.

3

The Day Before Yesterday I would suggest is a kind of modern midrash. But the text that it seeks to interpret is not the Akedah in isolation, but the Akedah viewed in its total context as the last trial of Abraham which completes the first. That is why Agnon did not think it necessary to cite the cancelled passage. The Akedah is seen as part of a larger narrative. And it is that larger narrative on which Agnon focuses our attention and which is actually reflected in the total design of his novel. Abraham's trials had begun at Genesis 12:1 where he was commanded to leave his father's house and go out to a new land of which he knew nothing. "Get thee out of thy land and thy place of birth and from thy father's house, to the land which I will show thee" (12:1). Agnon's reader is immediately alerted to this source by the very first sentence of the novel, already quoted, which reads in full:

> Like the rest of our brethren of the Dispersion, children of the Second Aliyah, Yitzhak Kummer left his land and his place of birth and went up to the Land of Israel in order to rebuild it from its ruins and to be himself rebuilt.[12]

(7)

It is not only that the Hebrew phrase translated as "his land and his place of birth" is an unmistakable echo of the language of Genesis 12:1 but that it evokes the whole biblical context, thus associating Yitzhak's "going up" to the Land of Israel with that of the patriarch Abraham who was commanded to "get thee out" (*lekh-lekha*) from his homeland and place of birth and journey to a new land which would be shown to him. This epic journey with its clear biblical overtones serves to point the direction which the novel will take.

Yitzhak Kummer's career thus evokes the first trial of Abraham as surely as it evokes the last trial, namely, the "Binding." Interestingly, the Rabbis of the midrash link these two commands together, basing themselves on several verbal affinities. In particular, we have in the command relating to the Akedah the same crucial term, *lekh-lekha*, a phrase which occurs nowhere else in Scripture except in these two places:

Take now thy son, thy one-and-only, whom thou lovest, Yitzhak, and get thee (*lekh-lekha*) into the land of Moriah: and offer him there for a burnt-offering upon one of the mountains which I will tell thee of.

It will also be noted that both passages speak of a location still to be defined – "to the Land which I will show thee," balancing "one of the mountains which I will tell thee of." And above all there is the same use of an unusual rhetorical configuration which we may term the decremental catalogue – "from thy land, from thy birthplace, and from thy father's house" matching, "thy son, thy one-and-only, whom thou lovest, Yitzhak" – each successive phrase defining the object of the trial more narrowly. In noting this the midrash on Genesis performs something like an exercise in literary analysis:

R. Levi said, Twice the term *lekh-lekha* occurs and we do not know which of the two is dearer [to the Almighty], the first or the second. Since in the second episode he added immediately "to the land of Moriah" it would appear that this was dearer than the first. R. Yohanan said, "Get thee out of thy land" – i.e. thy province; "from thy place of birth" – i.e. thy neighbourhood, "and from thy father's house" – i.e. thy parental home; "to the land which I will show thee." And why did he not reveal [his destination] to him at once? It was to make the land more precious to him and to give him a reward for every separate step. And parallel to this, we read: "Take now thy son." Said Abraham, Which of my [two] sons? He said to him, "thy only one." Said Abraham, Each is the only child of his mother. He said to him: "him whom thou lovest." Said Abraham, Are the bounds of love marked out? [lit. are there compartments in the bowels?]. He finally said to him, "even Yitzhak." And why did he not reveal [his identity] to him at once? In order to make him [i.e. Yitzhak] more precious to him and to give him a reward for each separate phrase. For R. Huna said in the name of R. Eliezer, the son of R. Yose the Galilean, The Holy One, blessed is he, keeps the righteous waiting and holds them in suspense, only later revealing his object to them. Thus it is written: "to the Land which I will show thee" and parallel to that: "upon one of the mountains which I will tell thee of."[13]

The novel may be seen as a fictional working out of this dialectic, the going-up to the new land and the Akedah bound together by affinity and contrast. The Rabbis were not interested in verbal parallels and symmetries for their own sake. What they are saying here is that both episodes have things in common. Both are trials. As the narrator says in the first Jaffa period of Agnon's novel: "The Land of Israel is only acquired through suffering" (45) – even the creative work of nation-building involved – for Yitzhak and his friends – tearing oneself away from one's family and surroundings and then there were the hardships and privations of a new and unknown land. This too was a kind of Akedah, calling for heroism and sacrifice and above all, faith. That is what was required of Abraham and those are the qualities shown also by the *halutzim* of the Second Aliyah. Modern Jewish history, we might say, imposes both kinds of trial on us – the trial of going up to the Land, "to build it and to be oneself rebuilt" and the darker trial of Yitzhak Kummer's biblical namesake, who is bound down on the altar in fear and trembling, his throat stretched out to the knife.

The symmetry which the Rabbis of the midrash found between these two chapters with their different kinds of trial will help us to understand the symmetry of Agnon's novel, consisting as it does of four blocks of narration: the first and third connected with Jaffa, the second and fourth connected with Jerusalem. There is here, we may suggest, a balancing of the two kinds of *lekh-lekha*: broadly speaking the two Jaffa portions, Books 1 and 3, together with the 40 introductory pages describing the journey from Galicia to Jaffa, belong to the first trial of Abraham, that which spoke of the going up to a strange and unknown land with all its risks and hardships as well as its promises. Interlocked with these and balancing them like a quadratic equation are Books 2 and 4 which belong to the other *lekh-lekha*, that which announced the last trial of Abraham. These Books, 2 and 4, situate Yitzhak appropriately in Jerusalem, the "place" which Abraham saw from afar when he went to sacrifice his son on the altar. We thus have a dialectical and balanced structure – as befits an epic composition.

But it is not simply a matter of a pleasing aesthetic design. The structure reflects a visionary history and a visionary geography. As we noted earlier in reference to Joseph Roth's novel, *Job*, the epic is essentially a type of narrative which brings the divine

and human orders together and explores the lines of communication between them. Men and women are commanded, tested;
there is an overarching divine plot. Roth's *Job*, like Agnon's novel,
also involved two contrasting locations and two contrasting spiritual
states. Such contrasts are likewise typical of the epic. We remember
the metaphysical geography of *The Divine Comedy*, or of *Paradise
Lost*, with their great balancing blocks of narration. Agnon's novel
is a tale of two cities in this sense. But it consists not merely of
two cities, Jaffa and Jerusalem, but of two alternating modes
of experience – the one associated with the trials and hardships
of "going up," of building and being remade, the other associated
with darker sufferings and trials, but also with "the spirit of tranquillity" which it seems Jerusalem is best able to provide. It is in
Jerusalem that Yitzhak will find his true soul's partner, the somewhat cloistered Shifra, but there he will also find his death, a
death mediated for us by the stray dog Balak. To Balak we then
return.

                                    4

The story of Balak was written in great part before the story of
Yitzhak Kummer had taken final shape. Parts of it were sepa-
rately published as early as 1935 and 1936.[14] But the idea of putting
the dog into the story of the Second Aliyah and connecting his
career with that of the hero must have come to Agnon relatively
late in the process of composition. It proved to be the novel's
most brilliant and arresting feature. We will be concerned not
with the history of the novel's composition and the genesis of its
separate parts but with the final product, its meaning, and its
effect on the reader. In particular we will ask ourselves how the
entry of Balak, his doings and the things done to him, affect the
design.
    Balak, a stray mongrel, enters the novel as a major character
in Book 2 during Yitzhak's first period in Jerusalem. Blaukopf
had taught Yitzhak to paint signs. Bothered one day whilst at
work by the friendly attentions of Balak, he had in a mood of
frivolity painted the words "mad dog" on the dog's back (275–6).
It was a whimsical, freakish and thoughtless action. Yitzhak thinks
no more about it but for Balak it marks a disastrous change in
his way of life. He is shunned and persecuted. Feared as a mad

dog, he is now hunted down by everyone who can read the words inscribed on his back. He seeks refuge in the non-Jewish neighborhoods where he finds himself less frequently molested, the reason being of course that the people there are unable to read the writing. In a word he is in exile. Grotesquely, his meditations, his wanderings, his sufferings, even his dreams (281, 571), become the subject of long stretches of narrative. Likewise his thoughts about human beings, about Jews, even his reflections on Jewish law, including the regulation allowing a dog to be fed with non-kosher meat. Balak prefers the Jewish setting; he pines for the Meah Shearim quarter where he enjoys listening to the discourses of Rabbi Gronam Yekum Purkan.

The baroque fantasies relating to Balak and his fate are wildly funny but nevertheless they are the key to the tragic denouement. After many weeks of reflection, Balak comes to the conclusion that his unique fate is somehow connected with the signs that the man with the paintbrush had painted on him. And he determines to take his revenge. As the weeks go by his condition deteriorates, he suffers hunger, thirst and disease until finally he does become actually deranged. His opportunity comes a week after Yitzhak's marriage to Shifra. Balak creates an uproar in Meah Shearim by appearing in the middle of one of Rabbi Gronam's open-air discourses just as he has announced – quoting a talmudic saying – that the face of the generation is the face of a dog (586). All the assembly flees in terror at the sight of Balak. The only one who isn't afraid is Yitzhak who now remembers that he was the author of the words on Balak's back and so he assures everyone that the dog is not really mad at all. However, he is wrong and as he stands fearlessly by his side, Balak, seeking out the final truth about himself from the flesh of the author of his troubles, turns and bites his leg and hand (595). After a few days Yitzhak becomes mortally ill. He dies in agony, bound down to his bed on the advice of a doctor called in by the community and left in isolation so that he should not be able to infect other people.

The figure of Balak has attracted more attention from the critics than anything else in the book. And understandably so, for he has a portentous symbolic weight and demands interpretation. But there is also a striking tonal contrast between this tragi-comic fantasy and the realism of the rest. Agnon is clearly making a major statement through the figure of Balak. It is a bit like the cat in Bulgakov's, *The Master and Margarita*. But Agnon is both more realistic and more inventive than Bulgakov. At the same time he deliberately covers his tracks, teasing those interpreters who might be inclined to propose allegorical readings of one kind or another. For instance, he tells us that rumors about the dog with the inscription on his fur had reached Tel-Aviv and were being treated there as political allegory, or as a satire on some local person or persons, or as a jocular beast fable like Mendele's stories of the horse or medieval tales about foxes and birds! (459–60).

The author is in short poking fun at his learned readers who will try to fathom the meaning of the dog in this incredible shaggy-dog story. It is all a little unnerving for students of Agnon. Nevertheless, it has been attempted. It has been suggested for instance that Balak is a demonic parody of Yitzhak.[15] The trouble with this notion is that Balak is not particularly demonic. He is rather a likeable dog with a warm heart and a capacity for patient long-suffering. We feel sympathy for him in his undeserved troubles. If he becomes mad and drives others mad, it is through no fault of his own.

What Agnon's Israeli critics seem to have missed is the utterly comic nature of the Balak episode. The critics are on the whole terribly solemn about something that is terribly funny. They are looking for an interpretation which might support a unified epic reading of this great novel, but what the Balak chapters do is basically to undermine, or as we might nowadays say, deconstruct all epic meanings whatever. Jews take history very seriously and Agnon is entirely Jewish in this respect. The story of the great historical reawakening which brought the first modern type settlers to Jaffa at the beginning of the century will be told, but it will also be turned upside-down to become the story of a man and a dog. Balak is Yitzhak's "secret sharer" in that they share the same kind of trouble. There is we may say a measure of transference between the two. But it is comic transference like Molly Seagrim's "Homeric" battle in the churchyard in *Tom Jones.* The novel had from its beginnings been the vehicle of the epic but it had also, from Cervantes and Fielding onwards, been the vehicle of the mock-epic. Agnon, by placing the story of Balak side by side with that of Yitzhak, is providing the scherzo movement for his symphony, transforming it briefly and at intervals into what Fielding called a "comic Epic-Poem in Prose." It is a reductive technique, serving to proclaim the vanity and absurdity of our highest endeavors as well as of the literary forms in which those same endeavors are celebrated. In the Bible this attitude is represented by Qohelet. He tells us, very much in the spirit of Falstaff, that it is better to be a living dog than a dead lion and later, after recounting the tale of a poor man who through his wisdom had saved a whole city from destruction, drily remarks that "no-one remembered that same poor man" (Eccles. 9:15). The general conclusion: all is vanity, even the greatest of epic achievements.

Here we may say is the non-heroic reading of history, as seen through the wrong end of the telescope, a "dog's-eye view" of human exploits and a dog's-eye view of the great fables in which those exploits are immortalized. Agnon does not demolish the Zionist myth. Quite the contrary. But he puts it in perspective. The midrash does the same in reference to the story of Joseph and Potiphar's wife. It sees him as nearly-but-not-quite capitulating to her charms. But we need not look beyond the text of the Bible itself for a non-heroic realigning of some of its most notable passages. In the continuation of the very same chapter in which Abraham receives and carries out the great command to leave his birthplace and go up to the new land "which I will show thee," we see him running away from that new land to Egypt on account of the famine and there somewhat ingloriously passing off his wife as his sister so as to escape death, whilst Sarai is seized for the harem of the local chieftain. We could argue that the introduction of Balak provides a reductive angle of vision not entirely foreign to the Bible itself.

Many have felt that there is something Kafkaesque about Balak. Hillel Barzel has suggested that Agnon was thinking of Kafka's *The Trial*. Joseph K. dies at the end, we are told, "like a dog."[16] Agnon may very well have had this episode in mind. A more suggestive parallel is with Kafka's shorter work "Investigations of a Dog."[17] Kafka is more allegorical, Agnon more realistic. But there is, it seems to me, a real similarity nevertheless. Like Balak, Kafka's dog, the first-person narrator in this strange fiction, is also in search of the truth about his existence and has philosophical reflections. Agnon's Balak is funnier and we seem to know him better as a fellow creature but, like Kafka's dog, he also carries out "investigations." He seeks an answer to the riddle of why he is hated (290) and will not rest until he discovers the truth. His sufferings, like those of Kafka's dog, do not deter him from his search (291). Why are the Jews suddenly his enemies and the

Arabs his friends (283)? He carries out a kind of scientific inquiry and when he gets results, he has, like Kafka's dog, the pride of a successful inquirer (588).

I would want to add that both dog fables have a similar metaphysical meaning. In Kafka's fable, the dogs do not see the human beings who give them food. They tend to think in terms of a divine agency. The scientifically-minded dog who is the subject of his story tries to find a more rational and empirically-based explanation for the phenomenon of the canine food supply, rejecting more traditional "religious" views. But his experiments actually endanger his life, for in seeking to disprove the existence of an outside agency who needs to be propitiated, he practices various forms of self-repression, such as refusing to paw the ground and to put his face up appealingly into the air. He waits to see if these changes in behavior will affect the food supply, and of course they do. He goes hungry and thirsty as a result. In short the key to Kafka's story is the equation which says: dog is to man as man is to God. The dog's existence is governed by certain conditions imposed on him by the will of an arbitrary deity (= Man).

The Balak story in Agnon works in a similar fashion. Eliezer Schweid suggested the parallel some 40 years ago, remarking that, like Balak, Yitzhak Kummer is also the object of a kind of practical joke perpetrated on him by a blind deity.[18] I should like to go further and suggest that Balak is to Yitzhak as the Jewish People as a whole are to the God of Israel who has sent them off on their journey through history. It was told them in connection with both the first and the last trials of Abraham that they would become a blessing to all the nations of the earth. In light of the disaster that overtook the Jewries of Europe in the mid-century, this promise does begin to look very much like a divine practical joke! Remember what Yitzhak does: he writes words on Balak's flesh and then sends him off with a kick so that he might wander round the city streets and thus publish his handiwork (276). Here it would seem is a bitter-comic reduction of the notion of the election of Israel for special trials, ordeals, and blessings. The God of Israel too had imposed on the people of Israel the burden of a written text. It was even, as a matter of fact, imprinted on their flesh! That indeed is how the prayer-book phrases it: it speaks of "the covenant which thou hast stamped on our flesh."[19] The election of Israel as related in the Bible comes to seem like a whimsical and inexplicable act. "How odd/ of God/ To choose/ the Jews" wrote William Ewer. He said it as a quip; Agnon in the story of Balak says the same out of pain and bitterness.

We noted earlier that in his short story "According to the Pain is the Reward" Agnon gave us an upward transcendence of the biblical paradigm. The Akedah is taken up into heaven. Here, arising out of the same historical crisis, we have instead a "downward transcendence." Again, the middle ground of the human has been lost and in its place we have a "dog's-eye view" of the covenant, its promises and trials, a kind of parody, or photographic negative of the ways of God to Man as presented in the Genesis narratives. The introduction of Balak thus provides, by way of inversion, a key to what might be termed the divine plot of Agnon's epic. This is done by means of a series of alternating and interlocking chapters in which we move from Yitzhak's world to that of Balak and then back again. Thus as well as being a tale of two cities, Agnon's novel is an account of the ways of God to Man seen from opposite directions, Balak's adventures in relation to the human world above him providing a dark simulacrum of Yitzhak's own situation and his relation to the metaphysical order. To be the object of God's special attention is to be, like Balak in Jerusalem, liable to mania. Far from being a blessing to the families of the earth, one becomes a disaster to oneself and to everyone around.

5

This would seem to be not very different from the conclusion that A.B. Yehoshua was to reach later on and which he would seek to demonstrate in *Mr Mani* where the family is driven to madness by the demons of the past, the central feature of which being the evil influence of the "Akedah" myth. But in fact the existential premises of the two writers are essentially different. The ironic shading provided by the Balak story by no means signifies for Agnon a denial of the fundamental ideology represented by the twin trials of Abraham. He remains committed to this ideology and bears testimony to it through the very structure of his masterpiece. Yehoshua seemingly dismisses the metaphysic of election, and explicitly, the divine ground of Israel's existence. At least he tries to do so. As a result he is left with the problem of explaining the sense of inescapable responsibility with which his characters are charged as well as the intensity with which his own imagination seizes on the Akedah and other signs of Jewish particularity. There is in Yehoshua no escape from this *aporia*.

It is true that Agnon and his characters are similarly seized by unwanted responsibilities, by unanswerable questions. But the novel itself gives us a kind of explanation: it is because they are text-haunted, still carrying a legend on their backs, that they draw on themselves suspicion, insults, sticks, and stones. If they take revenge, as Balak does, they have the world against them. What to Yehoshua are unresolvable contradictions are for Agnon paradoxes to be explored by means of a special kind of analogical discourse, a more intense hermeneutic effort, a more attentive listening both to the prime text itself and to the accumulated literature of interpretation and retelling to which it has been subjected.

Thus the two trials of Abraham, so dramatically realized in our time come together as a metaphysical paradox to be understood as we saw with the help of the midrash quoted earlier. In spite of the appalling distance between these two occasions, the midrash finds strange affinities, an arcane echoing. They have in common a deferring of aims and conclusions. It is in one case "the Land which I will show thee," and in the other case it is "the mountain that I will tell thee of." Not all our questions are going to be answered, and those that are will not be answered at once.

Above all the language of the two trials, each with a hidden objective to be revealed only when the trial is under way, each built on a catalogue which stresses the increasing difficulty of the enterprise, is the language of testing. The two trials of Abraham are not merely stories to be imitated but tests to be endured. This sense of a situation in which we are tested in new ways is clearly articulated in a comment made by the narrator towards the end of the novel. Yitzhak is lying mortally ill and his pious friends have exhausted all the verses of Psalms and all other modes of intercession customary in such cases, but to no avail "because the decree had already been sealed" (604). Agnon ends this chapter with a question as old as the book of Job and as old as the story of the Akedah. But though it is posed anew in every generation, it has never been so persistently and so terribly forced upon us as in our own time:

And now, good friends, when we contemplate the things that have befallen Yitzhak, we are struck with trembling and amazement. Yitzhak who was no worse than the rest of mankind, why was he so terribly punished?. . . . It is easy for those who, on account of excessive simplicity or excessive wisdom, do not trouble themselves much with such thoughts. But for one who is neither overly simple nor overly wise, what answer can he give and what can he say?

(604)

This is somewhat in the spirit of Job's great closing speech:

But where shall wisdom be found? and where is the place of understanding? Man cannot know its price; nor is it found in the land of the living. The depth says, It is not in me: and the sea says, It is not with me.

(Job 28:12–14)

There is a point where we reach the limits alike of art and wisdom. We are unable to find all the answers. But even here there is the hint of a vision deferred, of answers still to be disclosed in the long perspective of future time. Job will receive an answer of sorts out of the storm. And of Abraham it is said that "on the third day he saw the place from afar" (Genesis 22:4). The test is to remain faithful to the promise deferred, the destination still to be disclosed. In that way "the place of understanding" may yet be glimpsed.

Notes

1. Cf. Michael Walzer, *Exodus and Revolution* (New York: Basic Books, 1985), pp.4–7 and passim
2. Cf. Rashi, ad. loc., basing himself on *Mekhilta deRabi Ishmael*; and Menachem M. Kasher, *Hagadah Shelemah: The Complete Passover Hagadah* (Jerusalem: Torah Shelema Institute, 1967), p.27, note and comment no.298
3. Cf. Hayden White, *The Content of the Form: Narrative Discourse and Historical Representation* (Baltimore: The Johns Hopkins University Press, 1987), pp.24–5
4. On this second function, cf. J. Hillis Miller, "Narrative" in *Critical Terms for Literary Study*, eds. F. Lentricchia and T. McLaughlin (Chicago: University of Chicago Press, 1990), p.70
5. "The Human Experience of Time and Narrative" (1979), in *A Ricoeur Reader*, ed. Mario J. Valdes (Hemel Hempstead: Harvester, 1991), p.112
6. BT *Pesahim*, 116b
7. On the lack of closure in the creation narrative and elsewhere in the Bible, see H. Fisch, *Poetry with a Purpose: Biblical Poetics and Interpretation* (Bloomington: Indiana University Press, 1988), pp.21–5, 42
8. Most fully set out in English in *The Dialogic Imagination: Four Essays by M.M. Bakhtin*, trans. Caryl Emerson and Michael Holquist, ed. Michael Holquist (Austin: University of Texas Press, 1981). Hereinafter, *D.I.*
9. Cf. *D.I.*, pp.85, 97
10. Ibid., pp.301, 306–7 and cf. M.M. Bakhtin, *Esthétique de la création verbale*, trans. Alfreda Aucouturier (Paris: Gallimard, 1984), pp.146–56
11. *D.I.*, p.69. Bakhtin is not altogether consistent in this. In his study of Dostoevsky's Poetics he finds a profound analogy between Dostoevsky, an author who allows his characters to enact their freedom, and the figure of Christ in the gospels. On the other hand, the omnipotent deity of the Old Testament represents for Bakhtin the omniscient author whose point of view, external to the work of art, does not allow for true polyphony or true dialogue. See Katerina Clark and Michael Holquist, *Mikhail Bakhtin* (Cambridge MA: Harvard University Press, 1984), pp.248–51
12. Cf. Bakhtin, "Préface à Résurrection" in Tzvetan Todorov, *Mikhail Bakhtine: le principe dialogique suivi des écrits du cercle de Bakhtine* (Paris: Seuil, 1981), p.226; Ann Shukman, "Bakhtin and Tolstoy," *Studies in Twentieth-Century Literature* 9 (Fall 1984), 61
13. E. Auerbach, *Literary Language and its Public in Late Latin Antiquity*

and in the Middle Ages, trans. Ralph Manheim (New York: Bollingen Foundation, 1965), pp.34–7

14. Stephen Prickett (*Origins of Narrative: The Romantic Appropriation of the Bible* [Cambridge: Cambridge University Press, 1996], pp.120–30) following Hans Frei, argues, somewhat to the contrary, that it is the tradition of prose-fiction in England which tended to sanction a novelistic reading of the Bible, leading readers and Bible commentators to stress the real-life character of the biblical narratives. Whilst no doubt there is a two-way traffic in progress between the two modes in the eighteenth century, we must surely recognize the priority of the tradition of realism and simplicity going back to the medieval *genus humile* and receiving an enormous impetus with the arrival of the vernacular Bible in the sixteenth century – all this long before the rise of the novel proper.

15. Tzvetan Todorov, *Mikhail Bakhtin: The Dialogical Principle*, trans. Wlad Godzich (Minneapolis: University of Minnesota Press, 1984), p.77

16. Stephen Prickett, *Words and The Word: Language, Poetics and Biblical Interpretation* (Cambridge: Cambridge University Press, 1986), p.214

17. Walter L. Reed, *Dialogues of the Word: The Bible as Literature According to Bakhtin* (New York: Oxford University Press, 1993), p.15 and passim

18. Cf. Northrop Frye, *The Anatomy of Criticism* (Princeton NJ: Princeton University Press, 1957), p. 315 and idem, *The Great Code: The Bible and Literature* (New York: Harcourt Jovanovich, 1982), passim

19. M. Sternberg, *The Poetics of Biblical Narrative: Ideological Literature and the Drama of Reading* (Bloomington: Indiana University Press, 1985), pp.41, 44, 483, 504

20. Ibid., p.492

21. Critics have disagreed as to the exact mythological pattern intimated in these verses. J.W. McKay ("Helel and the Dawn-Goddess," *Vetus Testamentum* 20 [1970], 451–64) identifies Helel ben Shahar ("bright Star, son of the morning") with Venus whose equivalent in the Ugaritic legends rebels against Yam and Baal. There is possibly here a mixture of Greek and Canaanite myths.

22. Cf. M.M. Bakhtin, *Rabelais and his World*, trans. Helene Iswolsky (Cambridge MA: MIT Press, 1968), p.381f

23. E. Auerbach, *Mimesis: The Representation of Reality in Western Literature*, trans. Willard Trask (New York: Doubleday, 1957), pp.1–20

24. See S.D. Goitein, *The Art of Biblical Narrative* (in Hebrew) (Jerusalem: The Jewish Agency, 1956), pp.25, 27–8. And see, Fisch, *Poetry with a Purpose*, pp.8–14

25. See Katerina Clark and Michael Holquist, *Mikhail Bakhtin*, pp.27, 80. And see Nina Perlina, "Bakhtin and Buber: Problems of Dialogic Imagination," in *Studies in Twentieth Century Literature* 9 (Fall 1984), 15–20

26. Martin Buber, *I and Thou*, trans. Roland Gregor Smith (Edinburgh: T. & T. Clark, 1952), p.114

27. Martin Buber, *The Prophetic Faith*, trans. Carlyle Witton-Davies (New York: Harper & Row, 1960), p.201

28. Robert Alter, *The Art of Biblical Narrative* (New York: Basic Books, 1981), passim and Michael Fishbane, *Biblical Interpretation in Ancient Israel* (Oxford: Oxford University Press, 1985), passim; also George W. Savran, *Telling and Retelling: Quotation in Biblical Narrative* (Bloomington: Indiana University Press, 1988)

29. Reed, *op. cit.*, p.16. Adele Berlin has issued a salutary warning against exaggerating the phenomenon of narrative doubles and echoes. Many supposed parallels turn out to be, she says, not a "compositonal device" but simply an "interpretive strategy." ("Literary Exegesis of Biblical Narrative" in *"Not in Heaven": Coherence and Complexity in Biblical Narrative*, eds. Jason P. Rosenblatt and Joseph C. Sitterson, Jr. [Bloomington: Indiana University Press, 1991], pp.120–8). On the other hand, in the present climate of intertextuality such a distinction might be hard to sustain.

30. For some remarks on the relevance of midrash to contemporary literary theory, see the Introduction to *Midrash and Literature*, eds. Geoffey H. Hartman and Sanford Budick (New Haven CT: Yale University Press, 1986), pp.x–xiii. Other items are listed in the bibliography (pp.365–95)

31. See BT *Sotah*, 36b; L. Ginzberg, *The Legends of the Jews*, vol. II (Philadepha: Jewish Publicaton Society of America, 1910), pp.44–59; *Midrash Rabbah: Genesis*, vol.II (London: Soncino, 1939), pp.807–12

32. Thomas Mann, *Joseph and his Brothers*, vol. III ("Joseph in Egypt"), trans. H.T. Lowe-Porter (London: Secker and Warburg, 1968), pp.426, 455, 467–8

33. Ibid., p.471

34. Cf. David Stern, "Midrash and Indeterminacy," *Critical Inquiry* 15 (Autumn 1988), 132–61. Stern shrewdly notes the conjunction in midrash of interpretive pluralism and the sense, alien to the deconstructionists, of "a divine presence from which all the contradictory interpretations derive." In this respect midrashic polysemy is to be differentiated from the contemporay emphasis on indeterminacy (p.141).

35. *Joseph and his Brothers*, vol. III

36. Marthe Robert, *The Old and the New: From Don Quixote to Kafka*, trans. Carol Cosman (Berkeley and Los Angeles: University of California Press, 1977), pp.62, 56–7

37. Robert suggests elsewhere (*Origins of the Novel*, trans. S. Rabinovitch [Bloomington: Indiana University Press, 1980], pp.132–8) that in masking his true meaning in this way Cervantes reveals the mindset of the "New Christians," i.e. disguised Jews or marranos, of whom he may have been one. More recently Ruth Reichelberg, in *Don Quichotte ou le Roman d'un Juif Masqué* (Paris: Philippe Nadal, 1989), has taken up this notion again with a good deal of enthusiasm.

CHAPTER 2

1. Genesis Rabbah, I, 1. See *Midrash Rabbah: Genesis*, vol.I, trans. H. Freedman (London: Soncino, 1939), p.1
2. Cf. J. Hillis Miller, with special reference to the novel: "Whenever the interpreter thinks he has reached back to something original, behind which it is impossible to go, he finds himself face to face with something which is already an interpretation." "The Interpretation of *Lord Jim*," in *The Interpretation of Narrative: Theory and Practice*, ed. Morton W. Bloomfield (Cambridge MA: Harvard University Press, 1970), p.213
3. Tzvetan Todorov, *Grammaire du Décaméron* (Den Haag: Mouton, 1969), p.12
4. J. Hillis Miller, "The Interpretation of *Lord Jim*," p.227
5. Cf. Susan A. Handelman, *The Slayers of Moses: The Emergence of Rabbinic Interpretation in Modern Literary Theory* (Albany: State University of New York Press, 1982), pp.76–82, on the metonymic mode in rabbinic thought
6. Genesis Rabbah, LXXXVII, 7. See *Midrash Rabbah: Genesis*, ed. cit., vol.II, pp.811–12
7. Roman Jakobson, *Fundamentals of Language*, 2nd rev. edn. (The Hague: Mouton, 1971), p.94
8. Cf. G.A. Starr, *Defoe and Spiritual Biography* (New York: Goddian Press, 1971), pp.81–4, 97; see also Michael McKeon, *The Origins of the English Novel 1600–1740* (Baltimore: Johns Hopkins University Press, 1987), pp.317–19
9. Cf. J. Paul Hunter, *The Reluctant Pilgrim: Defoe's Emblematic Method and Quest for Form in Robinson Crusoe* (Baltimore: Johns Hopkins University Press, 1966), pp.89–90; see also Edwin B. Benjamin, "Symbolic Elements in *Robinson Crusoe*," *PQ* 30 (1951), 206–11. I take issue, however, with the overly typological emphasis of both Hunter and Benjamin.
10. Daniel Defoe, *The Life and Adventures of Robinson Crusoe &c.*, ed. Michael Shinagel (New York: Norton, 1975), p.14. Subsequent citations are from this edition; page numbers are given in parentheses in the text.
11. On this polarity, cf. George W. Coats, *Rebellion in the Wilderness* (Nashville TN: Abingdon Press, 1968), p.16 and passim
12. Cf. *Robinson Crusoe* (p.51): "Did not you come Eleven of you into the Boat, where are the Ten? Why were not they sav'd and you lost? Why were you singled out?"
13. This term for the interpreter within the text is usefully proposed by Naomi Schor in "Fiction as Interpretation," in *The Reader in the Text*, eds. Susan R. Suleiman and Inge Crosman (Princeton: Princeton University Press, 1980), p.168
14. See *Pirke deRabi Eliezer*, Ch.9; and cf. *Yalkut Shimoni* on Jonah, 550 (1)
15. Paul Fussell, *The Great War and Modern Memory* (London: Oxford University Press, 1975), pp.138–9

16. Cf. G.A. Starr (though without particular reference to *Robinson Crusoe*) in *Defoe and Casuistry* (Princeton: Princeton University Press, 1971); and cf. McKeon, op. cit., p.321

17. There is in general, it would seem, a parallel between Part II of *Robinson Crusoe* and Part II of *The Pilgrim's Progress*. The emphasis in both works is on the history of the salvation of the group rather than that of the lonely individual. In Bunyan's sequel too the role of the mediator of repentance is taken over by a pastor figure, as in the second part of Defoe's novel.

CHAPTER 3

1. *D.I.,* pp.308–9

2. Henry Fielding, *The History of the Adventures of Joseph Andrews...*, ed. Douglas Brooks (London: Oxford University Press, 1971), Book I, Chap. v (p.24). Subsequent quotations from this edition.

3. Martin C. Battestin, *The Moral Basis of Fielding's Art: A Study of Joseph Andrews* (Middletown CT: Wesleyan University Press, 1959), pp.26–35

4. Ibid., pp.41, 95 and passim. Douglas Brooks concurs, offering an exercise in numerology to support the view that *Joseph Andrews* is a "comic biblical epic" ("Symbolic Numbers in Fielding's *Joseph Andrews*" in Alastair Fowler ed., *Silent Poetry: Essays in Numerological Analysis* [London: Routledge and Kegan Paul, 1970], pp.246–51)

5. Robert Alter (*Fielding and the Nature of the Novel* [Cambridge MA: Harvard University Press, 1968], pp.125–8) writes insightfully on the "dialectical reversals" of the theme of clothing and nakedness in the novel but surprisingly fails to link this with the story of Joseph and his brothers and the wife of Potiphar.

6. See Genesis Rabbah, LXXXIV, 19 and LXXXV, 9 (*Midrash Rabbah: Genesis*, ed. cit., vol. II, pp.784, 795) where the Rabbis find a number of links between the story of Judah and Tamar on the one hand and the story of Joseph on the other. In both stories we have the expression *"haker-na"* – "discern, I pray thee" in reference to the identification of personal effects. In both there is mention of a kid of the goats – in Judah's case it is intended as payment for services rendered; in the case of Joseph, his brothers slay a kid and use it to bloody Joseph's coat (Gen. 37:31)

7. Cf. Herbert N. Schneidau, *Sacred Discontent: The Bible and Western Tradition* (Baton Rouge: Louisiana State University, 1976), pp.289–91 on metonymy as the characteristic mode of the Bible itself.

8. William Empson, "Tom Jones" (*The Kenyon Review*, XX, Spring 1958) reprinted in *Fielding: A Collection of Critical Essays*, ed. Ronald Paulson (Englewood Cliffs NJ: Prentice-Hall, 1962), p.129. I find no reference to snow in this chapter. Empson was evidently misled by the reference in the previous chapter to a brief hailstorm.

9. Stephen Prickett, however, (*Origins of Narrative: the Romantic Appropriation of the Bible* [Cambridge: Cambridge University Press, 1996] pp.124–5) plausibly suggests a debt in Laurence Sterne's sermons to novelistic touches in Josephus's commentaries.

10. *The Genuine Works of Flavius Josephus, The Jewish Historian. . . . Trans-*
    lated from the Original Greek . . . by William Whiston [folio] (London
    1737). Subsequent quotations from this edition.
11. Leo Tolstoy, "What is Art?" (1898), Chap. xvi, trans. Aylmer Maude.
    Reprinted in *The Great Critics*, eds. J.H. Smith and E.W. Parks (New
    York: Norton, 1951), p.686
12. *Mimesis*, ed. cit., p.15
13. Ian Watt, *The Rise of the Novel* (Berkeley and Los Angeles: Univer-
    sity of California Press, 1959), p.30
14. *St. Augustine's Confessions, or Praises of God . . . Newly Translated into*
    English . . . (Dublin 1807), Book III , Chap. 5 (p.67)
15. Edition of 1734, p.113
16. *D.I.*, pp.300, 326

CHAPTER 4

1. *Midrash Haggadol on the Pentateuch: Genesis*, ed. M. Margulies (Hebrew)
   (Jerusalem: Mossad Harav Kook, 1975), pp.675–7
2. M. Kadushin, *The Rabbinic Mind* (New York: Jewish Theological Seminary, 1952), pp.131–2; David Stern, "Midrash and Indeterminacy,"
   (see Chap. 1 above, note 34)
3. Cf. H.M. Daleski, *Joseph Conrad: The Way of Dispossession* (London:
   Faber, 1977), pp.150–1
4. N. Frye, *The Great Code: The Bible and Literature* (New York: Harcourt
   Brace Jovanovich, 1982), p.195
5. Cf. E. Auerbach, *Mimesis*, p.12
6. Cf. Bernard J. Paris, "George Eliot's Religion of Humanity," *ELH*, 29
   (1962), 418–43; letter to Mrs H.F. Ponsonby, December 10, 1874 in
   The George Eliot Letters, ed. Gordon S. Haight (New Haven CT: Yale
   University Press, 1955), VI, 98f
7. Cf. Walter Allen, *The English Novel* (Harmondsworth: Penguin Books,
   1958), p.227
8. E. Auerbach, *Mimesis*, p.10
9. J. Wiesenfarth, "Demythologizing *Silas Marner*," *ELH*, 37 (1970), 242.
   But the fact is that Eppie's arrival occurs not at Christmas, but somewhat pointedly, a week later, on New Year's Eve (see Chap. xii).
10. Cf. Q.D. Leavis, Introduction to George Eliot, *Silas Marner*
    (Harmondsworth: Penguin Books, 1967), pp.7, 13
11. David Carroll, "Reversing the Oracles of Religion," in *George Eliot:*
    The Mill on the Floss and Silas Marner: A Casebook, ed. R.P. Draper
    (London: Macmillan, 1977), p.212
12. Philip Fisher also recognizes the central importance in the novel of
    those reversals whereby "natural human bonds" – those of family –
    are denied and instead we witness the establishment of "true bonds
    that are independent of the formal relationships." ("*Silas Marner*"
    in *Making up Society: The Novels of George Eliot* [Pittsburgh: Univer-
    sity of Pittsburgh Press, 1981], pp.109–10). But Fisher finds no real
    compensa-tion to weigh against the loss and treachery which we
    have witnessed. The ending offers only deceptive satisfactions. This

it seems to me is to ignore the promise signified by Eppie w
edeems Silas from his barren and lonely state as surely as Rι
redeems Naomi.

13. Cf. John Holloway, *The Victorian Sage* (London: Anchor Books, 196.
p.114: "The little village [of Raveloe], off the beaten track in its woodeı
hollow, is half submerged in the world of nature. . . . The passage
of time and the rotation of the seasons affect humans and animals
and plants all alike."

14. Cf. H. Fisch, "Ruth and the Structure of Covenant History," *Vetus Testamentum*, 32 (1982), 425–37

15. See *Journals of Dorothy Wordsworth*, ed. Mary Moorman (London: Oxford University Press, 1971), p.42 (for 3 October 1800)

16. *Letters*, III, 382 (to John Blackwood). And see Lilian Haddakin, "Silas Marner" in *Critical Essays on George Eliot*, ed. Barbara Hardy (London: Routledge and Kegan Paul, 1970), pp.61–2

17. Cf. Wiesenfarth, pp.237–40

18. *Mimesis*, pp.7–9

19. Joan Bennett, *George Eliot: Her Mind and Art* (Cambridge: Cambridge University Press, 1962), p.138

20. Walter Allen, *George Eliot* (New York: Collier Books, 1967), p.118

21. Cf. *Letters*, III, 382 (to John Blackwood)

22. Cf. Matthew Arnold, *Culture and Anarchy* (1867), Chap. 3

23. *Letters*, III, 442

24. M.M. Bakhtin, *D.I.*, p.300

CHAPTER 5

1. Robert Payne, *Dostoyevsky: A Human Portrait* (New York: Knopf, 1961), p.13

2. *The Brothers Karamazov*, Book V, Chap. 1, trans. Constance Garnett (London: Heinemann, 1912), pp.256–7; hereafter cited in text

3. From *The Holy Scriptures*, the English text revised and edited by Harold Fisch (Jerusalem: Koren, 1989)

4. *The Writings: A New Translation of the Holy Scriptures according to the Masoretic Text* (Philadelphia: The Jewish Publication Society of America, 1982); *Ijob: Verdeutscht von Martin Buber* (Frankfurt am Main: Insel-Verlag, 1965)

5. Cf. Mishnah, *Sotah* 5:5

6. Cf. M. M. Bakhtin, *Problems of Dostoevsky's Poetics*, trans. Caryl Emerson (Minneapolis: University of Minnesota Press, 1984), pp.222–3, 256

7. E.g. G. Wilson Knight, *The Wheel of Fire* (London: Oxford University Press, 1937), p.209; Frank Kermode, Introduction to *King Lear: A Casebook*, ed. Frank Kermode (London: Macmillan, 1969), p.18; John Holloway, ibid., pp.213–17; Jan Kott, *Shakespeare Our Contemporary* (New York: Doubleday, 1964), p.104; Harold Bloom, Introduction to *William Shakespeare's King Lear: Modern Critical Interpretations*, ed. Harold Bloom (New York: Chelsea House, 1987), pp.1–2

8. Cf. Elizabeth Freund, "'Give the Word': Reflections on the Economy

of Response in *King Lear*," *HSL*, Special issue, 1982, 211–13. On Edgar's enhanced role in the Folio, see Michael J. Warren, "Quarto and Folio *King Lear* and the Interpretation of Albany and Edgar," in David Bevington and Jay L. Halio, eds. *Shakespeare: Pattern of Excelling Nature* (Newark: University of Delaware Press, 1978), p.105

9. Northrop Frye, *The Anatomy of Criticism* (Princeton: Princeton University Press, 1957), p.42

10. Cf. Evelyn Torton Beck, *Kafka and the Yiddish Theater* (Madison: University of Wisconsin Press, 1971), p.77

11. Ibid., pp.27–8

12. Yaakov Gordin, *God, Man and Devil* (in Yiddish) (New York: International Library Publishing Co., 1903), pp.9–10

13. Ibid. pp.89–90. The *Faust* reference is to Part 2, lines 7289–91

14. Erwin R. Steinberg ("The Judgment in Kafka's 'The Judgment'," *MFS* 8 (1962), 23–30) interestingly points out that Kafka records having written "The Judgment" during the night of September 22–3, 1912. This means that it was written in the hours immediately following the solemnities of the Day of Atonement which fell in that year from the evening of September 21 to the evening of September 22. On that day (*Yom Kippur*) according to traditional belief the judgment is "sealed" for all mankind. It is determined "who shall live and who shall die . . . who shall perish by fire and who by water." Georg belongs to the latter category.

15. Cf. by the present author, *A Remembered Future: A Study in Literary Mythology* (Bloomington: Indiana University Press, 1988), p.94

16. Cf. Max Brod, *Franz Kafka*, trans. G. Humphreys Roberts and Richard Winston (New York: Schocken Books, 1960), pp.172, 175–6, 180–4; David M. Kartiganer, "Job and Joseph K.: Myth in Kafka's *The Trial*," *MFS* 8 (1962), 31–43; M. Friedman, "The Modern Job," *Judaism* 12 (1963), 451; Herbert Tauber, *Franz Kafka: An Interpretation of his Works* (Port Washington NY: Kennikat Press, 1948), p.86; André Neher, *The Exile of the Word*, trans. David Maisel (Philadelphia: Jewish Publication Society, 1981), p.28; the critical discussion of the analogies is ably summed up by Rudolf Suter in *Kafkas "Prozess" im Lichte des "Buches Hiob"* (Frankfurt am Main: Peter Lang, 1976), pp.12–20. Suter's own contribution to the subject is to stress the important differences between Job and *The Trial* both in the matter of the ending and also throughout. Joseph K.'s relation to the Court is antagonistic whilst Job always sees himself in partnership with God. This *Gegenseitigkeit* (or what I prefer to call dialogue) is an essential dimension of Job lacking in *The Trial*. (See Suter, pp.29, 118–19)

17. On the likeness between these two works of Kafka cf. Heinz Politzer, *Franz Kafka: Parable and Paradox* (Ithaca NY: Cornell University Press, 1966), p.215n; Tauber, op. cit., pp.83, 88

18. D.M. Kartiganer, art. cit., 33, 39, 43

19. Franz Kafka, *The Trial*, trans. Willa and Edwin Muir (New York: Schocken Books, 1968), p.228; hereafter cited in text

20. Walter Benjamin, *Illuminations*, trans. Harry Zohn (New York: Schocken Books, 1969), pp. 120–1; and cf. Karl J. Kuepper, "Gesture

and Posture as Elemental Symbolism in Kafka's *The Trial*" in James Rolleston ed., *Twentieth Century Interpretations of The Trial* (Englewood Cliffs NJ: Prentice Hall, 1976), pp.60–9; hereafter, cited as Rolleston

21. Gershon Shaked speaks of the transformation of concrete Jewish historical experience (for instance, that of persecution) into the unparticularized, abstract world of Kafka's novels as an instance of "homology." (*The Shadows Within: Essays in Modern Jewish Writers*, Philadelphia: Jewish Publication Society, 1987, pp.8–11)

22. On the genesis of this trope, see E.R. Curtius, *European Literature and the Latin Middle Ages*, trans. Willard R. Trask (New York: Bollingen Foundation, 1953), pp.138–44

23. See note 13 above

24. In *J.B.*, a modern reworking of the Job story for the stage, Archibald MacLeish has schematized this situation by means of two different levels of action. We have the framed story of J.B. and his family, but it is observed and commented on throughout by the two old actors Nickles and Zuss. The audience shares in both levels of action – the human drama and the would-be metaphysical drama which frames it. The sign of this latter level, the code by which its presence is recognized, is its excessive theatricality. Nickles and Zuss we are told "gesture, [and] work themselves up into theatrical flights and rhetorical emotions."

25. See Martin Buber, "Job" in *Biblical Humanism*, ed. Nahum N. Glatzer (London: Macdonald, 1968), pp.195–6. (Cf. *The Prophetic Faith*, 1949, Chap. 8)

26. Northrop Frye, *The Great Code: The Bible and Literature* (New York: Harcourt Brace Jovanovich, 1982), p.195

27. Gerald L. Bruns, "Midrash and Allegory: The Beginnings of Scriptural Interpretation," in *The Literary Guide to the Bible*, eds. Robert Alter and Frank Kermode (Cambridge MA: Harvard University Press, 1987), p.634

28. *Der Prozess* in Franz Kafka, *Die Romane* (Frankfurt am Main: S. Fischer Verlag, 1969), p.436

29. Thomas M. Kavanagh, "Kafka's *The Trial*: The Semiotics of the Absurd," Rolleston, pp.91–3

30. Harold Bloom raises the uninterpretability of Kafka's fictions to a general principle. See *The Strong Light of the Canonical* (New York: The City College Papers, no.28, 1987), p.7: "My working principle in reading Kafka is to observe that he did everything possible to evade interpretation, which only means that what most needs and demands interpretation in Kafka's writing is its perversely deliberate evasion of interpretation."

31. Jacques Derrida, "Devant la Loi," trans. Avital Ronell, in Alan Udoff ed., *Kafka and the Contemporary Critical Performance* (Bloomington: Indiana University Press, 1987), pp.136, 146

32. Cf. Jill Robbins, "Kafka's Parables" in *Midrash and Literature*, eds. G.H. Hartman and S. Budick (New Haven CT: Yale University Press, 1986), p.268 (on the ways in which interpretation – as also the impossibility of interpretation – is thematized in Kafka's writings).

CHAPTER 6

1. See Chapter 2 above, pp.32–3 and note 15
2. Martin Heidegger, "Hölderlin and the Essence of Poetry," in *Critical Theory Since 1965*, eds. Hazard Adams and Leroy Searle (Tallahassee: Florida State University Press, 1986), p.761; Richard E. Palmer, *Hermeneutics: Interpretation Theory in Schleiermacher, Dilthey, Heidegger, and Gadamer* (Evanston: Northwestern University Press, 1969), pp. 155–6
3. Palmer, ibid. and p.136
4. See Robert W. Funk, *Language, Hermeneutic, and the Word of God: The Problem of Language in the New Testament and Contemporary Theology* (New York: Harper and Row, 1966), p.20 and passim
5. Ibid., pp.21, 26
6. Ibid., p.11
7. Ernst Fuchs, *Gesammelte Aufsätze*, vol.II (Tübingen: JCB Mohr, 1960), p.430. And see Funk, p.58
8. Translated by Michael Roloff in *Selected Poems: Abba Kovner, Nelly Sachs* (Harmondsworth: Penguin Books, 1971), p.91
9. All citations are from Dorothy Thompson's translation of 1932. References (hereafter in parentheses in the text) are to the East and West Library edition (Oxford, 1945)
10. *Anatomy of Criticism*, p.321
11. Preface to *The Reason of Church Government*, Book 2 (1641)
12. Cf. Mario Praz, *The Hero in Eclipse in Victorian Fiction* (London: Oxford University Press, 1956), passim
13. In her letter to John Blackwood, dated February 24, 1861 – discussed above, Chap. 4 (pp.72–3)
14. George Eliot, *Daniel Deronda* (Edinburgh: Blackwood, 1878), Chap. 50 (p.467). Subsequent references in parentheses in the text
15. Argued by F.R. Leavis, Joan Bennett, Edgar Rosenberg and many others. For a dissenting view see by the present author, "Daniel Deronda or Gwendolen Harleth?," *Nineteenth Century Fiction*, 19 (1965), 345–56
16. Leslie Mathew draws attention to the "rhythmic prose" with its balladlike effect. (See, *Ambivalence and Irony in the Works of Joseph Roth* [Frankfurt am Main: Peter Lang, 1984], p.126)
17. Roth's attitude to Zionism was, it appears, entirely negative. See Gershon Shaked, *The Shadows Within: Essays in Modern Jewish Writers* (Philadelphia: The Jewish Publication Society of America, 1987), p.47. It would seem that texts can bear witness independently of authors!

CHAPTER 7

1. Cf. Lillian Feder, "Marlow's Descent into Hell," *Nineteenth Century Fiction*, IX (1955), 281–90
2. Cf. Robert O. Evans, "Conrad's Underworld," *Modern Fiction Studies*, II (1956), pp.56–62

3. Cf. Louis H. Leiter, "Echo Structures: Conrad's *The Secret Sharer*," *Twentieth Century Literature*, V (1960), 159–75; Karl Miller, *Doubles* (Oxford: Oxford University Press, 1985), pp.255–7

4. For an excellent analysis of these echo-patterns see Nehama Aschkenasy, "Biblical Substructures in the Tragic Form: Hardy, *The Mayor of Casterbridge*; Agnon, *And the Crooked Shall Be Made Straight*," in *Biblical Patterns in Modern Literature*, eds. David H. Hirsch and Nehama Aschkenasy (Chico CA: Scholars Press, 1984), pp.85–94

5. Cf. Mark Goldman, "Comic Vision and the Theme of Identity," in *Bernard Malamud and the Critics*, eds. Leslie A. Field and Joyce W. Field (New York: New York University Press, 1970), pp.158, 159

6. S.Y. Agnon, *Works* [Hebrew] (Tel-Aviv: Schocken, 1953), vol. II, p.517

7. Cf. James M. Mellard, "Four Versions of Pastoral," in *Bernard Malamud and the Critics*, pp.70, 81; Gerald Hoag, "Malamud's Trial: *The Fixer* and the Critics," in *Bernard Malamud: A Collection of Critical Essays*, eds. Leslie A. Field and Joyce W. Field (Englewood Cliffs NJ: Prentice-Hall, 1975), pp.132, 138

8. Sandy Cohen (*Bernard Malamud and the Trial by Love* [Amsterdam: Rodopi, 1974], p.74) suggests rather improbably a link with the story of the near-sacrifice of Isaac. There a ram is offered up as a substitute (Genesis 22:13).

9. *The Fixer* (New York: Farrar, Straus and Giroux, 1966), p.240. Subsequent page references to this edition will be in parentheses in the text.

10. Cf. Mellard, "Four Versions of Pastoral," p.72 and Sheldon J. Hershinow, *Bernard Malamud* (New York: Frederick Ungar, 1980), p.72

11. Ibid., p.65

12. Robert Alter, *After the Tradition: Modern Jewish Writing* (New York: Dutton, 1969), p.125

13. On Joban features in *The Fixer*, see A.W. Friedman, "The Hero as Schnook," in *Bernard Malamud and the Critics*, pp.288–97 passim; Sandy Cohen, *Bernard Malamud and the Trial by Love*, p.74; Hershinow, *Bernard Malamud*, pp.73–4

14. Yosef Haim Brenner, *Breakdown and Bereavement*, trans. Hillel Halkin (Ithaca: Cornell University Press, 1971), p.32

15. Menachem Brinker ("On the Ironic Use of the Myth of Job in Y.H. Brenner's *Breakdown and Bereavement*," in *Biblical Patterns*, eds. Hirsch and Aschkenasy, pp.115–26) argues that the allusions to Job in Brenner's novel are purely ironic, a matter of "near parody" and that the story of Job "signifies nothing in the spiritual development of the main protagonist." This seems to me even less true of Brenner's narrative than it is of Malamud's. It is precisely the need felt to deny its relevance which so strongly foregrounds the Job motif. It becomes vividly present through denial. For a further example of this foregrounding see the conversation between Haim and Hanoch in a later chapter of Brenner's novel (ed. cit., pp.251–2).

16. On the link between the two novels see Sandy Cohen, *Bernard Malamud and Trial by Love*, p.82

CHAPTER 8

1. Saul Bellow, *Mr Sammlers Planet* (London: Weidenfeld and Nicolson, 1970), pp.230–3. Subsequent quotations are from this edition; page numbers given parenthetically in the text.
2. Erich Auerbach, "The Scar of Ulysses," *Partisan Review* 17 (1950), 411–32
3. Saul Bellow, *Herzog*, first published 1964. Quotations are from the Fawcett World Library edition (New York, 1965) – here at p.377. Page numbers, given hereafter parenthetically in the text, are from this edition.
4. Auerbach, *Mimesis*, ed. cit., p.6 – subsequently, page numbers given parenthetically in the text.
5. Robert Alter justly notes that in the Bible the term *hinneni* signifies the response of Abraham and Moses to the "imperative will of God." He goes on to suggest that for Herzog too it carries the sense of "an affirmation of identity and readiness to serve before the ultimate source of reality." (*After the Tradition*, p.114). I am arguing for a more ambiguous final stance on the part of Herzog.
6. Søren Kierkegaard, *Fear and Trembling* and *Sickness unto Death*, trans. W. Lowrie (New York: Doubleday, 1954), p.122
7. Elsewhere in the novel too he may have Hamlet in mind. Hamlet is much given to soliloquy also to writing his thoughts down on "tables." Hamlet's melancholy (and his soliloquizing) will cease after the sea-voyage in which he browbeats his enemies.
8. Edward Alexander sees Mr Sammler's experience of the Holocaust as "exploding forever the Enlightenment conception of man as naturally good." ("Saul Bellow: A Jewish Farewell to the Enlightenment" in *Saul Bellow: A Symposium on the Jewish Heritage*, eds. Vinoda and Shiv Kumar [Warangal: Nachson Books, 1983], p.1, reprinted from *The Resonance of Dust: Essays on Holocaust Literature and Jewish Fate*, 1973)
9. Cf. Ruth R. Wisse, *The Schlemiel as Modern Hero* (Chicago: University of Chicago Press, 1971), p.105. For further discussion of this aspect of the novel's debt to *Ulysses*, see by the present author, "The Hero as Jew: Reflections on *Herzog*," *Judaism* 17 (Winter 1968), at 46–8.
10. "Eli, the Fanatic" in Philip Roth, *Goodbye, Columbus* (New York: Bantam Books, 1963), pp.179–216 (at p.200). Subsequent page numbers are given parenthetically in the text.
11. The theory set out in the remainder of this subsection down to p.147 is developed in somewhat greater detail in *A Remembered Future*, Chap. 6, pp.102–13.
12. "Billy Budd, Foretopman" in *Selected Tales and Poems by Herman Melville*, ed. Richard Chase (New York: Holt, Rinehart and Winston, 1966), p.359
13. D.H. Lawrence, *Fantasia of the Unconscious* (1922; New York: Viking, 1960), p.174
14. From a letter to Edward Garnett, dated November 14, 1912 in D.H. Lawrence, *Selected Literary Criticism* (London: Heinemann, 1956), p.13

15. Philip Roth, *Portnoy's Complaint* (New York: Random House, 1967), pp.41–2
16. Marcel Proust, *Swann's Way*, trans. C.K. Scott Moncrieff (New York: Modern Library, 1928), p.44
17. "The Secret Sharer" in *The Portable Conrad* (New York: Viking Press, 1954), p.650. Subsequent page numbers given parenthetically in the text.
18. Cf. Martin Buber, *Biblical Humanism*, ed. Nahum N. Glatzer (London: Macdonald, 1968), pp.195–6; S. Terrien, in *Interpreter's Bible*, vol.III (New York: Abingdon Press, 1954), p.1173
19. Emmanuel Levinas, *Otherwise Than Being and Beyond Essence*, trans. Alphonso Lingis (The Hague: Martinus Nijhoff, 1981), Chap. V,2(e) and Chap. 6 (pp.149 and 175); and see idem, *Difficult Freedom: Essays on Judaism*, trans. Sean Hand (Baltimore: Johns Hopkins University Press, 1990), pp.8–10

CHAPTER 9

1. *The Paris Review*, no.61 (Spring 1975), 54–6
2. Robert Alter, *After the Tradition*, p.129
3. *Rights of Man*, Part I (1790), in *The Political Works of Thomas Paine* (London: Dugdale, 1844), p.285
4. *To Jerusalem and Back: A Personal Account* (New York: Viking, 1976)
5. On this there is now a considerable secondary literature. See, for instance, Yosef Melman in Zvi Levi, ed. *HaAkedah wehaTokheha* (in Hebrew) (Jerusalem: Magnes Press, 1991), pp.53–72; Abraham Sagie, "The Akedah and Its Meaning in Israeli Culture and in the Jewish Tradition," (in Hebrew) *Mehkere Hag* – A Journal of Jewish Culture (Bet Berl, September 1995), 66–85; Gabriel Hayyim Cohn, "Literary Analysis as a Gateway to the Bible" (in Hebrew), in David Cassuto, ed. *Judaism and Art* (in Hebrew) (Ramat-Gan: The Kotlar Institute, Bar-Ilan University, 1989), pp.195–239. In English there is a full-length study in microfilm (L.J. Wineman, *The Akedah Motif in the Modern Hebrew Story* [UCLA, 1977]); see also Michael Brown, "Biblical Myth and Contemporary Experience: The *Akedah* in Modern Jewish Literature," *Judaism* 31 (1982), 99–111. And see below notes 13, 14, 16, etc. and Chapter 10, notes 8, 9 and 10 for specific discussions of this topic in relation to Yehoshua and Agnon.
6. See in particular Claude Lévi-Strauss, *La Pensée Sauvage* (Paris: Librairie Plon, 1962). On the conjunction of death and marriage with reference to the cult of Dionysus, see Richard Seaford, *Reciprocity and Ritual: Homer and Tragedy in the Developing City-State* (Oxford: Clarendon Press, 1994), pp.266–80, 318–30
7. Some critics have sought to identify these two voices with two different components of the received text, known as the E and J documents respectively, E expressing the harsher doctrine of sacrifice and J, a more humane revision of this. Cf. Leslie Brisman, *The Voice of Jacob: On the Composition of Genesis* (Bloomington: Indiana Univer-

sity Press, 1990), pp.55–60. E.A. Speiser, however, who has rigor-
ously examined the editorial question, finds it impossible to disen-
tangle the different documents in this pericope. Whilst ELOHIM is
the divine name chiefly mentioned, the vivid style of the narration
is more suggestive of J. He suggests that perhaps we have here a
case of E superimposed on J (*The Anchor Bible: Genesis*, vol.I [Gar-
den City NY: Doubleday, 1981], pp.165–6). Nahum Sarna (*Understanding Genesis* [New York: Jewish Theological Seminary, 1966], p.162)
likewise feels that the text as a whole "is the product of a religious
attitude that recoils naturally from associating God with human
sacrifice." This also rules out the notion of opposed documents
constituting the story. I am not much concerned here with source
criticism, nor do I think that the supposed derivation of the Genesis
stories from different documents later put together by a priestly
"editor" has been a factor in the imaginative response of poets and
novelists to the received text. By "two voices" in the Akedah I have
in mind the kind of nuancing and ambiguity that we are accustomed to find in all great poetry and narrative and that we noted
earlier in the Joseph story. There the same source could sustain
different interpretations of Joseph's behavior – one would have
him impervious to his mistress's charms, another would emphasize
his human weaknesses. Here too the same source which
expresses horror and revulsion at the notion of human sacrifice may well
allow us to sense the still unsubdued fascination that the memory
of this enormity held for author and reader alike.

 8. Cf. *The Authorized Selichot for the Whole Year*, trans. Abraham Rosenfeld
    (London: Labworth, 1956), p.19, based on *Mishnah, Taanith* 2:4
 9. The Epistle to the Hebrews states that Abraham "by faith offered
    up Isaac . . . accounting that God was able to raise him, even from
    the dead, and from the dead, he did in a sense (*en parabole*) receive
    him back" (11:17–19); and see Augustine, *De Civitate Dei*, Book xvi,
    Chap. 32
10. See Shalom Spiegel, *The Last Trial . . . the Akedah*, trans. Judah Goldin
    (Philadelphia: Jewish Publication Society, 1967), pp.6–7, 46. For fur-
    ther comment, see *A Remembered Future*, pp.89–93
11. Published as an Appendix to Spiegel's book
12. A.B. Yehoshua, *Three Days and a Child*, trans. Miriam Arad (New York:
    Doubleday, 1970), p.54. (Page numbers hereinafter given parentheti-
    cally in the text)
13. Noted by Mordechai Shalev in his valuable commentary on this work,
    originally published in the daily newspaper *Haaretz* on November 8
    and 15, 1968 and reprinted (with supplementary essays) in *In the
    Opposite Direction: Articles on* Mr. Mani *by A.B. Yehoshua* (in Hebrew),
    ed. with introduction by Nitza Ben-Dov (Tel-Aviv: Hakibbutz
    Hameuchad, 1995), hereinafter referred to as "Ben-Dov". See pp.409,
    415.
14. Shalev in Ben-Dov, pp.400, 408. Nitza Ben-Dov cites written testi-
    mony from Yehoshua that he had not been aware of the Akedah-
    pattern during the writing of this story. (ibid., pp.36–7)

15. See A.B. Yehoshua, *On Behalf of Normality* (in Hebrew) – official English title: "Between Right and Right" (Jerusalem: Schocken, 1980), pp.16, 21 and passim
16. This episode (like everything else in the novel) is undoubtedly symbolic. Shalev (in Ben-Dov, p.413) sees it as the rejection of the false, alien versions of the myth and as marking the point at which the biblical version with its redemptive ending is affirmed. In a seminar which I gave at Yale in 1991, one participant, Meira Levinson, proposed the opposite interpretation. The old books with their hard words and their traditional tunes are the scriptural legends (specifically the Akedah) imposed on us and against which the narrator and his audience are – at one level – rebelling. I incline more to this view.
17. Examples of the sacrifice carried out are legion, typically in Wilfred Owen's war poem, "Parable of the Old Man and the Young" and in many Israeli fictions inspired by similar sentiments, e.g. Amos Oz's "The Way of the Wind" (1965). It often seems as though the paradigm of the murderous father who actually destroys his fair offspring has been adopted in Israeli literature as an (unconscious) importation from European writings where it came to answer needs and express impulses – for instance anti-Puritan impulses – which originated in non-Jewish societies.
18. See Shalev in Ben-Dov, p.411.
19. *Midrash Haggadol*, on Genesis 22:19. (Edition of M. Margulies [Jerusalem: Mossad Harav Kook, 1975], p.360)
20. *A Remembered Future*, p.87
21. Cf. Hyam Maccoby, *The Sacred Executioner: Human Sacrifice and the Legacy of Guilt* (London: Thames and Hudson, 1982), pp.88–9
22. Shalev sees the Passion narrative as well as the Passion play as a strong shaping influence in this story (see Ben-Dov, pp.427–8)
23. "Early in the Summer of 1970," trans. Miriam Arad (New York: Doubleday, 1977), p.43. (Page numbers hereafter in parentheses in the text)
24. See Ben-Dov, pp.419–26 and see note 22 above
25. Section 18 in the Hebrew text; in the English translation the subsections are not numbered.
26. Cf. Shalev in Ben-Dov, p.429
27. Published in the collection *Debits and Credits* (1926)
28. Abraham B. Yehoshua, *Mr. Mani* (in Hebrew) (Tel-Aviv: Hakibbutz Hameuchad, 1990). Quotations (hereinafter in parentheses in the text) are from the English translation by Hillel Halkin (London: Phoenix Books, 1994), first published by Doubleday, New York, 1992
29. In Ben-Dov, pp.339–47
30. And just that there should be no mistake, the use of the verb *la-akod* in the original Hebrew text at p.341 drives the point home.
31. In Ben-Dov, pp.395–6
32. Ben-Dov, Introduction, p.36
33. Shalev, ibid., p.435
34. Ibid., p.436
35. Yehoshua, ibid., p.396

CHAPTER 10

1. From *Sefer Hamaasim* ("The Book of Fables") in *S.Y. Agnon's Collected Fiction* (in Hebrew) (Tel-Aviv: Schocken, 1953), vol.VI, p.189. This is the standard edition of Agnon's writings, to be referred to hereafter as CF. To the seven volumes of this edition an eighth ("The Wood and the Fire") was added in his lifetime (see below, page 195.) Subsequent page references, given in parentheses in the text, are to this edition. A translation of this story by Anne Golomb Hoffman is included in S.Y. Agnon, *A Book That Was and Other Stories*, eds. Alan Mintz and Anne Golomb Hoffman (New York: Schocken Books, 1995). This and all other citations from Agnon in this chapter are, however, translated by H.F.
2. CF, vol. IV. An English translation by Misha Louvish appeared in 1968.
3. Page numbers given in parentheses in the text down to the end of this section (section 1) refer to this volume, i.e. CF vol.VIII.
4. B. Kurzweil, *Massot al Sippure S.Y. Agnon* ("Essays on Agnon's Fiction"), (in Hebrew), 3rd rev. edn (Tel-Aviv: Schocken, 1970), pp.316–19
5. The novel appears as CF vol.V. Page numbers in parentheses in the text from this point on refer to this volume.
6. Arnold J. Band, *Nostalgia and Nightmare: A Study in the Fiction of S.Y. Agnon* (Berkeley and Los Angeles: University of California Press, 1968), pp.414–15. Kurzweil pointed to the fundamentally epic character of Agnon's major writings in a highly influential essay which appeared in 1952 (reprinted in his *Essays on Agnon's Fiction*, pp.9–17) and he returns to this categorization in discussions of this novel. His position has generally been echoed by later critics, though definitions of "epic" have generally been lacking. I would wish to argue that as well as the epic, *Temol Shilshom* also gives us in the Balak chapters a powerful demonstration of the mock-epic. (On this aspect see below, p.210).
7. This is meant of the final design and composition only. Individual stories and parts of stories, later to be embodied in the novel, began to appear in journals and collections in the 1930s and earlier. Sarah Hager counts ten such prior publications and that, without counting the unpublished archival material which likewise belongs to an earlier period than the final version. (S. Hager, "The Day Before Yesterday: Evolving Structure and Unity" [in Hebrew], in *Shai Agnon: Researches and Documents*, eds. G. Shaked and R. Weiser [Mosad Bialik: Jerusalem, 1978], pp.154–93. And see below, note 11)
8. A.J. Band, "Crime and Punishment in *Temol Shilshom*," (in Hebrew), *Molad* 211 (May–June, 1967), 75–81
9. Idem, "Isaac Rebound: The Akedah Motif in Two Modern Jewish Writers," *The Nahum N. Glatzer Lecture in Judaism and the Humanities* (Boston University, 1988), pp.1–12
10. E.g. Gershon Shaked, *Hebrew Narrative Fiction, 1880–1980* (in Hebrew), vol.2 (Tel-Aviv: Hakibbutz Hameuchad and Keter, 1983), p.207; Hillel Barzel, *Agnon and Kafka: A Comparative Study* (in Hebrew), (Ramat-Gan: Bar-Urian, 1972), p.230; Michael Brown, art. cit., 108

11. Quoted by Hager, art. cit., pp.168–9
12. This opening sentence is a good example of the density of Agnon's biblical allusions. Apart from the echo of Genesis 12:1, there is also a subtler allusion infolded here in the phrase that I have translated by "our brethren of the Dispersion." The reference is to Ezekiel 11:15 where the exiles in Babylon, desiring to return to Jerusalem and finding difficulties in their path, are termed "thy brothers, the men of thy redemption" (*anshe geullatekha*). It is an odd expression. We would have expected rather *anshe galutkha* – i.e. "the men of thy exile." Here Agnon it would seem (and before him Ezekiel himself who was fond of such word-play) is punning ironically on the two like-sounding words with their opposite meanings. Are the exiles going to be redeemed or not? It is the question on which in a sense the whole plot of this novel will also turn.
13. *Yalkut Shimoni*, sect. 62; *Gen. Rabbah*, Chap. 39. Agnon had a near complete knowledge of the whole rabbinic corpus and his familiarity with this well-known text need not be doubted. This applies also to a great part of his readership, especially as the central portion of this midrash, that attributed to R. Yohanan, is cited in Rashi's standard commentary on Gen. 22:2.
14. See Hager, art. cit., pp.154–5 and Band, *Nostalgia and Nightmare*, pp.415–20, 432–7
15. B. Kurzweil, op. cit., pp.104–14
16. H. Barzel, op. cit., p.228
17. In Franz Kafka, *The Great Wall of China*, trans. Willa and Edwin Muir (New York: Schocken Books, 1970), pp.1–43. The link had been proposed by Shlomo Zemach (*The Two Doorposts* [in Hebrew] [Ramat-Gan: Massadah, 1965], p.131). Barzel discusses this parallel also (op. cit., pp.264–5) but tends to see essential differences between the function of the dog in Kafka and that of Balak.
18. Eli Shweid, "*Kelev hutsot, veAdam*" (in Hebrew), *Molad*, 120 (July, 1958), 381–8
19. Cf. "Grace After Meals" in *The Authorized Daily Prayer-Book of the United Hebrew Congregations of the British Empire*, trans. S. Singer (London: Eyre and Spottiswoode, 1957), p.280

Index

Abraham, testing of, 95, 205–7, 213–15; *see also* Isaac, Binding of
"Absalom and Achitophel" (Dryden) 47
"According to the Pain is the Reward" (Agnon), 195–8, 213
Agnon, S.Y., 159, 193–215; *A Bridal Canopy*, 199; *A Guest for the Night*, 194; "According to the Pain is the Reward", 195–8, 213; "Agunot", 26; "In the Heart of the Seas", 119; "Knots upon Knots", 193–4; *The Day before Yesterday*, 198–215; *The Wood and the Fire*, 195
"Agunot" (Agnon), 26
Akedah *see* Isaac, Binding of
Alexander, Edward, 227n8
Allen, Walter, 72
Alter, Robert, 16, 123, 156, 227n5
Amadis de Gaul, 21, 26
Amerika (Kafka), 92
"Ancient Mariner, The" (Coleridge), 4, 30, 32, 102
Apocalypse, 6–7, 13
Aristotle, 85
Arnold, Matthew, 74, 145–6
"Ascent of F6, The" (Auden and Isherwood), 184, 189
Assistant, The (Malamud), 118, 122
Auden and Isherwood: "The Ascent of F6", 184, 189
Auerbach, Erich, 9, 17, 53–4, 71, 102; *Mimesis*, 13, 136–41
Augustine, 9, 54
Austen, Jane, 34; *Pride and Prejudice*, 34; *Sense and Sensibility*, 34

Bakhtin, Mikhail, 7–14, 41, 46, 56, 76, 83, 189. 216n11
Band, Arnold J., 203
"Bar-Kokhba" (Goldfaden), 92
Barzel, Hillel, 211
Battestin, Martin C., 42–3
Baudelaire, 134
Beck, Evelyn Torton, 87
Bellow, Saul, 158; *Dangling Man*, 142; *Henderson the Rain King*, 117–18;

Herzog, 59, 136–42, 147, 151–2; *Mr Sammler's Planet*, 133–6; *To Jerusalem and Back*, 158
Ben-Dov, Nitza, 186–8
Benjamin, Walter, 92
Bennett, Arnold: *The Old Wives' Tale*, 59
Bennett, Joan, 72
Berlin, Adele, 218n29
Billy Budd (Melville), 145, 147, 160
Binding of Isaac *see* Isaac
Biographia Literaria (Coleridge), 69
Bloom, Harold, 224n30
Boccaccio, 26
Borges, Jorge Luis, 119
Branagh, Kenneth: *Dead Again*, 190
Brand (Ibsen), 145, 147, 160
Brenner, Yosef Haim: *Breakdown and Bereavement*, 128–9, 226n15
Bridal Canopy, A (Agnon), 199
Brinker, Menachem, 226n15
Brisman, Leslie, 228n7
Brothers Karamazov, The (Dostoevsky), 81–6, 90–1, 93, 152
Browning, Elizabeth Barrett, 145
Buber, Martin, 14, 83, 94
Bultmann, Rudolf, 101, 103
Bunyan, John: *The Holy War*, 48; *The Pilgrim's Progress*, 25, 27–8, 33, 39, 47–9, 64, 100–1
Butler, Samuel: *The Way of all Flesh*, 145–6

Cain, story of, 16
Call it Sleep (Henry Roth), 146
Carroll, David, 65
Cervantes: *Don Quixote*, 8, 11, 21, 26–7, 54, 100, 218n37
Chaucer, Geoffrey, 27
chronotope, 7, 14, 33
Cicero, 9
circumcision, 168
closure, absence of in Biblical narrative, 5, 141
Coleridge, Samuel: *Biographia Literaria*, 69; *The Ancient Mariner*, 4, 30, 32, 102

233